GOETHE'S IMAGE OF MAN AND SOCIETY

Drawing by K. A. Schwerdgeburth, Weimar, 1832

GOETHE AT THE AGE OF 81

Goethe's Image of Man and Society

by

Arnold Bergstraesser

HENRY REGNERY COMPANY
CHICAGO
1949

Typography by Philip Reed
Manufactured in the United States of America

JeK 12-10-63

Prefatory Note

THE BASIC CONCEPTION of this book dates back to lectures which the author gave at the University of Heidelberg in the early thirties. I have occasionally drawn on articles previously published in *Corona*, Zürich, 1936, *Monatshefte*, University of Wisconsin, 1945 and 1948, *Deutsche Beiträge*, Chicago, 1947, and *Modern Philology*, Chicago, 1949. I make grateful acknowledgement to the University of Chicago Press for permission to quote from *The Odes of Pindar*, translated by Richmond Lattimore (1947), pp. 50 f., and to Pantheon Books, Inc., for permission to quote from Curtius-Weigand, *Goethe, Wisdom and Experience* (1949), pp. 12 and 91. I am appreciative of the services rendered me in this work by the staffs of the University of Chicago libraries, of the Department of Germanics at the University of Chicago, and of Yale University Library. I am grateful to Professor Carl Schreiber, of Yale University, for facilitating the use of the *Speck Collection of Goetheana*. I feel especially indebted to the publisher and his associates for their generous co-operation and to my friends Professors Matthys Jolles and Max Rheinstein, of the University of Chicago, for their critical reading of the first draft of the manuscript. I wish to extend my thanks to Mrs. Fritz Caspari and to Miss Margaret McKenzie for their valuable advice on matters of style and to Miss Rita Blumenthal for her assistance.

Quotations from Goethe's prose are translated into English; Goethe's verse is quoted in German and paraphrased in English before or after the quotation. Thus the reader who is unfamiliar with the German language may follow the argument without a loss, whereas others may enjoy the original. Goethe's basic terms, such as *Entsagung*, "resignation," and *Wahrheit*, "truth," should be understood, even in the German, precisely within the range he assigned to them himself. Others, such as *Bildung* or *Gestalt*, are hardly translatable at all. Terms the colloquial usage of which is too far apart from Goethe's have therefore been included in the index in order to facilitate the understanding of their particular connotation by the comparison of passages.

A.B.

THE UNIVERSITY OF CHICAGO
May, 1949

CONTENTS

THE UNIVERSE AND MAN

THE IDEAL COMMONWEALTH

Introduction

AN IMAGE OF MAN AND SOCIETY IS EMBODIED IN THE MANI-
fold figures of Goethe's literary production. Through his
sayings and his metaphysical poetry he gave an insight into
the religious and anthropological bases of this image. He
verified the experience on which it rested by scientific inquiries into nature and strengthened its validity by his
critical consciousness of human thought. Thus he succeeded
in imparting a unity to his diversified pursuits which
amounts to a synthesis of faith and science, of philosophy
and art.

Goethe's image of man and society is a realistic one since
he faced the human situation with unprejudiced honesty.
It searches for standards and measures of life because Goethe
saw in the nature of man the tendency to find, to formulate,
and to follow an intrinsic norm. He regarded the meaning
of man's existence as a riddle to be solved by action and
thought from its constituent elements, and conceived of
his own life as a gift and a responsibility. Since he considered "life itself to be the purpose of life," the quest for
the best possible fulfillment of the human potentiality was
to him the worthiest task of man's cognitive faculties.

Goethe presented an affirmative answer to man's desire for "the good life" in the tale of the ideal commonwealth of emigrants in which his novel *Wilhelm Meister* culminates. The conceptions fundamental to Goethe's picture of the sound community grew out of his own personality and vocation. It is our intention in the present work to follow this genesis, to interpret the function of man, society, and history within his view of the universe, and to explain on this basis the symbolic model of the new community which he left as a challenge and as a warning.

With this tale Goethe entered the tradition of Western thought which since Plato has expressed man's desire for a healthy life of meaning and value: "the good life." This literature received its appellation, "Utopian," from the treatise of Sir Thomas More in which "the best state of the commonwealth" was attained on "the new island of Utopia." The English humanist, statesman, and martyr of the church by no means considered his imaginary isle to be a mere dream, although he confessed to have "wished rather than hoped" for the realization of the example of its institutions. Goethe was even more realistic than Thomas More in that he presented his ideal commonwealth as arising in the midst of the society of his day, as though to state that it could be realized at any time and wherever the reverence for life and the wisdom about nature and man which were indispensable to the new beginning were firmly grasped.

Goethe's image of man and society was in opposition to those tendencies of the nineteenth century which were to become fully manifest a hundred years later. His conception of man made him averse to the impersonal mechanization of social relations and to ideological passion. His reverence for nature made him antagonistic to the contempt for this life which had grown out of the religious reaction against the contemporary disintegration of faith. His own mental world was constructed upon the foundation of an organic idea of nature which he defended to the extent of defying its mechanistic counterpart. Seen from the point of view of twentieth-century conditions, his image of man and society seems indeed distant from present-day reality and implies a severe criticism of it.

Those moderns who advocate a philosophy of disillusionment will question the validity of Goethe's belief in the meaning of human existence. Modern skepticism is understandable in the face of the depravity and confusion which the living generations have experienced. Not so long ago we believed in the predestined progress of mankind, but we were to witness the most incredible cruelties of history. When we see ethical ideals turned into instruments of power and when events escape our control, we are tempted to abandon our beliefs and our efforts. Living in an age of insecurity we are unsure of ourselves. We are told that the existence of man is absurd and that truth is beyond reach. We are easily ashamed of faith, whatever may be its form of expression, and we excuse ourselves with the argument that our time is less conducive to constructive thought and action than the past to which Goethe belonged.

In reality, however, the dangers to which Goethe was exposed are much closer to us than we assume, and the solutions at which he arrived have meaning for ourselves. The epoch of his lifetime was similarly insecure, although not as brutal as ours; the philosophies and religions of his era were as conflicting as those of today; in his youth and early manhood he was often as uncertain as is twentieth-century man. He had no illusions about the contradictions within himself; he realized the contingent qualities of existence and suffered under the necessities to which man is inevitably subjected. Incapable of following mere convention, he set out to experience life in his own way and had to pay for this independence. More than once he found himself on the brink of despair, and he was aware of the destructive energies interfering, both from within and without, with the life of man.

Nevertheless, in the chaos of historical existence Goethe recognized the potentiality and the ever recurring task of man to form a cosmos. He overcame despair and grew firm in the conviction that a meaningful way of life is possible, that it is worth while to search for truth, that beauty is real, and that good can be distinguished from evil. Goethe experienced faith in himself, respected it in others, and confirmed it through study. Living in the succession of Greek thought within the Christian tradition, he saw man, a part of nature, as a manifestation of the universal creative power. He strove toward clarification of the common basis necessary for mutual understanding and constructive co-operation among men. He felt that men are related to the ideal of the human being through the core of man's self which he called the purely human in contrast to the merely human. Goethe regarded the triumph of the pure humanity as the meaning of his life and work. The realization of the purely human is the end to which he devoted his image of man and society.

LIFE AND VOCATION

Who has formed the figures of gods, raised us up to them, and brought them down to us, but the poet?

Wilhelm Meister's Apprenticeship II, 2

I

Personality

Nature, Character, and Conscience—Goethe's
Historical Moment—Chance, Genius,
and Self-Knowledge—Personality and *Gestalt*

THE LIFE OF Goethe, it has been said, is so universal a mirror
of human existence that, contemplating it, everyone can
find aid in understanding himself and the situation and
inner resources of man. No other poet of rank has left a
similar wealth of letters and diaries which give such insight
into his experiences, thoughts, and actions. Hardly any
other human being is reflected in so many records of conversations. The correspondence about him, by friends and
by enemies, and the discussion of his work and personality
in public and in private reveal him as a man who, already in
his own lifetime, belonged to the world and was regarded
as a touchstone of insight and judgment. Goethe himself
interpreted the growth of his personality in *Dichtung und
Wahrheit*, his autobiography, known in English as *Poetry
and Truth*, to which he added accounts of his Italian journey, of the campaign in France, of the genesis of his botanical studies, and of his relations to many of the men and
problems of his time. The history of his own life became
for him an object of study in which he was aided by a self-
knowledge developed from his early adolescence onward.
His literary, scientific, and philosophical work, his political

thought and activity, and his intimate relations of friendship and love, all illuminate each other and permit us to
touch the very fabric of his personality.

A keen and fortunate mind, Goethe gave meaning to experiences shared by every man; his life seems to us typically
human, since it was exposed to the fallacies and capable of
the best achievements of human nature. Above all, Goethe's
life bespeaks his strength in reaffirming the meaning of his
existence and in embodying it in his work and actions. To
those with whom he came in close contact, he meant more
as a man than as a poet, scientist, or philosophic mind. The
voice of human truth which resounds in his poetry, thought,
and wisdom drew them irresistibly to his personality.

From his youth to his death, Goethe's contemporaries felt
the impact of his strong and resilient power of being as it
was expressed in his way of living. His talk, his studies and
writings all seemed manifestations of one common source,
springing from one unmistakable and inalienable center.
Goethe believed this source to be the unity of his own existence, and he regarded this feeling of unity as typical of
the way in which nature proceeds with the creation of the
world of man.

Each being that feels itself a unity intends to preserve its own
inner self unseparated and unchanged. This is an everlasting
and necessary gift of nature. One might say that each individual has character, down to the worm which writhes when
stepped on. In this sense we may ascribe character to the weak-
ling and even to the coward; for he gives up what other men
value above all else, but what does not belong to his own nature:
honor, glory—just to preserve his personality. Ordinarily the
word character is used in a higher sense: to denote a personality
of remarkable qualities who insists on his own way and cannot
be deterred from following it by anything.[1]

Personality, then, in Goethe's conception, is the characteristically individual form and elemental energy of life

which nature bestows upon its creatures. As an outer form it is seen; as an inner form it is felt. Character is the constellation of qualities by which the individual personality becomes manifest; a great character is one whose strength "is connected with great, incalculable and infinite capacities, through which original and unexpected intentions, plans, and actions appear."[2] Man's ethical will is, however, in conflict with his character. A will toward the good is inherent in human nature and is potentially in opposition to other powers of the personality. Throughout his life the erring human being will have to face this tension. His nature can be modified but not basically changed. The margin of freedom granted to man in regard to himself is not large.

Goethe's friends saw him as a great character whose ethical will transformed into constructive activity the tension between it and the abundant nature of his personality. His knowledge of himself was just. It developed early and became an integral part of his way of living. At the age of fifteen he points to the strength of his personality, which breaks through "the trifles of etiquette," and to his inclination toward the constructive, which makes him forget personal injury. Thus he anticipates the conflict between selfhood and conscience and is already aware of the realm in which he will always seek and find an answer to this tension: the domain of unhindered human communication and understanding.

One of my chief faults is that I am somewhat impetuous . . . on the other hand no one forgets an injury more easily than I. Moreover, I am very much given to laying down the law, yet, when I have nothing to say, I can let things alone. . . . I write as familiarly to you as if I had already known you a hundred years; but what of that? this is simply something I cannot unlearn.[3]

Eight years later, Kestner, the fiancé of Werther's Lotte, describes Goethe and his first meeting with him when, on a walk, he found him lying under a tree and talking with friends. It was the freedom of Goethe's personality that struck Kestner most:

His emotions are passionate; often, however, he has great control over himself. He is of a noble spirit; free from prejudice, he does whatever comes to his mind without considering whether others like it, whether it is fashionable, or whether custom permits it. All compulsion is hateful to him.[4]

Kestner describes this "man of true genius" with observant understanding; he notices his love of children and his gift for dealing with them, his respect for women, the bizarre traits of his conduct. He finds him reluctant to speak of essential things except to a few friends. He observes in him the independence of a strong religious impulse, a hatred of skepticism, and a striving for truth, "although he values more highly the feeling of truth than its demonstration." Goethe appeared to Kestner as a man on a road of his own, concerned with the arts and sciences rather than with the practice of law. Even in the state of ferment in which Goethe was at Wetzlar, the resolution which was latent in his very being made itself felt, although he could not yet give it conscious form.

A character of such vitality was not spared the full experience of both the depths and the heights of human existence. One sometimes feels that Goethe lived life anew and wholly on his own, brushing aside convention and acquiring tradition in his own way, without tolerating a spot in his world which could not be integrated with his personality. In the exuberant days of his youth he did not simply live his nature; he lived the tension of his nature. In his crises of faith and love he came close to despair of the possibility of a constructive life: Werther, Mignon, Tasso, as well as Götz and Egmont, are figures of his own blood. Slowly Goethe developed the self-observation of his boyhood days into self-control: he gave strictness of form to his language, measure to his action, and clarity to his thought. Inclined by nature toward spontaneity of communication, he learned from experience to impose restrictions upon himself in order to further his work and to protect his creative sensitivity.

The mature Goethe, of the time after the Italian journey, followed a responsible way of living, with a high regard for time and an aversion to superfluous or disturbing talk. His "Olympian" reserve often offended others by its seeming detachment, but his personality and his humanness left a deep impression even on those who at first approached him with hesitation and prejudice.

Thus Jean Paul Richter—the poet on whom Herder set his hope, particularly when he was in disagreement with Goethe—visited him in 1796. He came "without warmth, out of mere curiosity"—for good reason, because Goethe was well aware of the incompatibility of his own classical aims with the baroque reveries of Jean Paul. Friends had described Goethe to him as stiff and icy, especially toward strangers, and proud as one of the patricians of an imperial free city. When Jean Paul entered the house in Weimar, the "pantheon of statues," it gave him a cold nightmare. There he awaits the Olympian.

Finally the god appears; cold, laconic, without accent. Knebel says for instance: The French enter Rome.—Hm! says the god. His figure is pithy and fiery, his eye is a light (but without an agreeable color). In the end, however, not only the champagne, but the conversations on art, on the public and so on, stir him up and then—one is with Goethe. He does not speak with Herder's flowing spontaneity but calmly and with sharp precision. He read us, rather he acted before us, a magnificent unprinted poem, and thereby his heart drove the flames through the crust of ice.[5]

While the skeptical critic or the merely social visitor might find it difficult to penetrate the formalities by which

Goethe preserved his freedom to determine for himself his relations to others, a sympathetic mind could elicit a warm response. Even Hölderlin, whose genius remained unrecognized at Weimar, speaks of one of his few conversations with Goethe as "the highest enjoyment of life in finding so much humanity combined with so much greatness."[6] And Wieland, after twenty years of acquaintance, still loves "this curious and marvelous mortal being whose personality is so much of a piece, so bona fide."[7]

Schiller regarded his meeting with Goethe as the most beneficial event of his life. The human radiance of Goethe's personality was, he confessed in 1800, the strongest bond of their friendship.

Nature has been more bountiful to him than to anyone who has arisen since Shakespeare. Besides what he *received* from nature, he has *given* to himself, through restless search and study, more than anyone else. . . . It is not these high qualities of mind by which I am bound to him. If I did not value him as a human being more highly than anyone else, I should admire his genius from a distance. In his nature are truth and honesty, and the most earnest concern for the right and the good.[8]

In the memory of the Western world, Goethe lives on as a personality of ineffable charm, with a versatility reminiscent of the *uomo universale* of the Renaissance, an authoritative humanistic mind, and a unity of being which makes his life appear a work of art. When, today, there is doubt as to the significance of the solution he gave to the problem of human existence, the question usually arises whether we have truly understood his conception of personality and have not, perhaps, read into it an alien meaning. It may be that the image we cherished of Goethe's personality has interfered with our insight into the ends to which he devoted it. To him personality was the riddle to be worked out through the course of life in awareness of the universal context of man's existence. He accepted life as a gift of nature and as an ethical responsibility. His view of the universe was not man-centered; he strove rather for a cosmic understanding of the human situation. His experience of the creativity of genius and of the productivity of love formed the basis of his work. Through both these energies he was taught to accept transcendental reality; he conceived of the potential immanence of the divine in the temporal as a reflection of its transcendence. The catholicity of Goethe's thought was built upon the comprehensive and metaphysical character of his mind.

Each individual's personality is, then, a means toward attaining truth. In this perspective, Goethe's life appears as an independent experiment, permitting the formulation of laws which he believed were valid beyond his own existence. The young Goethe, whose spontaneous genius attracts our sympathies, and the old Goethe, whose impersonal and objective wisdom demands our study, do not stand in contradiction to each other. Goethe's eighty-two years were an essay in living and thinking which concerns not only the individual but the human community.

It is only in moments of historical crisis that such catholicity of pursuits as Goethe undertook is necessary and possible for an independent personality. The classical era of German literature coincided with the beginning of the disintegration of modern society. European culture, disrupted by the conflicting forces of the Renaissance and the Reformation, had experienced a brief consolidation in the thought and style of the baroque. But the time of synthesis had passed. In Goethe's youth, old established orders had lost their validity, and soon after his adolescent years the intellectual conflicts and uncertainties of the eighteenth century became manifest through the breakdown of Europe's ancient social and political organization. The young Goethe, who accepted with enthusiasm the liberty of his growth from within and tended to take nothing for granted, shared the longing for spontaneity of which Rousseau's "return to

nature" was the epitome. It was not only by his own choice
and capacity that he set out on the dangerous and burdensome road of independence. If, ever and again, he felt
thrown back upon the resources of his personality, and was
prevented by a deep inner restlessness from leaping to pre-
mature conclusions, it was because the historical moment demanded the reliving and rethinking of the human situation.[9]

Eras of transition are eras of both disintegration and renewal. Before Goethe was able to give a firm and constructive response to life he had to experience its ultimate
problems. Hamlet's question, "To be or not to be," was
Goethe's in his youth. His deep awareness of man's exposure
to uncertainty, error, and suffering challenged his resources
of creativity and affirmation. This aspect of Goethe's life
was rather obscured in the mind of the generations following him by the image of his radiant genius. It was not easy
to grasp the functional relationship between his suffering
under the problem of man's existence and his constructive
view of the good life, between the inwardness of his youth
and the objective projection of his experience in his mature
work.

We are coming to realize the contrast between a conception of literature as a product of fancy for the purpose of
entertainment, and Goethe's understanding of poetry as a
form of truth; we no longer see Goethe as a writer "confessing" his feelings in beautiful form; we see him as a poet
creating, with a full sense of metaphysical responsibility,
a mental world. We understand that he rejected traditional
forms of cult and dogma only to give forms of his own to
genuine religious experience and philosophic cognition. The
young Goethe met life with only the guidance of his nature, without the shelter of definite convictions and without
a firm direction. His unprejudiced but at first wholly subjective insight into the human situation was the precondition for his renewal of impersonal norms of individual and
social existence. At the time when, on the new continent

and in France, the solution of the problem of liberty was
sought in new political forms, Goethe experienced and
formulated an answer to the universal human quest for freedom.

Goethe lived in his time with all his vitality; he responded
to the time's needs, yet he reached beyond it, leaving much
of the results of his life to what he knew to be a still distant
future. The historical rhythm of time is often different on
the level of social and political action and on that of thought
and poetry. The problems of his own time took on a significance in Goethe's mind which only gradually revealed
itself through the ensuing course of history. His vision
penetrated to the core of the conflicts between science and
faith, authority and freedom, individual and community.
He recognized the uncertainty about the normative bases
of literature, art, and government characteristic of his age
as of ours. By pointing out the tension between the organic
and mechanistic conceptions of nature and the conflict between man and machine, he anticipated problems which
determined the further course of the century. Through the
historical roots of his thinking, Goethe was related to an
aspect of Renaissance humanism which was neglected by
most nineteenth-century interpreters because of its religious
impulse. By his insight into the incalculable character of
history and the fragility of human existence he anticipated
a basic element of twentieth-century consciousness. The
core of his work belongs to the timeless achievements of
Western culture.

Chance, genius, and self-knowledge united in making
Goethe what he became. With a naïve self-assurance he accepted the favors of nature and fortune as coming rightly
to him; he was neither burdened by them nor did they make
him conceited. He early realized that he had to "earn" what
chance gave him.[10] He grew up as the son of a burgher family of some means; with his sister Cornelia he was given a
private education of high quality; his family was close enough

to trade not to be cut off from the people, and had, at the same time, social standing. Goethe's maternal grandfather, Johann Wolfgang Textor, who his grandson tells us had the gift of second sight, was a city magistrate and a man of influence. Goethe's social origin pointed to a future of care-free circumstances, of a not too burdensome profession, and of intellectual interests within a fairly wide horizon.

In *Poetry and Truth* Goethe describes the city of his birth, Frankfurt-am-Main, where everything reminded one of a time of unrest long gone by: the towers and city gates, the bridges and walls, the place where Charlemagne's fortress was said to have stood, the town hall called *der Römer*, where the emperors were elected and crowned. He tells of the foreboding with which, in his youth, people were aware that only one more space remained in the imperial hall for an emperor's portrait. The picture of this surviving past is blended with the impressions of the city's commercial activities, the traffic on the river, the fairs held in spring and autumn, the ceremonies which at regular intervals interrupted the daily life with their festivities and linked it again to past centuries.[11] In Frankfurt, medieval Europe had merged with eighteenth-century open-mindedness. This center of west German commerce was one of the few towns which had survived the decay of city life in the wake of the religious wars. Bordering on the territory of the archbishop of Mainz and on various secular principalities close to the Rhine and on the route to the south of Europe, the free city of Frankfurt, in spite of the many narrow aspects of its life, had a wider horizon and a freer atmosphere than most of the small duchies, counties, and cities into which eighteenth-century Germany was divided.

Goethe's father, a tailor's son, had studied law and bought the title of Imperial Councilor. He rebuilt the house, located in the midst of the city on the Hirschgraben, in which Goethe spent his youth. As long as he was healthy, Goethe's father occasionally practiced law without much of an effort.

He loved his books, and the diary of his own travel in Italy reveals his desire to understand the historical bases of art and civilization. His eagerness in collecting works of art and specimens of natural history foreshadowed Goethe's own zeal as a collector. Goethe found his father pedantic and all too fond of teaching; the father's exacting demands may have prompted the son's irony about his own didactic inclinations. The elder Goethe is described in *Poetry and Truth* as an affectionate and well-meaning though grave man, a man who, "because he had a very tender heart, externally maintained an iron-clad severity."[12]

In terms of modern standards the education which the councilor gave to his children was demanding, and yet it permitted the freedom of the son's growth. Early mastery of the ancient and modern languages was regarded as indisputably necessary, and the boy's imagination came to the aid of his father's educational zeal when he tried to unify his various linguistic studies by inventing a story about a dispersed family who corresponded with each other in French, Italian, Latin, and Greek; Goethe wrote all the letters himself in the various languages. The instruction in religion was reduced to a deistic ethic, so that Goethe early became interested in the dissenting groups of pietists and separatists, called the "Quiet in the Land," who flourished in the city, along with the Lutherans, Roman Catholics, Calvinists and Jews. The father had his son round out his gentleman's education by lessons in fencing, riding, and dancing, and in drawing, etching, and music. In his early boyhood the puppet show which his grandmother provided for the children kindled Goethe's dramatic imagination. Theater- and concert-going and acquaintance with local artists and the intellectually significant men of Frankfurt—jurists, physicians, theologians, and humanists—were part of his life. A wealth of impressions, vividly renewed in *Poetry and Truth*, centered around the house in the Hirschgraben.

The father's principles were thoroughly classical, and,

whereas Homer and Virgil, the Old Testament and French drama were read in the original languages, "modern" literature—which, in Goethe's boyhood, meant Klopstock—was banned by the Imperial Councilor. We are told how the conspiracy of Wolfgang and his mother and sister in keeping, reading, and memorizing a borrowed copy of the *Messias* led to a family catastrophe. On overhearing Cornelia's passionate recitation of Klopstock's hexameters, the barber who was shaving the older Goethe was so startled that he dropped his bowl of soap into the councilor's lap; this resulted in an inquisition which led to Father Goethe's horrified discovery that Klopstock's verse had invaded his household. For him there was no such thing as poetry without rhyme.[13]

As we recognize and admire the vitality with which the young Goethe made his own the world surrounding him in books, in personalities, and in the monuments of the past, we are tempted to interpret this spontaneity and richness of mind as a foreshadowing of genius. In retrospect, Goethe himself kept in modest balance the relationship between the time and himself. He expressed his conviction of the organic unity between youth and old age when he prefixed to the second book of his autobiography the saying: "The desires of our youth are the riches of our old age." In our first attachments to the outer world and in the wishes and dreams of youth Goethe saw the premonitions of the capacities latent in ourselves: "We feel a longing for that which we already secretly possess." He considered this inner compulsion, which acts as though it were obeying a plan of nature, as most likely to be productive when, "in a creative time, man is sensitive to the needs of the epoch" and his desires coincide with these needs.[14] Then he may find it possible to console himself even about frustrated efforts and unfinished projects by realizing that his individual self is only part of an all-encompassing process:

life comprises friendship and love. Through them a
of communication is possible which surpasses the realm
gns, reflects the existence of one being in that of the
, and increases the awareness of the transcendental
nd from which all human existence arises.

he portrait of Cornelia in *Poetry and Truth* shows all
lepth of this conception of personality through the re-
truction of the one person who was Goethe's closest
panion in childhood and adolescence. Her outward
s come alive through the description of the natural dig-
of her demeanor, of the disharmonious expression of
face, of her physical and psychic inhibitions in human
ons. We are led to see the hidden excellence radiating
her mind and through her eyes in significant moments,
dir the indestructible bond of confidence between
li er and sister and, finally, the incomprehensible ground
or which even the brother could not penetrate. In this
ait, as in the others, Goethe's power of grasping out-
l forms joined with his ability to reproduce the inner
n by analogy to the most fundamental experience of his
self. His capacity for understanding others was gov-
ed by a reverence for the inaccessible and given center
any human being, for man's character as a creature, for
point in the depth of personality where it touches upon
transcendent.

rom this depth of his personality Goethe responded to
realm of chance. A severe physical and psychological
sis made him ready for the experience of genius in him-
f. The faith in genius was commonly accepted in the
riod of the *Sturm und Drang*, the literary movement of
hich Goethe became the protagonist during his year of
dy at Strassburg. "Every great man of genius," someone
rote in 1773 with reference to Lavater, "has his own
ay, his own expression, his own tone, his own system, and
en his own costume."[20] In retrospect, Goethe saw this
onception of genius

Only mankind in its entirety is the true man, and the individual can find joy and satisfaction only when he has the courage to feel that he is within the great whole.[15]

The characteristics of Goethe's personality are first evident from his relations to the inner circle of his childhood and early adolescence: a strict father, insisting on his prerogatives as the master of his children's education; a beloved sister, for years sharing study and play and the growth of physical and moral energies with her brother; a congenial mother, married as a child and "growing up to consciousness with and in her children," cheerful, imaginative, of a sound wit and a natural talent for narration—this was Goethe's family. A bond of affection and understanding united the mother with the only two of her six children who survived infancy, and this bond grew stronger as the father withdrew more and more into sickly, demanding, and self-centered isolation.

Elisabeth Goethe told Bettina von Arnim of the lively imagination with which her little boy followed her tales, took the telling into his own hands, or informed his grandmother how he wanted the story to go on, so that the old lady could discreetly inform the storyteller:

There I sat and he stared at me with his big black eyes, and if the fate of some hero of the tale was not to his liking, I saw how his vein of wrath swelled and how be suppressed his tears. Sometimes he interfered and said, before I had taken the next turn: "Is it not so, mother, the princess does not marry the cursed tailor, not even if he kills the giant?" When I stopped and postponed the catastrophe until the next evening, I could be sure that before then he would have straightened out everything, and thus, where my power of imagination was not sufficient, it often was replaced by his; . . . to his grandmother . . . whose favorite he was, he always confided his views, and I learned from her how I should proceed in my text according to his wishes; . . . thus I had the satisfaction of presenting my fairy tales to the joy and astonishment of the listeners, and Wolfgang, without ever confessing that he was the originator of all these curious events, anticipated with glowing eyes the fulfillment of his keenly drafted plans and welcomed their execution with enthusiasm.[16]

To his companions of his own age, the boy was a marvel of experience and imagination. They especially liked his stories, one of which, "The New Paris," Goethe inserted as an example in his autobiography. The boy Wolfgang is described as handsome, somewhat precocious, quick and yet penetrating in learning, inventive in play, of some resolution and propriety in appearance. As he grew older, he came more and more into the foreground of the household. He helped his mother and sister maintain a way of living different from the father's, with his inclination toward withdrawal. For his father, however, Goethe retained understanding and respect.

In his sister, he found a second self. As for Cornelia, she had boundless confidence in her brother; otherwise, she tended to seclude herself in an inwardness "which was not, and could not be, in harmony with itself."

Her eyes were not the finest I ever saw, but the deepest, behind which one expected the most; when they expressed affection or love, their radiance was unequaled; and yet this expression was not tender, as though it came from the heart and carried longing and desire with it: it came from the soul, it was full and rich, it seemed as though it intended only to give with no need to receive.[17]

Cornelia was of an exterior which Goethe called "in some measure repulsive." Others sought her advice, but she herself never overcame the feeling of strangeness toward outer life, and she died early after an unfortunate marriage. Goethe once planned to give, in the form of a Richardsonian novel, an idea of her personality and a feeling of "the wonderful depth which was its source," by reconstructing

---

from innumerable details the im[a...] incomprehensible being."[18] That [...] ality which made it difficult for [...] flected in the character of his siste[r...] he first experienced the producti[ve...] furthered human growth.

In his "Contributions to Morphol[ogy...] cluded some reflections on human [...] illustrate his view of human relatio[ns...] of existence he used the term "mo[nad...] named the basic unit of life, and a[c...] tions. "The rotating movement of t[he...] is the source of man's certainty of hi[s...] highest gift he receives from God [...] living and mobile monad touches [...] world, it "becomes aware of itself as [...] its and as outwardly restricted." Inev[...] acts upon us with either affection o[r...] nize what our enemies undertake aga[inst...] make it a part of our inner experien[ce...] friends do with us and for us touche[s...] of our existence. The living mona[d...] through friction with the outside real[ity...] from within; it is furthered by frien[ds...] inner experience becomes so much a [...] one can take it away.

Personality is seen as a series of circ[les...] an indestructible and unfathomable c[enter...] pulsing life emanates. From the depth o[f...] solitude, his urge to live tends to fulfill [...] inherent in himself by means of his [...] through this depth of solitude he touch[es...] sonal infinity; the character of his exist[ence...] him a part of an encompassing whole. [...] differentiated in depth; it oscillates bet[ween...] and the divine, between immanence and [...]

as manifesting itself by trespassing against the existing laws, by overthrowing the rules that were introduced, and by declaring itself unrestricted. . . . It took a long time before it was possible to assert that genius is the energy of man which, through action and deed, gives measure and law.[21]

However, the very subjectivity that was essential to Goethe's first experience and conception of genius had a specific function in the genesis of his personality. It forced him into a path entirely his own; it supported him in the spontaneous immediacy of his spoken and written word; it made his growth in the implementation of his potentialities as thorough as it was slow.

The crisis from which this development received its original impetus occurred toward the end of Goethe's three years of study at Leipzig and continued after he had returned home, just nineteen years old and, as he says himself, like one who had suffered shipwreck. The self-conscious, bold, and vivacious young man had made great efforts to adapt himself to the elegance of "Little Paris," as Leipzig was called. He had brought himself to learn card games and to acquire other social virtues considered less provincial than the Frankfurt habits. He had fallen in love and had written Anacreontic poetry. He had lived with some critical independence in the atmosphere of the late Gottsched's waning literary dictatorship. Through his friend Oeser he had received a deep and lasting impression of the archaeologist Winckelmann's personality and work.

The decisive event of his Leipzig years was, however, the illness during which he found himself in the balance between life and death. Sickness and convalescence led Goethe to a prolonged experience of the fragility of human existence—an experience induced by the unbalanced exposure to the extremes of exuberant gaiety and deep melancholy which he relates as characteristic of the preceding months. In his home he had been used to churchgoing and prayer, and from childhood he had known the Bible thoroughly. He had early been fascinated by the character of Moses, and among the youthful poetical efforts which he destroyed was one on the biblical figure of Joseph. In Leipzig he had exchanged his religious conventionalism for a sophisticated irony until the break-through to a genuine religious experience occurred, of which his letters to Ernst Theodor Langer are eloquent testimony.[22] The style of the exchanges between Goethe and Langer was that of pietism; it was "the true gospel which Langer as the first man on earth preached" to Goethe. Upon his return to Frankfurt the convalescent was encouraged on his new way by his mother and by the pious canoness Susanna von Klettenberg, friend of Elisabeth Goethe and her son, the *Schöne Seele* of *Wilhelm Meister's Apprenticeship*, the model of Makarie in *Wilhelm Meister's Travels*. Goethe became acquainted with the theosophic tradition of Renaissance Neo-Platonism, which combined a mystic religiosity with the alchemistic study of nature. Saved apparently by the elixir of the pietist family doctor he even began, in a laboratory he installed at home, a Faustian study of the secrets of nature.

In the following years, the pietist forms vanished in which Goethe had clothed his discovery of the ultimate dependency of human existence. However, the experience of the separation of man from the creator and of man's intensive desire for reunion had left an indelible mark on him. In *Faust*, *Prometheus*, *Mahomet*, and *Werther*, Goethe touched upon the riddle which human existence is in itself.[23] He abandoned his Faustian alchemism when he began at Weimar his serious and consistent studies of nature, but he retained the fundamental concepts and terms of the Renaissance philosophers of nature, and their understanding of the organic universe as an emanation of the divine spirit remained the core of his own thinking. Thrown back upon the ultimate resources granted to the human being, he accepted the best part of his self as a gift, with that genuine piety which came to form the basis of his own religious expression. During the crisis of his twentieth year he had learned to resign himself completely "to the wisdom of his God which flows in everywhere";[24] the mystic way of life had taught him to distinguish between man's own wishes and ideas and those thoughts which appear to come to him from a higher source.

Thus was laid the ground on which Herder's inspiration and criticism could bring about the last step toward independence and creativity. Goethe could then proceed from the experience of himself as a creature to the recognition of the forms of nature and culture as parts of a dynamic universe. He began to realize that the formative energies which produce nature and culture were identical with the spirit for which he was longing and even praying, and which, finally, came to speak "through him." Two seemingly contrasting aspects of his character could now unite: the vitality of his attachment to nature and men, and the sensitivity of his inner consciousness reaching to the depths of solitude. The religious experience of the marginal situation of man had opened up an ultimate depth in himself; the discovery, in Herder's stimulating companionship, of the universal origin and significance of art, language, poetry, and prophetic religion, strengthened his faith in the legitimacy of his own poetical inspiration.

From now on, Goethe experienced inner and outer life with the immediacy characteristic of the poet who is unprotected by the shells which are most men's indispensable safeguard against the overflow of their inner and outer sensitivity.[25] Goethe needed to develop all his power of self-observation and self-control before he could balance his excessive receptivity and his expansive energy with a firm cognition of nature, man, and society and their interrelationship within the encompassing whole. The poise of his later years was won through a self-education which reconciled his creative urge with the measured form by deliberate mastery of both. He learned to balance the burden of his sensibility to grave and overwhelming experiences by inventiveness in working out a free and yet sociable way of living.

What chance and genius gave him, Goethe tried to hold, to develop, and to render productive through self-knowledge and self-discipline. In *Poetry and Truth* he tells of the stoical training in bearing physical pain which he gave himself as a boy. Later on he took courses in anatomy to overcome his horror of dissection. The writing of *The Sorrows of Young Werther* was the final act in his struggle against a passionate love and a powerful temptation to despair. The letters to Charlotte von Stein and the diaries of his first decade at Weimar reveal the effort and thought necessary to reach a balance which he could consider sound and productive. Many a strange habit of his later years—such as his high regard for time, his formality in social relations, his esteem of work as a remedy against suffering, his self-isolation in moments of distress—was an economy to protect him from the consequences of his fame and position as well as from impressions which, without such protection, might become overpowering and destructive. The sensibility of Goethe's inner organization was the source of his troubles as well as of his creative achievements; his capacity for love and friendship and his piety arose from the same depth of feeling which impelled him to free himself through the creative act of the artist.

Goethe focused his self-knowledge on his contacts with the world: the maxim "Know thyself" should not lead to a false introspection.[26] His experiences of men and nature, of historical tradition and poetic motives took on an objective character in his memory. He could carry them within himself "for forty or fifty years"; he could reconstruct them without changing their substance, until they had attained the mature form in which they could be presented to the world. This detachment of his mind from his own experience and creative products illustrates Goethe's relation to himself as that of one who assists himself in his natural growth, almost as one friend helps another. Goethe consciously observed his own subconscious being with the reverence he had for all the phenomena of life and with an irony and distance which lifted him above himself. Irony and, especially in his youth, self-irony were as much the support of his self-objectification as were his talent for friendship and his religious impulse.[27]

The most striking quality of the young Goethe was, perhaps, his elasticity in exhausting the significance of the lived moment. This capacity mirrors the outstanding characteristic of his mother, who knew how to find in life stimuli to thought and action of which others, lacking her uninhibited devotion to life, never became aware. To Bettina von Arnim, who elicited from her the story of Goethe's youth, she spoke of occurrences which seem so small outwardly that they are not even mentioned, while within they do their work so skillfully and secretly that they are hardly felt and, precisely therefore, often determine "a person's heart and hence his whole fate."

When I enter a group of bores to whom the rising sun is no longer a miracle, to whom the approach of the evening is no joyous confirmation that God has not yet abandoned the world, then my soul says to itself: Yes, yes, go right on believing you know all about the world. If you only knew what the councilor's wife has experienced today![28]

The son responded with the same attentiveness and with stringent self-discipline to an even greater sensitivity. What nature bestows on man, he felt, is unmerited, and for it he owes praise to the creator. Only the severest test of life, his victory over himself, is to man's own credit. Through it he attains freedom from the forces which dominate all beings in the conflict between the expansive energies of the individual and the dynamism of the world resisting them:

Denn alle Kraft dringt vorwärts in die Weite,
Zu leben und zu wirken hier und dort;
Dagegen engt und hemmt von jeder Seite
Der Strom der Welt und reisst uns mit sich fort.
In diesem innern Sturm und äussern Streite
Vernimmt der Geist ein schwer verstanden Wort:
Von der Gewalt, die alle Wesen bindet,
Befreit der Mensch sich, der sich überwindet.[29]

This insistence upon freedom through self-mastery, expressed in the fragment "Die Geheimnisse" (1785), is the
ethical epitome of the experience and resolution which
Goethe gained from the first decades of his life. It pronounces the principle of resignation, *Entsagung*, which he
had come to recognize as an imperative inherent in the
structure of human life and as the precondition of a wholesome way of existence. The sorrow accompanying the
necessity of resignation reverberates in *Werther* and *Faust*;
Tasso's inability to obey this law is his tragedy; the art of
resignation is the supreme aim of education and communal
life in *Wilhelm Meister*, the work whose second part bears
the subtitle, "The Resigned Ones," *Die Entsagenden.*

The object of this resignation is the impetuous self. The
aim of resignation is the fulfillment of life, and of individual
life in so far as it forms a part of the idea of mankind. The
personality of the individual attains its highest value through
self-surrendering devotion. Throughout his life, Goethe
learned that man's own self attains and receives value only
by lavish giving, as Hatem, in the *Divan* poem, says of
Suleika's love:

Wie sie sich an mich verschwendet
Bin ich mir ein wertes Ich.[30]

Love leads the individual beyond himself. The exigencies of
fate bring forth our inner potentialities if we face necessity
and, instead of wanting what we desire, use our capacity

"of wanting that which we know should be." "Duty means loving that which one makes imperative upon one's self."[31] The demand that man recognize and formulate for himself his ethical responsibility is part of his freedom. The strictness of Goethe's conception of resignation, saturated with life-experience as it is, transforms the mystic teaching of obedience which he learned to understand in the religious crisis of his youth, into a maxim guiding the life of the individual and of society. Personality is an instrument in the hand of the ineffable core of Being, the demiurge, rather than an end in itself. The longing for union with the original pure source of being will never be silent: "What is alive keeps longing for death in the flames." Personality is, in fact, a dynamic process, a continuous rhythmical interchange between inner core and outer expansion. By accepting the law of his existence, man recognizes that he is subject to a universal rhythm. In his poem "Selige Sehnsucht," the old Goethe praised such acceptance of the flux of life between birth and death.

> *Und solang du das nicht hast,*
> *Dieses: Stirb und werde!*
> *Bist du nur ein trüber Gast*
> *Auf der dunklen Erde.*[32]

By a Rousseauan outburst of independence, the young Goethe liberated himself from conventional forms for the sake of inner truthfulness. What he gained, however, was not an arbitrary freedom but liberty in the search for man's nature and destiny. Through the study of nature, he tried to confirm and to clarify the experience of the norm, the guiding standard which, he felt, was the intention of nature in himself. The development of his morphological thought and knowledge made it possible for him, at the age of sixty, to approach the history of his own life in the spirit of a student of man. He tried to see the typical in his individual growth and to approach the universal law of formation to

which man, like the rest of nature, is subject. The child
which Goethe described in *Poetry and Truth* "had become
important." Goethe, however, considered great men to be
different from others only in their scope. "They have virtues and vices in common with the smallest man, only they
have them in greater quantities."[33] Thus his autobiography
came to be simultaneously a confession, a historical narrative, and a book of philosophic contemplation.[34]

Goethe's morphological conception of personality is
based upon his conviction of the correspondence of outer
and inner form. We have an inner feeling of unity. We approach this unity in others like the portraitist, by concentrating on the essential, "original," form of a being and
distinguishing it from its contingent variations. By this art
of intuition, which Goethe calls morphological, we arrive
at an image of the other person and we presume that it
comes close to the unity which the other one feels in himself. This entity of life, subject to organic growth from
within and to interference from without, is called *Gestalt*.
Nature produces species and individuals of species, each of
which has its unmistakable and determining form. Through
individuation, the universal creative power manifests itself.
The germ of each creature determines the basic law of its
future transformations. *Gestalt* is a living form, unfolding
through evolution, changing and yet remaining identical in
its essence. It is, in the human world, the carrier of a "demonic" energy which from the day of birth inescapably
fashions man's way of being, feeling, and acting:

> *Wie an dem Tag, der dich der Welt verliehen,*
> *Die Sonne stand zum Grusse der Planeten,*
> *Bist alsobald und fort und fort gediehen*
> *Nach dem Gesetz, wonach du angetreten.*
> *So musst du sein, dir kannst du nicht entfliehen,*
> *So sagten schon Sybillen, so Propheten;*
> *Und keine Zeit und keine Macht zerstückelt*
> *Geprägte Form, die lebend sich entwickelt.*[35]

Through all the kingdoms of nature, Goethe studied the manifestations of the basic formative power from which all forms derive their existence. Man is part of nature and subject to the law of evolution inherent in his typical and individual form of being. On each level of nature Goethe observed a law of compensation which balances the shortcomings of a species by other qualities. Man's physical shortcomings are balanced by his mental power. As the highest product of organic nature he is given the privilege, within definite limitations, of forming himself with the aid of his cognitive faculties. He is capable of grasping the highest thought to which nature creatively elevated itself. Related to the whole of the created universe, he is able to think in terms of the universe. Harboring in himself the universe, as a microcosm corresponding to the macrocosm, he may approach, in the depth of his self, a spiritual certainty which is outside his conscious reach. It manifests itself as "given" and forms the basis of man's feeling of selfhood. Man attains fulfillment by transcending his personality in devotion to forces emanating from a higher order.

With Goethe, this religious experience, mystic in character, took the form of a guidance which acted upon him as an inner compulsion beyond hope and despair. The life of man is a venture; he takes his most important steps into an unknown and dangerous future. Wind and waves may play with his boat, they must not play with his heart:

> Mit dem Schiffe spielen Wind und Wellen,
> Wind und Wellen nicht mit seinem Herzen,
> Herrschend blickt er auf die grimme Tiefe
> Und vertrauet scheiternd oder landend
> Seinen Göttern.[36]

Whatever his fate may be, Goethe exclaims in this poem, he keeps his trust in his gods. From them comes a command which is unconditional, although its full content is disclosed only in the course of life.

Goethe was able to live on the basis of his personality because he had arrived at a lasting religious certainty. The strength of faith released in him was fundamental to the course he took. He confirmed it in his work by many symbols through which he sought to name a nameless experience. The very strength of the religious phenomenon which he discovered through the consciousness of his own existence, made him sensitive to the anthropomorphisms of established formulations and guided him in the creation of independent expressions of his faith.

2

The Experience of Faith

The Urge to Form—The Eye—God in Nature
Pietism and Goethe's View
of Christ—Communication and Solitude

MORPHOLOGICAL INTUITION and the inner feeling of personality helped Goethe to understand the intention inherent in
the nature of man, and became a guide for him in the conduct of life. His destiny revealed itself to him through the
process of life, his personality was involved in a rhythm of
self-alienation and return, and the integration of his self was
a never-ending task. Many of his lyrical poems were produced as acts of reintegration; the problem of reconciliation, recurrent in his dramas, emerged from his own life. He
conceived of the poet, to whom "a god granted the gift of
saying what he suffers,"[1] as a being that lives vicariously.
For Goethe himself, his creative work often had a liturgical
function. It was a resilient spiritual strength which enabled
him to regain balance and confidence and to render error
and guilt productive.

In a description of himself, written in the third person at
the age of forty-eight, Goethe defined the urge to form as
primary in his personality:

A constantly active poetic urge to give form to both the
inner and the outer life is the center and basis of his existence.
Once one has understood this, all the other apparent contradictions dissolve.[2]

The urge to form was the one quality that he dared attribute to the deity, which in its transcendence and infinity otherwise remained, he felt, beyond human definition:

What do we know of the idea of the divine, and what could our narrow concepts convey of the highest being! If I wanted to name it like a Turk by a hundred names, I would fall short, and would not have said anything in comparison with such boundless qualities.[3]

Goethe's conviction of the correspondence between the human microcosm and the universal macrocosm explains why he considered his own urge to form as similar in nature to the creative urge he saw at work in the demiurge.

In this "Self-Description" of 1797, Goethe further characterized his own personality as

determined by a sensibility and flexibility which is immediately affected by the atmosphere of the object and, consequently, must either flee it or unite with it.

In other words, he emphasized his tendency toward a decisive and active response to the outer world. The functions of cognition, feeling, and judgment co-operate in Goethe's urge to form, which is the organ of his experience. It compels him to learn through practice, and also leads him into false tendencies:

toward the fine arts for which he has no talent, toward active life for which he has no adaptability, toward the sciences for which he has not enough persistence.

In this merciless and penetrating account of himself, Goethe recognized that even his false tendencies had not been without productive results. Thus he realized his lack of talent for the fine arts only when he had worked at them long enough to grasp their objectives and methods comprehensively: "Only thereby did his sympathetic observation attain its purity." His scientific studies taught him that in this field the formation of the investigating mind is more important than the subjects themselves, and he confesses that as a consequence he had organized better what theretofore had been "merely an indefinite and accidental aspiration."

Unfortunately his nature unfolded in regard to content and form through many obstacles and difficulties, and only later, when the time of the greatest energy had passed, could it work with any consciousness.

His slowness in arriving at full consciousness of his own potentialities and limitations, which Goethe regretted in this autobiographical account, appears to be an inevitable consequence of the experimental way of living which he chose.

As we have seen, Goethe discovered the significance of this urge as the power of genius after the religious crisis of his adolescence. Many of his early writings reveal that Goethe's formative power arose from a realm of religious inwardness, the purity of which was in tension with the outer world and even with his own outer activities. His susceptible senses, his exuberant youth, his brilliant mind drew him into life and yet each of his activities also had the aspect of a separation from himself. From this inner tension there arose his first poetical figures. Prometheus and Faust insist on their independence, and suffer under it; Mahomet begins with the purest intention and is inevitably involved in guilt; the returning Christ, in Goethe's epical fragment, "The Eternal Jew," is no more acceptable to men on his second coming than he was when he was crucified for the first time.[4] Ganymede, the incarnation of man's longing for union with the divine, and Prometheus, the epitome of independence, date in all likelihood from the same year. In Goethe himself this tension lasted far into his first years at Weimar: In August, 1780, he completed the satirical comedy *The Birds,* and in the beginning of September he withdrew into an ultimate of inner calm in the poem "Über allen Gipfeln ist Ruh."

To work out the tension between inner and outer experience and to arrive at a synthesis of his personality, meant for Goethe to aim at forming a cosmic view of life on the basis of his own experience and thought. He was driven toward universality by the exigencies of his own character. In retrospect, his growth toward it appears to him as organic; its individual steps, however, were taken without foreknowledge of their function in the whole of his life until, in the years following his Italian journey, his self-knowledge attained a degree of certainty permitting the "calmer flow" of existence which characterizes his later years. The productive tension of Goethe's personality made itself felt in his earlier life as a conflict between his genuine and unprejudiced religious sense and the organs with which he addressed himself to the outer world: eye and language. When Goethe's inner sense which, in the manner of mystics, he associated with the quality of "purity," discovered a corresponding purity in the outer world, his own nature succeeded in the reconciliation it sought.

Goethe's urge to develop the art of seeing early became manifest in, for instance, the intensity with which he grasped the language of the visible form in art and architecture at Dresden and responded to the inspiring experience of the cathedral of Strassburg by his essay on "Ancient German Architecture."[5] His perception, however, had the peculiarity of proceeding from the whole to the details, from the essential to the peripheral, and his efforts in design were devoted to bringing into harmony the strong intuition of the totality of his subject and the disciplined observation of the particular—a task which was repeated in his study of nature. What Goethe's eye perceives is already being transformed into an image in his inner vision before his attention is blurred by detail.[6] His morphological intuition, his art of conceiving *Gestalt* and "original phenomenon" in things and people, his impulse to penetrate to their "inner meaning," are implicit in his way of seeing. On the other hand, Goethe's thinking did not become separated from his seeing:

the elements of the objects and the perceptions become a part of my thinking and are thoroughly penetrated by it, so that my intuition itself is thinking, and my thinking, intuition.[7]

The inner sense, the "eye of the spirit," in continuous co-operation with controlling perception, is the mediator between the inner and outer world and the creative agent of Goethe's thinking in images. His eye produced these images and brought them before his mind, and he was able to call them forth in his visual memory. These visions, moving on the borderline between dream and reality, were essential to his way of poetic production and to the expression he gave to his religious experience. From a letter to Charlotte von Stein, written ten weeks before his departure for Italy, it is evident how great an importance the achievements of his art of seeing in botany took on for him in general:

The infinite domain [of the world of plants] becomes simplified in my soul so that soon I can delineate the most difficult problem. If I could only tell someone of the vision and the joy, but it is not possible. And it is no dream and no fantasy; it is a way of becoming aware of the essential forms with which nature, as it were, plays and in playing produces manifold life. If I had time in the short span of life, I am confident that I could extend this study to all the kingdoms, to the whole realm, of nature.[8]

The eye, however, is also the most eloquent expression of man's self. Through its outward radiance it reveals the inner light. With the light of his vision man responds to the light of the universe. It is because his inner vision creatively mirrors the universe that he becomes aware of the normative content of the phenomena around him, of the intention which creative nature pursues. The eye is able to grasp the light of the sun because it is akin to the sun.

The eye owes its being to the light. Out of insignificant organs of the animal body, the light calls forth an organ which is to become its equal; thus the eye forms itself through the light for the light, so that the inner light may face the outer light.

Thereby we are reminded of the ancient Ionian school which ever and again repeated with so much emphasis the belief that only equal can know equal, and also of the words of an ancient mystic which, in German rhymes, we may express as follows:

> *Wär nicht das Auge sonnenhaft,*
> *Wie könnten wir das Licht erblicken?*
> *Lebt' nicht in uns des Gottes eigne Kraft,*
> *Wie könnt uns Göttliches entzücken?*

No one will deny this immediate kinship between the light and the eye; it is more difficult to think of them both as one and the same thing. This is more comprehensible, however, if we say that, in the eye, there dwells a resting light which is aroused by the smallest cause from within or from without. In the dark we are able to call forth, at the demand of our power of imagination, the clearest images. When we dream, objects appear to us as though in clear daylight. When we wake, we sense the slightest outer impact of light; even if the eye receives a mechanical impulse, light and colors emerge.[9]

The eye is the agent of reconciliation between inner and outer experience. It is the seat of creation for a language of images through which the human microcosm realizes the universe latent in man. Therefore, to Goethe, the act of seeing has a religious significance; the praise which Lynkeus gives to the eyes in the fifth act of *Faust II* expresses the religious conception of nature as a divine manifestation.[10] Goethe's urge to form found productive scope in the intuition of this archetypal world of manifestation; through it, his religious inwardness was reconciled with his sensitivity for the living phenomenon and his personality developed toward integration.

On his way toward the realization of these potentialities, Goethe passed through a critical and important phase of friendship with Johann Kaspar Lavater, the Zürich preacher and pietist, and Friedrich Heinrich Jacobi, the philosopher and writer. Lavater was a noble character full of missionary zeal, intent upon converting great numbers, as well as the outstanding individual Goethe, to his cult of Christ and his view of mankind. Incessantly active in public for his religious mission, he had wide connections in the world of letters. On his talent for psychological intuition and his interest in face and figure, he based an extensive work on physiognomy, in which Goethe collaborated. Jacobi, the son of a merchant family on the lower Rhine, was a correspondent and friend of Johann Georg Hamann, the East Prussian mystic, and of Franciscus Hemsterhuis, the Dutch philosopher. He himself was to become a leading figure in the irrationalist movement pervading European thought toward the end of the eighteenth century. On the basis of his conviction that through feeling we are immediately given a certainty of faith beyond proof, he opposed Kant's transcendental criticism and, later, Schelling's philosophy of nature. Through the contact with both these men the results of Goethe's religious crisis were brought into a new focus; each of them was strong enough to challenge Goethe's own convictions and thus to contribute to their further development.

The pietist communities, with which Lavater had more direct contact than Jacobi, emphasized inner feeling rather than theological dogma. They were in agreement with the Protestant churches in that they judged worldly life as inextricably sinful, considered man a potential recipient of divine grace, and accepted the Bible as the revealed word of God. They envisioned Christ, however, in terms of the spiritualistic interpretation of John's Gospel, and cultivated the practice of religious brotherhood according to the example of early Christianity. They kept aloof from the established doctrines and from church communities, or else formed separate groups within them. The attention which, in opposition to ritualism and theological rationalism, the pietists gave to religious feeling, refined their capacity for observing and judging these inner processes. With a frankness almost incomprehensible to twentieth-century men, the pietist brethren were concerned for each other's religious development.

Since the time of his friendship with Langer, this atmosphere was by no means strange to Goethe, and in the earlier parts of his correspondence with Lavater he fell in with this concern for the most intangible movements of the soul and spoke the language which arose from it. He concurred with the pietists in their criticism of the established churches. In charging the church with the persecution of "the dearest witnesses and messengers of Christ," Gottfried Arnold[11] had exercised a lasting influence upon the young Goethe, who understood the idea of the church as the invisible church, the *ecclesia spiritualis*, and shared the hope that "the church of the Cross would transform itself into the church of the Spirit."[12] The vision of an evangelical communion of "those good and wise to the highest degree"[13] was to become the nucleus from which his ideal of a good society developed. The distinction between the religion of Christ and the Christian religion, which was fundamental for Arnold as well as for Lessing, Goethe made his own, and the pietist emphasis on the conduct of life rather than upon doctrine was in accord with his inclination toward tolerance. In the "Ephemerides,"[14] a diary begun with an entry on Paracelsus in 1770, Goethe notes Thomas à Kempis' interpretation of life as a test of that fragile creature, man; and another passage, in which he defends Giordano Bruno against Bayle's misinterpretation, reveals his deep-seated distrust of rationalism.

In the same diary, however, are found entries which fore-shadow Goethe's mature convictions about the relations between God and Nature, and thereby the difference which arose between him and Lavater as well as between him and Jacobi.

It is difficult and dangerous to speak separately of God and the nature of things, and, likewise, to think disjointedly about body and soul. We do not know the soul except through the mediation of the body, nor God without the cognition of nature; therefore it seems absurd to accuse those of absurdity who, with the best philosophical reasoning, associate God with the world.

The Neo-Platonic system of emanation had left its impact on Goethe through the various writings which, as he tells in the eighth book of *Poetry and Truth*, Susanna von Klettenberg and his mother had studied with him. His concern with the Renaissance philosophy and theosophy of nature had developed his sense of universal unity; now it confirmed him in his inclination to go his own way.

He discovered that his closest pietist friends did not agree with each other, whereas he had already formed his own view of Christ. From the meeting of Susanna and Lavater, Goethe learned "how one and the same confession is transformed according to the attitudes of different persons."[15] His religious sensitivity was strengthened by his contacts with pietism; his mental acumen aided him in distinguishing faith from its expression; his sense of soundness warned him against losing himself in religious emotionalism. In the long run, a rift with Lavater was inevitable.[16]

Their friendship and their co-operation in physiognomy were not strong enough to bridge their religious differences. Goethe never doubted that Lavater pursued the noblest aims. But he also observed that Lavater's missionary activity compelled him to conform to the secular realm in order to work for these aims, and he foresaw that his friend would finally have to sacrifice the higher to the lower, the end to the means. The *Mahomet* drama was a reflection of this insight into the tragedy of religious leadership in the course of which, of necessity, "the earthly grows and expands, the divine recedes and is dimmed." For "the heavenly and eternal is immersed in the body of earthly designs and is carried away toward temporal destinies."[17] To Lavater, however, as later to the Stolbergs, Goethe appeared incapable of a decisive step beyond himself. In faithfulness to his own conscience, Goethe had to resist Lavater's urgent demand to follow him in his excessively emotional practice of Christianity.

In his early manhood Goethe considered individual religious experience as hardly compatible with organized religious community. In his old age, as we shall see later, he gave this problem a different solution in the example of the religion practiced in the Pedagogic Province of *Wilhelm Meister*. On the basis of the religious philosophy he developed, however, Goethe retained the view of Christ which he had formed in his contacts with spiritualist tradition and pietist Christianity. In the fragment of "The Eternal Jew," which presents Christ as returning to earth, he opposes the pure Christ to the abuse of power and the misunderstanding of the Savior in which Goethe, like the spiritualists before him, saw the churches involved. From his early poem on Christ's descent into hell to his last conversation with Eckermann, Goethe gives his image of the pure Christ an affirmative meaning. Historically, he sees Christ as the wise teacher and the victor over suffering, and it is as such an exemplary being that the God-man is described in *Wilhelm Meister*. There he is the model of man's potential devotion to the purest and highest spirit. From a cosmic standpoint, Goethe sees Christ as the spirit of a pneumatic energy, as he is represented in John's Gospel. Goethe's Christ, however, is not the exclusive mediator between man and God. It was precisely at this point that Goethe differed from Lavater's piety and Jacobi's supernaturalism.[18]

Ever and again Goethe refers to John's Gospel. His experience of the spirit as transcending personality suggested the use of symbols which ultimately derive from Plotinus' intelligible world of pure spirits.[19] The ascension of Faust forms an integral part not only of the drama but of Goethe's view of the universe. The magic formula which Faust uses to elicit from the poodle his true being, Mephisto, applies spiritualist theology.[20] Christ as the "Uncreated" is identical with the creator and inherent in the sphere where the reconciling act of the world drama occurs; "poured forth through all the heavens," he is identical with the Holy Spirit; as the Spirit, he is "unexpressed," ineffable. The indestructible reality of the spirit—this is the meaning conveyed by the resurrection of the triumphant Christ. Goethe understood the resurrection to be "the basic result of the Christian religion, the core of the gospel."[21] To him the spiritual dimension of man is incontestable; hence he retains a spiritual conception of Christ, over and above his criticism against, and his distance from, church and dogma. His conception of nature certainly excluded a supernatural understanding of Christ; his conception of the spirit as inherent in the universal polarity excluded also a magical relationship to Christ. The Johannine Christ of the spirit, however, was and remained significant for Goethe.

The religious side of Goethe's personal development was not easily understood until recent times. For he remained the "child of the world"; in his youth he was just as secretive about decisive matters as in his old age, and he balanced any temptation to attach himself to formulas, or even to dwell on moments of great emotional significance, by critical observation and irony. Continuously thrown "from one extreme to the other"[22] by his own nature, he periodically looked through his papers and "burned all old shells." He did so in Leipzig, in his landlady's kitchen stove, radically resigning what he had loved and judged good to the moment, which demanded a complete change of mind. He re-

peated this auto-da-fé before his departure for Strassburg:
fragments and outlines of plays, poems and letters went up
in flames. At the age of thirty, in his Weimar garden house,
he surveyed his life while going through the documents of
the pre-Weimar years and destroying most of them: "Other
times, other worries."

A calm backward glance on life, on the confusion, the activity, the thirst for knowledge of youth which roams everywhere
in search of something satisfactory. How I especially liked to
indulge in secrets, in dark, imaginative situations. How I approached everything scholarly in a halfhearted fashion and
let it go again. How a kind of humble self-complacency pervaded everything I then wrote. How shortsightedly I ran in
circles in regard to everything human and divine. How little
there was of action and purposeful thinking; how many days
were wasted in time-destroying feeling and the shadow of passion; how little of it proved helpful. And now with half of life
already past, no headway has been made but rather I stand like
one who has just managed to save himself from the water and
whom the sun kindly begins to dry.[23]

Goethe balanced this verdict by the "idea of purity"
which he felt in himself and on which he prayed that "more
light" might be thrown. Others looked on him with suspicion or cool hostility. An ally of his literary enemy
Nicolai reported that Goethe might become "a freethinker
as easily as a Herrnhut pietist—were it not for his pride."[24]
Nicolai's correspondent had at least discovered Goethe's ob-
stinate energy in his literary pursuits, but otherwise was
unable to find any philosophic steadiness in the versatile
youth who seemed to switch from one extreme to the other:
he used the same words which in retrospect Goethe himself
used. In fact, Goethe at this age with equal spontaneity expressed his capabilities in poetic productions and literary
fights, in the life of society and intimate relations with
friends. Intent upon experiencing life with the totality of
his being, he came to know it in all its contrasts.

In regard to the development of Goethe's personality, this epoch of ferment seems like an illustration of a statement by which, in his old age, he intended to emphasize the active and dynamic nature of man's relation with the outer world:

Man comes to know himself only in so far as he knows the world; he becomes aware of the world only through himself, and of himself only through the world. Each new object, well observed, releases a new capacity in us.[25]

He was a devoted friend of such opposite characters as the devout Susanna and the "Mephistophelian" Merck, the Darmstadt entrepreneur and art critic. With the same inner freedom he traveled with members of the high aristocracy or brought to his mother's house a poor boy who had impressed him. The quickness of his mind prevented him from tolerating anything stale; the depth of his feeling made it impossible for him to lose himself in anything trivial. Goethe's energy in seizing upon life in its most diversified aspects was accompanied by a genuine affection for people. It was easy for the young Goethe "to let everyone pass for what he was or even for what he pretended to be."[26] In his youthful spontaneity, he was not domineering; his friends felt themselves understood, and Goethe was too considerate to touch unnecessarily upon deeper divergences. When, in Strassburg, he met Jung-Stilling, the pietist eye doctor, religious writer, and political economist, he quickly learned to distinguish between Jung's doctrine of divine providence, which he could not share, and the significance which this particular experience of faith had for Jung himself as the center of his vitality.[27] By instinct, Goethe looked for the productive possibilities of human relationships and avoided useless strife.

On the other hand, his irony was a strong means of detachment. In his "Satyros" Goethe attacked the prophetic rhetoric of the enthusiasm for nature from which he was not so distant himself.[28] When the people follow the deified Satyros' teachings and discover a universe in eating raw chestnuts, Goethe puts in the prophet's mouth words which reflect his own and lasting cosmogonic views. In the end, he unmasks Satyros as "an uncouth, shameless animal." In Satyros we find a satirical portrait of Herder; in the hermit, who discovers the truth, an ironical treatment of Goethe himself. But along with this ridicule of human credulity, there is a sincere tone of conviction.

This sense of contradiction and paradox is actually "Mephistophelian." In Goethe's development it had a function not unlike that of Faust's companion in the drama—the negating function which stimulates the more vital abilities. Goethe's irony is the other pole of his reverence, and in matters religious it accentuated his sense of the discrepancy between the lived faith and its representation. In his youth, Goethe did not care how one thought about faith, if only one had it. Thus he could say concerning the sons of a friend: "Whether they believe in Christ or in Götz or in Hamlet does not matter. Only let them have faith in something. A man who does not believe in anything, despairs of himself."[29] Goethe experienced faith as an energy, and he regarded thought about faith as prone to emotional and intellectual anthropomorphism. He early sensed the danger that man, giving the relative forms of his symbols to his thought of the absolute, may come to the point where he identifies words with the absolute.

Both the power and the depth of Goethe's personality are revealed in the outstanding moment of his meeting with Jacobi. It led to communion at the most profound level. Goethe speaks of this meeting in a somewhat veiled fashion in the fourteenth book of *Poetry and Truth*, and Jacobi's description of it in letters corresponds to Goethe's few but eloquent hints. Traveling down the Lahn River with Lavater and other friends, Goethe dictated verses. As the boat floated by the castles that lined the banks, the knights who once lived in them came to life in his mind and he improvised the poem "Geistesgruss," which anticipated the ballad "Der König in Thule," recited a few days later in Düsseldorf.[30] He met the Jacobis in Cologne, and together all of them visited the house of an old Cologne family, the Jabachs, which had been carefully preserved as they had left it, with a portrait of the old Jabach and his family that showed them in the fullness of life. This whole experience seems to have effaced Goethe's consciousness of time. With "the most tender and beautiful emotion," past and present merged into one.

I do not know how to recount my reactions to these overwhelming impressions. Through the infinite motion of my heart, the deepest ground of my human gifts and my poetic talents was uncovered, and everything good and loving was disclosed and broke forth.[31]

This was a meeting of souls and minds which surpassed the ordinary and rationally comprehensible. The feeling of the temporality of human existence and the vivid re-emergence of lives long past released Goethe's "prophetic" spontaneousness with overwhelming strength. His silence about his own words is as significant as their distinct echo in the others. A human relationship arose which was beyond expectation and surpassed prior experience. With the barriers between the individuals broken down, Goethe's creative thought began to flow unhindered toward his friends. The secret of the freedom of creative speech, the immediacy of the active spirit, manifested itself with revealing strength. When the barriers of man's personality fall, it seems that he is lifted to a higher level.

In this communion of minds Fritz Jacobi acted as the releasing and responsive partner. An exchange of thoughts followed, for which Spinoza's conception of the universe served as a medium. Under the impact of these days, Jacobi described how Goethe's genius impressed itself irresistibly upon him. He characterized Goethe to Wieland as "one possessed, who is almost never permitted to act arbitrarily."[32] Shortly before, Lavater, applying to Goethe the term which Michelangelo's friends had used to describe his impact upon them, had said: "You would adore the doctor Goethe. He is the most *terrible* and the most amiable human being." Jacobi, however, felt that through his meeting with Goethe his soul was, as it were, renewed. The radiance of Goethe's personality and the restraint exercised over it by his genius impressed other contemporaries with equal force. But only of Jacobi did Goethe himself say that "his nature like my own operated on the deepest level."

Goethe's faithfulness to the moment which had broken his inner solitude and to the man who had brought this about outlasted the divergence which, soon afterward, arose between them in matters religious and philosophical and endangered and restricted their relationship. Even then, the inner truth from which their friendship had emerged kept them united, though the development of their thought separated them. But Goethe's tolerance came to an end when Jacobi, in his attack on Schelling in 1812, turned against convictions which Goethe himself had "taken as guiding principles of his life and endeavor." Goethe replied with the poem "Gross ist die Diana der Epheser."[33] In a letter of the same period, he expressed the hope that their differences might be balanced as before "by affection and love." But he made it unmistakably clear where the points of irreconcilable difference lay. The Ephesian goldsmith continues to work on the statue of his goddess, undisturbed by the alarming news that a new god has seized the public mind, a god in man's foolish brains—

Als gäbs einen Gott so im Gehirn
Da! hinter des Menschen alberner Stirn,

Der sei viel herrlicher als das Wesen,
An dem wir die Breite der Gottheit lesen.

Goethe sees divinity at work in the whole of creation and
he reads it in the breadth of its manifestations. He himself
feels that he is engaged in the religious act of adorning the
symbol of the divine, and he asks only for unhindered freedom in working out his reverence in his own way. The
uniqueness of Christ as the mediator between man and God
was the core of Lavater's worship. Goethe could not share
this simple faith, in spite of his profound conception of the
"pure Christ." He shared with Jacobi faith in the immediacy of the spirit. But Jacobi's insistence on the exclusion
of nature from the divine revelation brought about the tension between them. Slowly their active interest in each
other subsided and finally vanished altogether.

It was the spirit which Jacobi had in mind, and nature which
I had in mind. What should have united us, separated us. . . .
Whoever aims at the highest must aim at the whole: whoever
deals with the spirit must presuppose nature, and whoever
speaks of nature must presuppose the spirit.[34]

Faith revealed itself to Goethe as an integrating power
beyond argument, as the ultimate source of creativity, of
wisdom, and of hope. He experienced in it the strength of
the spirit which he saw manifest in all the realm of nature.
The image which came closest to expressing his own understanding of divinity was that of God as an artist. Thus he
could not exclude nature from divine revelation, which he
recognized even in plants and stones, *in herbis et lapidibus.*[35]
His inner experience taught him that there is a bond between man and the supreme power of the creator. Man
becomes aware of this bond in the purity of his heart. But
his finite cognition cannot penetrate to the infinity of Being; he can only contemplate the manifestations of Being.
Goethe's experience of the spirit, the "prevalence of the

higher guiding power of man,"[36] helped him to reach a constructive synthesis of his manifold pursuits. This experience was for him the center in which the inner and outer worlds converged; it made it possible for him to conceive of the action of poetry and thought as a creative reflection of the universe; it revealed to him a criterion of judgment in the free encounter with nature, men, and their creations. To the experience of the transcendent he gave forms of his own, and he considered it wise to conceal his deepest convictions behind the figures and symbols through which he conveyed them to the sympathetic mind. The immediate and creative character of Goethe's experience of faith makes his productivity as a religious genius a part of the history of faith. He was able to relive in religious personalities and ideas of the past—in the Mosaic legislation, in Greek mythology, in the cult of the ancient Persians, in Indian legend—the fundamental simplicity by which faith responds to the human situation. His own religious independence engendered the universality of his religious thought.

All epochs which are governed by faith, whatever its form, are brilliant, heart-stirring, and productive for contemporaries and for posterity.[37]

3

Art and Poetry

The Wanderer—Man and Time—Genius and Language
The Artist and the Original Phenomenon

GOETHE'S RESOLUTION to live and to speak out of an independent religious faith thrust him upon ineffable ground. Much as he made his own the religious thought of the Christian heritage, deeply as he came to understand non-Christian religions, it was his personal experience that he made the arbiter of decisions about religious and philosophic personalities and ideas past and present. When he conveyed to Lavater as a momentous discovery the phrase *individuum est ineffabile*,[1] he added that from this word he derives "a world." He renounced for himself the sheltered way of life which organized religious communities offer and ventured upon the open sea of unhindered and unprotected encounter with inner and outer life. We sense in him an urge to experience the ultimate reality of human existence in his own way, to expose himself to this experience, and to take the risk it involved. His resoluteness made him impatient with convention in spite of the tolerant tribute he could pay to society; it made him impatient with his own actions and works and prompted him ever and again "to burn the old shells." This unsheltered existence was the price of the freshness of his productivity, of his capacity to put new life into old poetic forms and to create new ones, of the releasing and formative effect of his personality on his work.

The consequence of this inner freedom was an ultimate solitude. A personality able and willing to experience its own ineffable depth cannot feel attached to places or circumstances. Goethe, who conceived of himself as a wanderer, was wholly at home nowhere but in his creative activities. His sense of the temporality of human existence, his conviction that "time is the highest gift we receive from God,"[2] was an essential part of the value he attached to life in general. The conclusion he drew from this awareness of the everlasting flux of time was the conviction that man ought to live fruitfully. For himself fruitful living consisted in the acceptance of the fate of the creative mind, of his homelessness in the temporal and his wandering through it. In *Poetry and Truth* he tells how he was described by his friends in the years before Weimar:

I often was called the confidant or, because of my strolling about in the region, the wanderer. As I walked, I used to sing hymns to myself, of which one survives under the title "Wanderers Sturmlied."[3]

The wanderer's awareness of the human situation makes him a trusted and disinterested friend. When Goethe, in *Wilhelm Meister's Travels*, resumed the symbol of wandering as generally representative of human existence, he formulated an experience basic to all his life. The poem "Wanderers Sturmlied"—this "half nonsense," as he called it in his autobiography—reveals where he sought a sanctuary to shelter the poet.

The free rhythms of this poem, sung in a hail- and rainstorm, invoke the transcendent source of the poetic genius. Genius gives the poet shelter and energy, a ground to stand on, the warmth in the snowstorm which attracts the muses. The muses are "pure like the heart of the waters and like the pith of the earth"; soaring like the gods, the poet is lifted up to them. If genius is with him, he is charmed against rain and storm, like the lark.

Wen du nicht verlässest, Genius,
Nicht der Regen, nicht der Sturm
Haucht ihm Schauer übers Herz.
Wen du nicht verlässest, Genius,
Wird dem Regengewölk,
Wird dem Schlossensturm
Entgegen singen,
Wie die Lerche,
Du da droben.

Goethe appeals to a genius who may abandon the poet, to an inspiring power not of his own making. This he feels to be the source of poetry and of that enthusiasm which reaches the sphere of purity. Two divinities are named who, opposed to each other, govern the realm of poetry: father Bromius, the "genius of the century," an epithet of Dionysos as appearing in orgiastic uproar; and Phoebus Apollo, the "prince" of poetry, the classical divinity of lucidity and form.

The first two parts of the poem disclose that Goethe believes the substance of poetry to be the gift of genius. The proper home of genius is the realm of purity, a sphere which throughout Goethe's work stands in contrast with the troubled and perturbed domain of actual life, in which inner and outer forces mingle. He sees Bromius, the Dionysian divinity, rule his age; he hints at the "return to nature" in the figure of "the small, dark, fiery peasant" who expects only Bromius' gifts. Him alone the poet is not able to follow; so he calls upon the "warmth of his soul" to aspire to union with the Apollonic forces. In this poem of 1772, Goethe anticipated the classical tendencies of his later years, and detached himself from the *Sturm und Drang* while he was still in the midst of it.

The third part of the poem, however, determines the rank and breadth of the poet's aspiration by the invocation to Jupiter, "from whom the song set out, in whom it ends, out of whom it rises." Anacreon and Theocritus, singing to please idle mortals, were not inspired by this storm-breathing godhead. Pindar is the poet whom Goethe sees as his model; in the last stanza he paints a Pindaric picture of the heroic championship of Greek youth mastering the fiery horses and of Pindar's love of the courage that seeks and responds to danger. Jupiter, however, to whom the poem is ultimately dedicated, is the universal and all-embracing godhead, addressed as the biblical "Beginning and End" and understood as the poet's shelter and master:

> *Der du mich fassend deckst,*
> *Jupiter Pluvius!*

Near the universal heavenly power the poet feels that at last he will find himself.

> *Dort auf dem Hügel,*
> *Himmlische Macht!*
> *Nur so viel Glut:*
> *Dort meine Hütte,*
> *Dorthin zu waten!*

In a letter to Herder, written early in July, 1772, Goethe revealed how in a personal inner crisis he had taken Pindar as his guide toward realization of the longing for the high aims of poetry he had expressed in the "Sturmlied." The integration of inner aliveness with Olympian universality and Apollonian clarity which the poem demands is a problem of living rather than of technique. This way of living presupposes that order of the faculties which helps obtain the freedom for which Goethe prays "like Moses in the Koran: Make room, O Lord, in my narrow breast." Pindar says of poets:

> *They speak to the understanding; most men need interpreters.*
> *The wise man knows many things in his blood; the vulgar are taught.*

They will say anything. They chatter vainly like
crows against the sacred bird of Zeus.[4]

These words about the immediacy of wisdom, the innate
knowledge which makes man an interpreter of the hidden
truth, pierced Goethe's soul like swords. "All that there is
of doing in me revives, for I feel nobility and know what
purpose is." "Poor man to whom the head is everything."
Together with the vision of the born poet arises the demand
for totality, anticipating the totality which came to be the
basic conception of the classical to Goethe and Schiller:
"thought and feeling form the expression." It is Pindar's
symbol of the best man that strikes Goethe as the secret of
mastery: the image of the chariot-driver who masters his
"four fresh horses, wild beyond measure, . . . until all six-
teen feet in simultaneous tread attain the goal." He concludes the letter with a humble hint at the inner reason of
his hope:

There is in the depth of my soul much premonition, often
only a flickering, which makes me feel that if only beauty and
greatness interweave themselves more with my feeling I should
without knowing why speak and write what is good and beautiful.[5]

Both the man who "is nothing but head" and the "dark"
man untouched by the light of Apollo are rejected by the
young Goethe, who considers emancipated feeling as insufficient as the intellect for dominating man. When he finds
himself setting as a goal the mere ability to speak without
knowing why, he resolves to follow a higher guiding power.
This power reveals itself in the poems of Pindar and in the
figures of the young Greeks whom the poet praises in his
hymns. It belongs to the energies which bestow mastery
upon man although they are not at his command. In "Wanderers Nachtlied," Goethe conceives of peace as such an
energy of inner calmness descending upon him. In the

"Sturmlied" he sees it as coming to those who are courageously active in exposing themselves to the encounter with inner and outer existence: "To grasp, to seize, is the essence of all mastery," says the letter to Herder.

In "Seefahrt" Goethe knows that guidance is given to him who entrusts himself to the divinities. The "purity" of the poet is, however, the necessary precondition which makes it possible for the element of grace to enter into his poetry. The *Divan* poem "Lied und Gebilde" expresses this paradox of the poet's existence by the image of water forming a ball in the poet's pure hand:

> *Löscht ich so der Seele Brand,*
> *Lied, es wird erschallen;*
> *Schöpft des Dichters reine Hand,*
> *Wasser wird sich ballen.*[6]

The creative process which occurs in the poet is half his own work, half that of a higher force which works through him. A transcendent reality reaches into his temporal existence and strengthens him in reaching beyond the temporal. He is to realize the parallelism of immanence and transcendence and to devote his unprotected self to life as it is with the calmness and resignation which the mystics called *Gelassenheit* or obedience. This mystic simplicity comes wholly to the fore in the *Divan* poetry; the reverence for life which is its basis is also the core of Goethe's early poetry.

The "Wanderer" of the dialogue which bears this name and which was written in the same year as the "Sturmlied" takes a brief rest at the hut of a mother nursing her boy at her breast. They live in the ruins of a temple in the midst of fragments betraying the artistic mastery that had formed them. On this "grave of a holy past" a new life has grown, simple as that of the birds; the wanderer, looking with reverence at the rise of life out of destruction, realizes the double-sidedness of nature which gives birth and destroys, and he dreams of a *temenos*, a sanctuary in the bright but tempered midday sun. The moment of undisturbed happiness he shares while the young mother is his hostess, stands out against the everlasting flux symbolized by the ruins of the ancient temple. Was it Goethe's intention to hint at the common basis of the calm life of mother and child and the sanctuary of bygone times, the pious hope of the living and the devotion of the dead? Seeing both in their universal significance the poet feels a universal sympathy.[7]

The wanderer Faust experiences the bliss of this sympathy in the sublime moment of solitude in "Wald und Höhle," when he praises the spirit who gave him whatever he asked for:

> *Erhabener Geist, du gabst mir, gabst mir alles,*
> *Warum ich bat. Du hast mir nicht umsonst*
> *Dein Angesicht im Feuer zugewendet.*
> *Gabst mir die herrliche Natur zum Königreiche,*
> *Kraft, sie zu fühlen, zu geniessen. Nicht*
> *Kalt staunenden Besuch erlaubst du nur,*
> *Vergönnest mir, in ihre tiefe Brust,*
> *Wie in den Busen eines Freunds, zu schauen.*[8]

In this moment Faust is no longer the despairing seeker he was when he encountered the earth spirit; he has learned to face the phenomena through which nature, the creative spirit, manifests itself—to feel them and to view their depths. The gap between inner and outer experience is narrowed. This monologue was written after Goethe had confirmed his feeling for nature by the study of nature, after the "grasping and seizing" of his letter to Herder had proved to lead him ahead. His advance toward the depths of existence reached its catholicity in the first *Divan* poem, in which the poet "announces the meaning and intention of the whole [work]." There he considers himself as a traveler.[9]

> *Dort im Reinen und im Rechten*
> *Will ich menschlichen Geschlechten*

In des Ursprungs Tiefe dringen,
Wo sie noch von Gott empfingen
Himmelslehr in Erdensprachen,
Und sich nicht den Kopf zerbrachen.

Wo sie Väter hoch verehrten,
Jeden fremden Dienst verwehrten;
Will mich freun der Jugendschranke:
Glaube weit, eng der Gedanke,
Wie das Wort so wichtig dort war,
Weil es ein gesprochen Wort war.[10]

Once more it is in the realm of purity, now united with that of justice, that Goethe looks for the "original" reality of human existence, its *Ursprünglichkeit*. The German prefix *ur* carries connotations not only of time but of value. The intention of the creation, which is original in this sense, is the formation of that society in which the spoken word is the vessel of the word of God and which has significance because of its prophetic origin and character. It arises where the realm assigned to faith is wide and that assigned to thought is narrow. The word becomes the vessel of the higher power when it transcends the human situation out of which it arises; in other words, religious faith is the origin of poetry and art—the faith which makes itself felt as the ultimate guiding element in the life of man.

The impatient craving of the youthful Goethe for the inspiration of genius was answered by the wealth of the poetic creativity that, as he reports in his autobiography, overwhelmed him. The man Goethe, when he studied the forms and transformations of nature and conceived of the whole of nature as the expression of God, was as it were searching for proof in the outer world of his inner experience. The old Goethe widened his reverence to include the universal process as a whole, in its constructive and retroactive, its fathomable and unfathomable qualities. Throughout the stages of Goethe's life it was faith, the nonderivable inner certainty he had in common with the mystics and the simple faithful of all religions, in which he found the justification of the poetical calling. On faith too is based the capacity to recognize the purity which manifests itself through the troubled medium of the phenomenal realm and thus interprets the temporal as a parable of the eternal.

The brief moment, then, which is given to human existence, calls for the proper response through fruitful action. In order to describe man's constructive relation to time, Goethe liked to turn to metaphors from the realm of nature. His relation to the world at large is like that to a living organism, and he regards each of its phenomena, including man himself, as an entity subject to growth and decay, and accessible to the constructive help only of those who possess not merely knowledge of, but reverence for, this organic character of life. Within the limits of man, possibilities are open to make the moment last through the works of the mind and to bring divergent forces together into a fruitful harmony. In the poem "Grenzen der Menschheit," Goethe contrasts the gods who dwell above the waves of time with men who, carried on these waves, are bound to sink into them in the end. In "Edel sei der Mensch" he points to the sources of dignity accessible to the human being within the circle of life granted him. In "Dauer im Wechsel," a poem written around the turn of the century, he brings to completion the theme of time and of man's response to his own temporality.[11]

Nowhere and never will the flow of time halt. We ourselves and the world around us "speed to the elements"; all form is fleeting, like the moment which is unique and never returns: "One never swims twice in the same stream."

> Jene Hand, die gern und milde
> Sich bewegte wohl zu tun,
> Das gegliederte Gebilde,
> Alles ist ein andres nun.
> Und was sich an jener Stelle

Nun mit deinem Namen nennt,
Kam herbei wie eine Welle,
Und nun eilts zum Element.

In the face of the irretrievable moment, however, Goethe calls upon the mind for the significant action of "drawing together into one the end and the beginning." He demands that we conceive of the whole of our life as a unity. Then we will become aware of the promise which the muses give and which lasts imperishably beyond the moment: the living essence in man's breast and the form in his mind.

Lass den Anfang mit dem Ende
Sich in Eins zusammenziehn!
Schneller als die Gegenstände
Selber dich vorüberfliehn.
Danke, dass die Gunst der Musen
Unvergängliches verheisst,
Den Gehalt in deinem Busen
Und die Form in deinem Geist.

In this poem a tone of firmness carries the images of floating time, which swiftly follow each other as moment follows moment. The perspicuity with which Goethe faces the universal law lifts him above the sorrow temporality causes to the reality of substance and spirit, which last above change. The edifice of Goethe's mental world, growing from the creative depth of his personality, had finally achieved its unity. The longing invocation of the earlier poems is transformed in the later one into the certainty of testimony.

This growth toward unity had, in fact, begun with the religious crisis of his last year in Leipzig. It made him ready to create the means by which he could give expression to his formative urge. Only a few lyrical passages of his Leipzig time anticipate the union of word, rhythm, and intuition at which he was later to arrive. The *Sturm und Drang* supported him in his rise above the conventional forms toward mastery of his own form, confirmed his independence in the realm of poetry, and led him to a conception of language congenial to his inner experience of the spoken word. "When looking for a confirmation of independence, I found my productive talent to be its safest basis"—thus he characterized his beginnings in this era.

The revolutionary outburst of the *Sturm und Drang* was directed against the rule of pedantry which, until the sixties, governed the aesthetics of German literature. This pedantry was based on rationalistic theory and encouraged the continued adaptation of poetry to forms of the late baroque era. The young writers and poets who resolved to obey nothing but their genuine inner impulse, did away with the inherited conventional standards in the realm of letters. In religion they were ready to question the authority of the churches; in politics, the theory and tradition of absolute government. Seen within its wider European context, the literary *Sturm und Drang* formed a part of the rising eighteenth-century antirationalism. It was, in its way, as much a preparation for the French Revolution as was enlightened freethought. As one who had already removed himself from the authority of the Protestant church, Goethe was easily drawn into the movement toward literary liberty which helped to free his own genius from oppressive fetters.

The fact that Goethe shared in the drive toward literary and religious freedom influenced the attitude he later took in regard to the French Revolution. He understood the general significance of human actions even if they belonged only to one particular aspect of life. Thus, as a revolutionary in the world of letters, he came to experience the psychology of revolution in himself. He became aware of the gap between intention and achievement, ideology and realization. The critical attitude which he soon took toward his own works of the *Sturm und Drang* fostered his growth beyond it. It was indispensable for the liberation of his innermost faculties that he joined this movement toward the unhindered rule of feeling and genius in poetry. It was essential to the fulfillment of the promise inherent in his nature that he set out to create his own classical forms, which served to hold and to heighten the aliveness released by his *Sturm und Drang*.

Soon after his arrival at Weimar, he began to reach out beyond his own revolutionary stage toward a way of living and an art of writing which could be measured by standards of perfection. The old Goethe speaks of revolution as "intending a state of nature." "Before the revolution," he also says, "striving was everything; after it, everything was transformed into demand."[12] Such statements result from self-knowledge as much as from observation. Since Goethe had to overcome his own revolutionary stage, as a man and as a poet he could later build his judgment of the political crisis engulfing the whole continent upon an evaluation that originated in his personal history.

The most auspicious moment of Goethe's *Sturm und Drang* era occurred when, at Strassburg, he found in Johann Gottfried Herder the critical and stimulating pedagogue and friend who could assist the flowering of his creative genius. Herder, who was five years Goethe's senior, had just attained his first literary fame as a critic and was about to finish his inquiry into the origin of language. Thus Goethe came under his attractive and repelling, electrifying and penalizing influence in the moment when there had crystallized in Herder's mind the germs of those future writings through which he exercised his infinitely stimulating impact on the literature of the central and eastern European nations, on the comparative study of languages and cultures, on the rediscovery of folksong, folklore, and mythology. Herder was more of a scholar than a poet and he was, above all, a teacher who impatiently demanded from his younger friends a critical interest in literary form. To them, on the other hand, what was essential was the life which they encountered in their common readings, such as, Oliver Goldsmith's *Vicar of Wakefield*.

I felt as a human being, as a youth; to me everything was living, true, and present. He [Herder] paid attention only to content and form and, when he realized that I was overwhelmed by the subject . . . he would not permit this. He regarded the work merely as a product of art, and demanded the same viewpoint from us who still lived in a fashion allowing us to receive the impact of a work of art as that of a product of nature.[13]

Goethe's relations with Herder never attained the immediacy of his friendship with Jacobi. Actively helpful as he was to all his friends, Goethe suggested and obtained for Herder a call to Weimar before he was sure that he would stay there himself. In the mid-eighties, their relations grew closer again after a period of coolness, but in the end the disharmonies in Herder's character proved too strong even for Goethe's faithful tolerance. Herder's mind was "bent upon the dialectical rather than the constructive." His thought had an insistently polemic quality, an inclination toward contradiction. "He could ridicule somebody who repeated with conviction something that, shortly before, he had taught and conveyed as his own opinion."[14]

In Strassburg Goethe was so eager to share in Herder's creative energy that he took in his stride all the inconveniences which then already accompanied his friendship with him. Yet it is significant, in regard to Goethe's sensitivity in matters of poetic production, that he withheld from Herder his more important and daring projects until he had gained an objective distance from them himself. Herder's impact on Goethe brought to fruition the seeds of his earlier philosophic and mystic experiences, inasmuch as it enabled him to reconcile his attachment to the world with his religious sense. Under the impact of Hamann, Herder had developed his conception of language as a product of the subconscious. As soon as Goethe permitted himself full freedom in the use of his gift for the word, his own experience with it seemed to him evidence for Herder's view. Goethe's con-

sciousness of his talent and its bearing in the light of Herder's theory encouraged his bringing it to realization.

The dramatic figure in which Goethe, in 1773, first crystallized the experience of his productive genius, was Prometheus. In his autobiography he associates this figure directly
with his self-discovery. The productive talent, he says,

for some years did not leave me for one moment. What I became aware of in the daytime, while awake, often formed itself even during the night into regular dreams, and when I
opened my eyes there either appeared a curious new whole or
the part of something already existing.[15]

The Promethean experience of the young Goethe had its
theoretical counterpart in the conception of genius and inspiration as it re-emerged in the mid-eighteenth century.
Thought and form "come" to the poetic genius from a
sphere outside will and consciousness. The relation of the
poet to the word is primarily that of reception and is closely
parallel to the process of religious inspiration.

Hamann conceived of language as an emanation from the
divine. He held that God crowned the manifestation of his
glory with the creation of man and, most important, he
gave speech to this creature made in his image. Man's speech
translates "from an angel's language into man's language, it
transforms thoughts into words, things into names, images
into signs."[16] Language is by no means merely a medium of
intellectual orientation. On the contrary, it serves as the
instrument of creative communication from the eternal to
the temporal, a medium for the immanence of the divine.
It emerges from the immediacy of Being, on a level beyond
the intellect. It is "given" to the poet, whose language,
prophetic and mythopoetical, is a revelation of the divinity.

Even Herder's more cautious secularization of Hamann's
ideas upheld the subconscious origin of language and its religious significance. Goethe read Herder's essay *On the*

Origin of Language while it was being written. At the same time, through daily contacts, he became acquainted with the fundamental tendencies of Herder's mind as these were later successively expressed in his writings. The point in this theory of language which left a lasting impression on Goethe was Herder's conviction that "the art of poetry is a gift to mankind and for all peoples, rather than a private inheritance of a few refined and educated men."[17] The conventional view of language as the medium of a cultured aristocracy was broken down by him, together with the rationalistic theories of French classicism. Goethe came to realize that language is nature in man himself. He considered his own poetical talent as nature all the more because he "was led to conceive outer nature as its object."[18] The poet is, as the "Sturmlied" says, the son of water and earth. When we combine Goethe's conception of man as nature with his conviction that God manifests himself through nature, we understand his thesis that, in man himself, an organ is alive through which God may speak. In its full significance Goethe's position reveals its kinship with Hamann's prophetic philosophy.

Goethe and Hamann concur in emphasizing the involuntary and subconscious factor in the process of poetical production. Moreover, in so far as the poet acts under inspiration, his work transcends the sphere of mere subjectivity. Although Goethe, in contrast to Hamann, refrained from speculative exploration of genius, he was convinced that poetry is the manifestation of the objective being of the poet. The poet's signature is revealed in every motion of his work. It cannot lie. Man is born a poet or he is never a poet. Goethe's concern for literary form, which grew in proportion to the development of his philosophy of art and criticism, took away nothing from this insight but rather confirmed it. As a poet, a "favorite of the gods," he felt that he was given the full measure of life, its joys and its pains, and it was his work as a poet which justified the experience.

Alles geben die Götter, die unendlichen,
Ihren Lieblingen ganz,
Alle Freuden, die unendlichen,
Alle Schmerzen, die unendlichen, ganz.[19]

Proceeding beyond his own *Sturm und Drang*, Goethe transformed into a new order the freedom which this era had granted him. From the beginning, the discovery of order was inherent in his experience of genius. The genius "is the first one out of whose soul the parts emerge, grown together into *one* eternal whole."[20] Goethe's first visit to the cathedral at Strassburg revealed to him the normative power of genius together with the role of art in mediating between the gods and men. The spirit exists within the nature of man as the power to form. It makes manifest an inherent norm. The normative character of genius was the object of Goethe's praise of Erwin von Steinbach. Goethe conceived of self-education as the search for the normative measure latent in the urge to form.

When recalling his essay on the Strassburg cathedral, the author of *Poetry and Truth* regretted the obscuring strangeness of expression which he had adopted under Herder's and Hamann's influence.[21] Like his criticism of Herder's deficiencies in method, this statement reflects Goethe's consistent striving for lucidity. The integration of his personality was the precondition of his attainment of style.

Goethe arrived at the mature form of his language when he succeeded in reconciling his experience of outer and of inner nature. He understood both as emanations from a universal ground, from which the law and measure of all existence arises and to which man's feeling of reverence is to be primarily devoted. The measure inherent in our inward sense will permit us to grasp the inner meaning of what we see. Thus our understanding of works of art and letters depends upon the extent to which we can penetrate to

the inner meaning, the intention of the work; here lies the
original, the divine, the effective, untouchable and indestructible
part of it, and no time, no outer interference or condition can
damage this original inner essence.[22]

Like the personality of man, the work of art is morphological in character, which means that it is *Gestalt*. It has an
inner form and demands intrinsic interpretation. In the
realm of culture in general, *Gestalt* becomes the agent of
communication between the living creature and the mind of
the past. The works of man disclose themselves to our
understanding if both emotion and intellect co-operate in
seizing upon their "inner essence." Goethe's sense of the
historical was fashioned after the example of his own poetic
experience. The depth of this sense and its universal intention he had in common with Herder, whose stimulating
power resulted from such a capacity for historical perspective. In the search for the measure inherent in genius
and nature, Goethe went beyond Herder. It was, however,
Herder's and Hamann's "obscurity" which had encouraged
Goethe in the art of perceiving the "inner meaning," fundamental to all his future work.

The discovery of the genius of Shakespeare was the most
powerful single element to give impetus to Goethe's own
productive potentialities, in spite of the difference between
their styles and purposes. Goethe saw Shakespeare as the
epitome of the spirit of poetry. He speaks to the "quickness
of the inner sense." He is able to penetrate from the particular to the whole, because the whole is latent in him.
"Shakespeare is 'the greatest wanderer'; he creates man as
nature creates him," Goethe said in 1771; and in 1813 he
stated, "He joins the World Spirit; in the same way he penetrates the world; to both of them nothing is hidden." Herder had made Goethe aware of "the poverty of German
literature" at the beginning of his career, and had aroused
in him a responsibility which he sometimes felt as a burden.

In this situation, the discovery of Shakespeare occurred almost as a revelation of kinship. From reading the first play, says Goethe,

I got up like one born blind, to whom in one instant a miraculous hand had given sight. I recognized, I felt most vividly, my existence infinitely extended. . . . all his plays circle around the secret point—which no philosopher has as yet seen and defined —in which the peculiarity of our self, the pretended freedom of our will, coincides with the necessary course of the whole.[23]

Goethe sees Shakespeare as the genius through whom the law of the universe becomes manifest. This is the poet's calling, and he can obey it because the universal law is inherent in his own genius. In *Götz von Berlichingen*, Goethe, true to the intentions and interpretation of the *Sturm und Drang*, adopted the "Shakespearean" liberty from the French interpretation of the Aristotelian rules. He turned to Shakespeare and the Greeks until, in the era of *Iphigenie* and *Tasso*, Racine's classical strictness revealed its significance to him. What appealed to the innermost urge of his own poetic self was the vision of Shakespeare as the universal poet who presents "the history of the world passing along the invisible thread of time." In Shakespeare he had discovered a model. He seized upon its inner essence and found himself encouraged to be faithful to his own genius.

Goethe's understanding of the Plotinian concept of "inner meaning" and his interpretation of the work of genius as the revelation of law, explains the freedom with which he handled literary form. The function of form is the adequate manifestation of inner meaning. It grows from within. Thus the history of Goethe's literary form reflects his evolution from the stage of self-liberation to the increasing consciousness of the normative character of art. The meaning of wandering is the discovery and manifestation of law through the course of life.

During his first decade at Weimar, in correspondence

with his studies of nature and his experiences in government, Goethe's verse turned from the free rhythms of the *Sturm und Drang* to stricter measures. Soon they were no longer adopted as mere outward shells, as he had used them at Leipzig. Without loosing a fine but imperative bond, the strictness of his verse was later reduced again. Goethe mastered the forms of poetry in the way that each creative purpose demanded. Each poem is born together with its own rhythmical law. Goethe's poetical work attained style, but a style of his own. With new phases of life, new forms of verse emerged; or, on the other hand, established forms, such as the sonnet, were molded by Goethe's own tonal power. Sometimes a new tone announced a metamorphosis. The verse form of *Iphigenie*, about which he corresponded with Herder just before leaving for Italy, anticipated the "hegira," the beginning of a new phase, in 1786. The rhythm of the *Divan* verses came to him as he set out on his way to southwestern Germany in 1814.

The style and structure of Goethe's epic and drama are equally dominated by his ever moving creative personality. They arise together with the core of each theme and develop jointly with its growth. In consequence, they are scarcely compatible with conventional patterns. *Wilhelm Meister*, describing an educational evolution in the first part, a didactic image of society in the second, does not harmonize with any established scheme of the novel. The *Novelle*, charged with symbolism, introduced a new literary type. Goethe's autobiography is interspersed with tales which form units in themselves. It contains vistas of the history of culture and of literature, and the story of Goethe's religious growth is given as a paraphrase of the morphology of religion. And yet in its clear plan of wide though firm ramification the edifice reveals an organic unity. *Pandora* is a unique composition evading any "normal" aesthetic rules. The unity of the conception and structure of *Faust* proved the most difficult to grasp. Its first part is often read without

the second, although the end of the Gretchen tragedy offers
no solution to the universal and inquisitive unrest which im-
pels Faust to conclude his pact with Mephisto. The second
part is often read without the end, Faust's ascension,
although without it the unity of the whole, and thereby its
significance, cannot reveal itself. Only the whole *Faust*,
taken, in spite of its growth over a period of sixty years, as
an integrated unity, conveys its architecture and its meaning.

The mature Goethe remained and wanted to remain the
creator of his style. He understood the poet as the master of
the laws of poetry. Since the conscious and deliberate part
of his activity is subordinate to the voice of his inward nature, this lawgiver in turn formulates laws according to the
truth which is given him, and he is therefore the opposite
of arbitrary. He divines an objective law in his subjective
experience. This mediating function of the poet has its analogy in that of the statesman, as we shall discover from
Goethe's thoughts about public administration. Both poet
and statesman, while operating in the world and within the
secular realm, can operate well only from a transcendental
point of reference to which they have access through their
own inner selves. The ultimate wisdom of the artist, the
statesman, and the philosophic mind is one.

Goethe's theory of art and the artist corresponds thoroughly to his conception of man and human life. The artist
who exercises the mediating function of art will develop
style—his highest achievement. Goethe does not use the term
"style" in a historical and comparative sense. He does not
speak of "styles" but of "style" as the ultimate perfection of
the mission of the artist. Style arises neither from simple imitation of nature nor through mannerism. The calm and consistent devotion of the artist to the object of nature teaches
him to imitate; out of his desire and ability to produce an
individual language of forms, grows his personal manner of
representation. The devoted intuitive study of the objects
of nature will lead the artist to awareness of their universal

interconnection. Such study will prepare him for entering the sanctuary of style itself.

Style rests upon the deepest foundations of cognition, upon the essence of things, in so far as we are permitted to recognize it in visible and tangible things.[24]

By this significant formulation, written shortly after his return from Italy at the time of his co-operation with Moritz, Goethe defined art as an act of cognition. From the artist he required the study of nature in the spirit in which he pursued it himself. The inner sense of the artist is called upon to penetrate into the essence and inner form of things. The "subjectivity" of the artist and the "objectivity" of outer nature then meet on a common ground. The dialogue between art and nature is, so to speak, a dialogue between nature and itself. Man is a part of nature; nature is spirit embodied; and spirit is the inner meaning of nature. The phenomenon of art and its production are possible because man's nature forms an organic part of the universe and is able to reflect the cosmic whole. The universe is engaged in a process of dynamic individuation; it builds and destroys in order to build again. Man, who is involved in this process as a microcosm, was given the faculty to grasp and express the "inner meaning" of things. Therefore, naturalistic realism never approaches truth.

Above the imitator of outer nature and the arbitrary artist who follows his subjective impulse, Goethe places the perfect artist. In him, inner and outer nature merge through the productive co-operation of his eye with his inner sense. Through working, he undergoes "intensification," the heightening metamorphosis which is throughout the law of nature in evolution. By surrendering himself to both the nature without and the genius within him, he attains the perfection of style. "Nobody is master of what is truly productive"[25]—but precisely therefore it is possible for the work of the artist to surpass individual arbitrariness, if

genius speaks through him. Then the inner form of the artist
and the inner form of his object will elucidate each other.
The artist will be able

to produce, in competition with nature, something spiritually
organic, and to impart to his product a content and form
through which it appears natural and supernatural at the same
time.[26]

The creativity which brings forth independent works of
art is given to the artist through nature. "It is only individual generative energy that drives forth independent works
of art as it does the creatures of nature."[27] The life of the
artist requires the whole of his personality and leads him
beyond it toward objectivity.

Like his poetry on man's relation to time, Goethe's
thought on art and the artist proceeds from the emphasis
upon the emotional truthfulness of the productive self to
the discovery of the higher and objective law which is inherent in the creative process and becomes manifest through
it. In the realm of art, nature produces, through the medium
of man, a second revelation. "Beauty is a manifestation of
secret laws of nature which, without the appearance of
beauty, would have remained concealed forever."[28] The
artist's love for the beautiful leads him onward to his cosmic
function. In the artist's response to the object, his highest
activity is called forth, and it in turn elucidates the highest
and most perfect elements of his object. The artist's personality is to serve as an instrument toward higher ends.
His work—to dissolve the dualism between idea and phenomenon—is the highest achievement of genius. Through
his creativity God-in-Nature intends another manifestation.
The highest works of art

are produced by men according to true and natural laws. Whatever is arbitrary and fanciful collapses. There is necessity, there
is God.[29]

When writing this sentence in Italy, Goethe disclosed the motives of his love for the art of antiquity. The best of Greek art revealed to him the idea of the perfect. It reconciled his religious interpretation of God as the supreme artist with his conception of man as the highest creature of nature. It showed how the production of the artist, on the level of human existence, follows the law inherent in all formations of nature. Because the Greeks were responsive to the divine which they felt was immanent in nature, they attained style. The "Juno Ludovisi," the "Aldobrandinian Nuptials," and the Elgin Marbles were to Goethe not only specimens of perfect art, but they permitted him an insight into the creative process and the cosmic meaning of great art. He was convinced that the Greeks possessed the secret of perceiving the normative core of phenomena and rendering it visible through the creation of their own language of symbols. In his essay on Winckelmann, Goethe defined the realm of art as producing the highest lasting achievement. Art represents the outstanding evolution of the spirit. It operates through the totality of the living energies of man. By the work of art "man is lifted above himself, the circle of his life and action comes to completion, and he is deified for a present in which past and future are implied."[30]

By interpreting the artist as called to formulate, through his life and work, the norm latent in nature and spirit, Goethe relates his theory of art to his morphology. The "original phenomenon," *Urphänomen*, is the concept in which Goethe's metaphysics, his study of nature, and his theory of art converge. Man is able to penetrate from the sense-perception of the manifold to the simplicity of the original phenomenon by means of a devoted and disciplined intuition which gives him certainty. The "inner form" corresponds to the outer form as the inner meaning corresponds to the literal surface of a work of poetry. By grasping the inner forms of things man gains constructive insight into the creative process out of which they emerge. During the *Sturm und Drang* Goethe expected the achievement of art and criticism to rise from "the feeling of this inner form, which comprises in itself all forms."[31] Consolidating his intention by the study of nature, Goethe discovered that to man is given the faculty not only to feel but to intuit as an inner form the original phenomenon.

The phenomena perceived by our senses are in continuous flux. The morphological intuition, however, approaches the unity underlying the process of metamorphosis. It grasps its *Gestalt.* We can draw into one the beginning and the end of life. Thus Goethe described this act of the mind in the poem "Dauer im Wechsel." Such an act of reconstructive intuition draws into one the phases of life to which, for instance, a rosebush is subject; we become aware of the climax toward which these phases strive and we "see" the bush completing its cycle. On a still higher level of generalization, Goethe conceived the principle of unfolding that governs the vegetable kingdom as the original plant, *die Urpflanze.* He tells how, in the first momentous conversation he had with Schiller, he designed for him "a symbolical plant." Whereupon Schiller replied: "This is not an experience, this is an idea."[32]

For a long time Goethe was averse to having the original phenomenon called an idea, for he rated the inner sense equal to outer perception as a means of seeing. When Schiller called the *Urphänomen* an idea, Goethe objected, realizing at once the divergence between their ways of thinking. In retrospect, long after the exchange of thought on philosophic problems which he and Schiller carried on for ten years, Goethe saw the original plant as the sensual form of a metasensual reality. Through it he felt able to intuit the original identity of all parts of the plants in a more living fashion. He could reconcile himself to Schiller's conception of the original phenomenon as an idea as soon as this word had lost for him its lifeless, merely intellectual connotation and took on. instead, a creative and organic significance.

Goethe studied nature as an artist, and he saw the artist and his work as a manifestation of nature or, rather, of God in nature. For the artist touches upon the numinous, as we do when perceiving original phenomena. The intuition of original phenomena means to Goethe the possible climax of cognition. They inspire

awe increasing to anxiety: we feel our insufficiency; only when enlivened through the continuous play of the empirical world do they give us joy.[33]

Beyond the original phenomenon is the realm of the unsearchable, the realm into which Faust takes a glance when he descends to the "Mothers." Out of this unfathomable ground Faust calls forth the symbol of the highest beauty, the original phenomenon of Helena. The original phenomenon has the quality of an idea, because it is the last object accessible to cognition; it is real, in so far as it becomes a part of cognition; it is symbolical, because it includes all individual cases, and it is identical with all cases.[34] We ought to content ourselves, Goethe holds, with intuiting the original phenomena. Facing them, our cognitive faculties make us aware of the intentions inherent in the universal dynamics of formation and transformation.

We have advanced far enough in the comprehension of nature when we encounter the original phenomena which we see face to face in their inexplorable glory; then we can turn back to the world of phenomena where the inconceivably simple reveals itself unchanged in all changeability in thousands upon thousands of manifestations.[35]

The original phenomenon causes Goethe to experience the *numinosum tremendum,* the sublime which makes us tremble. At the limits of mankind Goethe takes the Platonic turn from the realm of ideas to the realm of phenomena. Life is to be lived, whereas its ultimate secret is hidden. The

Homunculus in *Faust*, the brain child of the giant scientist
Wagner, sacrifices himself to the elements in order to obtain life. Body is indispensable to life although it is transitory
by nature. Through the passing forms of life, however, a
miraculous reality becomes manifest as a patent secret. Penetrating to the original phenomena man is struck by a transparent, ideational fact which is given and cannot be pursued any further: the rose, as such, is and remains a miracle.

> *Vernehme der göttlichen Stimme Schall!*
> *Unmöglich scheint immer die Rose,*
> *Unbegreiflich die Nachtigall.*[36]

Out of the process of life the work of the artist arises.
Like the sculptor, the poet devotes his personality to his
work without restriction and thereby surpasses his personality. His mediating function is in need of the concreteness
of life, the "occasion" of the moment from which the poem
should be born. The poet's power to penetrate to the inner
meaning of the occasion then transforms his experience into
a self-sufficient and meta-individual product. By imparting
form to the inner meaning of human existence, it articulates
and clarifies the confused and confusing phenomena of experience. The universal intention of this poetry is reflected
by its art of connecting the moment with its lasting significance, the particular with the whole, man with the universe. Eye and urge to form finally converge in the creation
of poetry which is praise,[37] the praise of the glory of the
creation. Such is the religious poetry which is born of
faith and in which metaphysical cognition is inherent. The
universality of his vision enables Lynkeus, the watchman of
Faust II, to praise all that he sees.

Out of his love of man the poet Goethe felt the urge to
communicate to his brothers what was granted to himself.[38]
The work of art extends its effect back into the process of
life toward an unforeseeable end. Its self-sufficient perfection calls forth the sense of the perfect in others. The per-

fect work of art never leaves us untransformed. It exercises
a formative, liturgical impact.

The best work of art deprives us of our arbitrariness; we
cannot do as we like with the perfect; we are compelled to give
ourselves up to it in order to receive ourselves back from it
heightened and improved.[39]

The artist, then, compels the recipient of his work to repeat, in his way, the process which with himself resulted in
a product of style. On first sight only, the subjectivity required from the friend of art as from the artist seems to
transform the objective function of art into the psychological. Because of the meta-individual objectivity which
Goethe recognizes as inherent in the nature of man, however, the work of art leads man beyond his psychological
individuality to the recognition and appropriation of objective standards and values. Aesthetic perfection reconciles
love and cognition. The work of art speaks to the totality of
man, to this whole of manifold and interrelated forces, because it is itself an organic whole and presents, together
with the individual manifestation, its meta-individual significance, "in the end no longer the creature, but the idea
of the creature."[40] Therefore the work of art has the power
not only to satisfy our limited affection and our curiosity,
but to awaken "the higher part latent in ourselves."

The urge to form leads the artist beyond the subjective.
His craft demands that he practice his art with the aid of
scientific consciousness. The seriousness of his mediating
function requires an increased strictness of self-education;
it demands community with others and the intensification
resulting from his joining a school, even a world, of art and
artists. This strictness is postulated in the essay "On Dilettantism";[41] it is once more reflected by the life of the artists
in *Wilhelm Meister*. Even the amateur will never attain a
sound relation to art so long as he conceives and re-enacts it
merely by emotion through its "pathological reality." He

ought to leave intact the "ideal" character of art by lifting himself to the cognition of its fundamentals and traditions.

Goethe demands for art a place of its own in society. It shall serve, but only according to its own autonomous and inherent law. "Art has an ideal origin; one can say that it emerged out of, and together with, religion."[42] It surpasses the beauty of nature, and its own beauty resides in its measure. Art is the epitome of freedom because it is subject to the laws of the human spirit in its highest formation.

The beauty of nature is subject to the laws of necessity; the beauty of art is subject to the laws of the human mind, in so far as the mind has attained the highest form; therefore the one appears to be determined, the other to be free.[43]

Art appears free precisely in that it discovers and articulates the law inherent in the entelechy of nature.

Goethe's concern about his own consciousness of the objective standards of art and its function in society formed an integral part of the cultural problem that was raised by his reliance upon the resources of his own personality. The art of the baroque age had given expression to a universal view of the world and of man's existence within it. The liberation from the standards of the past called for another creative formulation of objective truth. Goethe attempted to achieve this by considering his own personality the organ of such cognition. Thus his life and work attained unity and catholicity. To an age whose faith was dismembered and whose society was beginning to disintegrate, he could convey his message that personality finds achievement when it turns to the cosmic whole of which it is a part.

The firmness and clarity which Goethe attained in the decade following his return from Italy were the fruit of his acceptance of the wanderer's destiny. There was no sheltering home for him but the daily rhythm of thought and action in fulfillment of the law inherent in the process of life. The phases of his youth and early manhood now appear as organic steps in his growth. Undisturbed by his solitude he continued to pursue his aims as a poet, a student of nature, a theoretical thinker, and a friend. Rarely did a contemporary become aware of the unity of his pursuits, but to Goethe these pursuits represented the way in which he exercised the mediating function of man: the reconciliation of the personality with its universal origin and end.

My whole inner activity turned out to be a living heuristic which, acknowledging an unknown law, tries to find it in the outer world and to introduce it into the outer world.[44]

He recognized and confirmed the nature and meaning of man's wandering. He continued in the active consummation of his calling and pursued it to the end. "I have nothing more important to do," he wrote five days before his death, "than to enhance as much as possible that which is and remains in me and to distill my properties."[45]

4

Government and World Affairs

The Friend of a Prince—Government and
Self-Control—World Affairs
The Desirable and the Idea of Justice

Poetry and Truth comes to a close with a description of
the moment in the fall of 1775 when the messenger of Duke
Karl August of Sachsen-Weimar reached Goethe at Heidelberg, where he was making his first stop on the way to Italy.
This Italian journey was one which Goethe had planned
since childhood; nevertheless he resolved to turn north to
visit at Weimar. "No result had as yet emerged out of my
life," he says. He had the feeling of stepping into an unknown future, as though "goaded by invisible spirits" into
a course not chosen by deliberate will, and he expressed his
sense of the fateful moment with the words of Egmont:
"Whither he is hasting, who knows? He hardly remembers
whence he came."[1]

Goethe came to Weimar as the friend of the young duke
whom he had met a year before in Frankfurt and whom he
had visited in Mainz, to the dissatisfaction of his father with
his ingrained burgher's distrust of princes and courts. The
son, however, was not wholly unprepared for living in the
realm of government. Jurisprudence and legislation had
more of a place in his early life than his occasional practice
of law in Frankfurt would lead one to expect. His father's
tutoring and his own studies had given him the knowledge

of positive law required to pass the examinations. He had early come to realize the opposition between the "right which is born with us" and the laws and privileges which "continue like an everlasting sickness from generation to generation."[2] He sought the source of legislation and legal institutions in their historical growth rather than through a system of natural law, and the theses he wrote for his promotion at Strassburg anticipated, with the aid of Schlosser's and Möser's ideas, his view of the organic nature of man as the foundation of any thought on justice and right.[3] Justus Möser's *Patriotic Phantasies* had been the subject of Goethe's first conversation with Karl August, which had focused on problems of society and government rather than of letters.

When, some months after his arrival at Weimar, Goethe decided to stay on, he entered state politics, unlike Wieland and Klopstock, whose position at the courts of Weimar and Karlsruhe was that of poets and men of letters only. The young duke included his friend in his cabinet, the "secret council," and explained this decision to the experienced bureaucrats on the ground of Goethe's unusual talents, which should not be wasted in mere routine work. As a member of the council he was to participate in the meetings and take over some branches of administration; as a friend he would, after the meetings, criticize Karl August's conduct of affairs. Chance had brought Goethe, friendship held him—a responsible friendship accompanied by a sense of inner obligation to support and further the development of an exceptional character.

The beginnings of this common life were stormy enough to become the subject of nationwide gossip. Even Charlotte von Stein joined more sedate observers in their anxiety about the dangerous influence this wild man of the literary *Sturm und Drang* might exercise on the young ruler.[4] Both prince and poet had to grow into the world of affairs and the mastery of human relations. They had in common essential problems of maturing and, in spite of eight years' difference in their ages, their friendship was one of reciprocal gains. Seven years after his arrival, Goethe wrote the poem "Ilmenau,"[5] in which he looked back upon the personalities of Karl August and of himself as they were when still governed by the spontaneous impulses of their youthful nature. The pure fire which Goethe brought was not, he says, used to kindle a pure flame, and the storm fanned it into a dangerous blaze.

Ich brachte reines Feuer vom Altar;
Was ich entzündet, ist nicht reine Flamme.
Der Sturm vermehrt die Glut und die Gefahr.
Ich schwanke nicht, indem ich mich verdamme.

Karl August lived out of the demonic ground of his nature. His character was pervaded by tempestuous contradictions and, at this early time, he was "passionately devoted to error." In the poem Goethe recalls the moment when he observed the prince in his restless sleep and hoped that Karl August through the innate strength of his nature would yet fulfill the promise of his personality. He concludes this retrospective poem with the quintessence of ethical wisdom distilled from his experience with government. The ruler does not live for himself; he is called upon to restrict his free soul; he who strives to govern others well must be able to renounce many of his own desires.

Der kann sich manchen Wunsch gewähren,
Der kalt sich selbst und seinem Willen lebt;
Allein wer andere wohl zu leiten strebt,
Muss fähig sein, viel zu entbehren.

During the weeks in which this poem was written, Goethe entered in a visitor's diary an expression of his sorrow over the ever-recurring errors of man which, it seems, cannot be prevented by the transmission of past experience.

Will der Knabe nicht hören, was der erfahrene Mann
spricht?
Muss der Jüngling stets irren? und schwerbetrogen
die Männer
Wieder zu Knaben sich wünschen, nur um sich selber
zu folgen?[6]

From his life with Karl August, Goethe had learned that the demand of life to overcome one's subjective self for the sake of a higher truth is also the precondition of the art of government.

Self-mastery as the duty of the perfect ruler was the central theme of the "Prince's Mirror" of the Renaissance. This type of literature flourished with the emergence of the modern state. From Castiglione's *Cortegiano* through Elyot's *Governor* to Friedrich II's *Anti-Machiavel*, the education and moral self-control of the executive formed a central theme of political thought. The nineteenth century, involved in the constitutional issue of modern government and in the social problems accompanying the rise of industrialism, paid little attention to the question confronting Goethe at Weimar. Because he could relive the issue of "the perfect ruler" on the basis of human companionship, he was able to deal with it as a human problem and to detach it from the particular constitutional form of the absolute monarchy. It merged with his inquiry into the nature of man and of a healthy society. Goethe's experience was thus integrated into his conception of social leadership. As in his intimate personal contact with the problem of the ruler, so in the social realm of his utopian communities the education toward self-mastery is a corollary of man's growth toward useful membership or leading service in society.

Even though it arose in the atmosphere of small-state absolutism, Goethe's thought does not belong only to the past. The question of the human quality of those in public service is a perennial problem, independent of the form of government. The complicated ramifications of modern administrative machinery make it difficult, however, to realize the part personality still plays today in public affairs. In Goethe's time the duchy of Sachsen-Weimar was a state of one hundred thousand inhabitants, which permitted immediate government, and therefore could provide an experimental station for Goethe.

Goethe had approached his new situation with the confidence of a somnambulist, the confidence of Egmont, and had soon learned that, like Karl August, he also had to earn "by pain and sweat" what destiny seemed to present as a gift. His position in Weimar society and his place in public administration were due to his personality; for a long time his most personal qualities were the main source of his influence. His relations with the duke were such that from the outset he could have restricted his public duties to a less demanding range, yet he did the opposite. Year by year his obligations increased, for he made the duke's cause his own. He needed all his tenacity and self-discipline to carry through a work which, for the time being, prevented him from pursuing poetic projects with the intensity they required. His urge to form was now primarily applied to public affairs. Three months after his arrival, Wieland wrote of him:

He does the possible and, in addition, what would be impossible to a hundred others. . . . But, lo! how much more this magnificent mind could and would do had he not sunk into this our chaos, out of which, in spite of all his will and capacity, he will not create a tolerable world.[7]

Goethe was able to attempt the impossible because within the narrow confines of Weimar state and court life his personality had a chance for free action. His inborn talent for enlivening the atmosphere around him found new domains for expression, and he could rely on Karl

August's confidence. Merck, the sharp observer, when he visited Weimar in 1777, recognized at once the firmness of the duke's character—"He is one of the most respectable and clearheaded men I ever saw"—and he knew of Goethe's faithful love for Karl August.[8]

He is as completely at home in the house of the duke as he would be in mine; he has given up none of his previous poetic productivity, as the silly asses claim, but he has as a man increased his hunger and thirst for the knowledge of men and affairs and he has gained in wisdom and prudence.

Goethe often sought unhindered contact with social conditions by roaming the country incognito, or asking one of his protégés to provide him with observations made unobtrusively on the spot. He carried through every practical task to the minutest detail, whether it was to write a public document, to save on soldiers' uniforms, to enlarge the university library, or to restore mining at Ilmenau. In his close contact with the dynamic life of society, he intended to impart to it the sympathy and reason latent in himself and, at the same time, to gain an insight that he needed. He was convinced that "a significant writing, like a significant speech, must be the consequence of life."[9] For ten years he continued to divert his poetical fountains "to the mills and irrigation works," because this offered a universal experience to the universal inclination of his mind. One of its results was his recognition of laws conducive to a fruitful human community.

At the beginning of his years at Weimar, Goethe approached his task without foregone conclusions and almost in a revolutionary spirit. Soon he found himself within a sphere of necessities which imposed definite rules of procedure upon the conduct of public life. His conception of public responsibility was revolutionary in so far as it resulted from his faith in man as a mediator between his innermost resources and the outer world. The concept of

Humanität, which in these years Herder developed in
community with Goethe, supported his tendency to focus
on man's inner intentions rather than on legal rights, on
ethical action rather than on the reorganization of institutions, on the "inner form" of personalities rather than on
the outward formulation of rules of conduct. Born a citizen of a free city and never a monarchist in principle,
Goethe considered the state as a human problem of ethics
and of culture.

In a restrospective letter written to Karl August from
Italy,[10] Goethe regrets that "at the beginning of his interim
administration he did not have more knowledge of detail,
more resolution, and more firmness." He had started as an
improviser, convinced that his good mind, his strong personality, and the purity of his intentions would make up
for his lack of practical training. In this respect he was not
different from any citizen elected to a high position in a
democracy without previous administrative experience.
But it is essential to an understanding of his ideas and later
decisions to realize that Goethe never entered public service as a career, not even on the highest level, in the sense of
abandoning his literary work. His venture into the "world"
widened his experience but did not change his personality.
He never considered the political realm as his exclusive
medium. His later withdrawal from political administration was not the result of a frustrated mission, nor was his
participation in politics merely an occasional side line.

The life of most diversified interests and activities which
Goethe led at Weimar required extraordinary elasticity of
mind. Even his use of time became an art with Goethe; he
could turn from one aspect of his life to another with no
loss of intensity. Some of his studies, such as geology, were
assisted by simultaneous work in branches of administration assigned to him. He found time to progress in anatomy
and botany, using for this end his connections with the
University of Jena. By writing, conversation, reading

aloud to the court, and staging plays, he provided a substantial part of the court's intellectual and social life. Nevertheless, the portion of his poetic projects which he had most at heart did not suffer a complete standstill. He often isolated himself in his "garden house," or out of town in Ilmenau, at the Wartburg, in the Harz Mountains. A new world of personalities and situations opened up for him. He knew his way in the realms of letters and science; now he had to live in the world of affairs, with men of action—officers, administrators, diplomats, in the circles of the aristocracy.

In the midst of all these new impressions he remained faithful to his old friends. Lavater, Jacobi, the Stolbergs, as well as Merck, came to visit him. He tried to help his Strassburg companion, Klinger, back on his feet, while at the same time providing for the education of a Swiss orphan boy, Peter im Baumgarten, whom another friend had left to his care when he died.[11] Even the most gifted personality could attempt to integrate this ever-widening and manifold range of personal and public duties only by an increasingly strict and conscious self-control. In this situation, where he was often torn between his expanding outward life and his longing for inner calm, Charlotte von Stein provided for him a sphere of unhindered communication which helped him ever and again to recover his equilibrium.

The diaries of these years give ample evidence that Goethe by no means underestimated the difficulties in his way, which arose both from within and from without. "I become aware of general confidence, and may God grant that I earn it, not the easy way but the way I wish it to be. Nobody realizes the burden that I carry in regard to myself and others."[12] He felt alone in the central aim of his activities. Obstacles from the outside he tried to meet with tenacity and penetrating study. In significant moments his charismatic powers succeeded in breaking "through the

thick skin" of other persons. Thus misunderstandings
could be removed and developing projects furthered. In
balanced moments, however, he found obstacles mainly in
himself. Carefully observing the mistakes of Karl August,
he sometimes discovered that he made the same mistakes.
He controlled the orderliness of his technique, the con-
ciseness of his thought, and the logic of his conduct. He
realized how often sheer selfishness motivates the giving of
advice by subordinates and advisers, and he balanced this
experience, which is inescapable for anybody "in power,"
by increasing his caution. He tried to be silent at the
proper time in order to allow others the degree of initiative and freedom conducive to the best results. Deeply disgusted by the narrowness which "poverty of mind and
purse" caused in others, he turned to a reckoning with
himself in which he was far more merciless than any of his
critics. He brushed aside theory and history as "ridiculous
to the one who gains experience through actions." He was
incessantly at work to establish an immediate relationship
with the world of affairs, to attain a comprehension of
government which would exclude self-delusion, and to
acquire a steady hand in his administrative assignments.

In spite of the many anxieties Karl August caused Goethe, he remained Goethe's central concern in these years,
both as a person and as a ruler. He alone, Goethe once said,
was in the state of becoming, whereas the others were "like
puppets who, at best, lack paint."[13] Regarded in the context of Goethe's conception of life, this meant that the
duke alone really lived. Thus Goethe found himself, together with Karl August, in conflict with society. He realized how difficult it is "to get earthly machines going" and
keep them going. There is no achievement that lasts: an
unceasing renewal of effort is necessary. Perhaps the atmosphere can never be cleared which "boredom conserves
among men." An immense struggle is needed to produce
even a "small result." "What the patriarchal ruler has to

suffer," Goethe wrote to Lavater,[14] "no tongue can express. No one is born for rulership, and whoever inherits it must conquer it as bitterly as the conqueror." And he added: "No one understands this who has had the chance to create and to widen the realm of his action out of his own self." A ruler finds himself in a most restricting predicament; to live creatively out of his own self is more difficult for him than for anyone else.

In accordance with Karl August's own instincts, Goethe had helped the young duke to rise above formalism and outward appearance. In summing up Karl August's personality after his death in 1828, Goethe described him as a human being whose activities emerged from one single, great, and good source.[15] What matters in regard to princes, he said at this time, is "what one weighs against the balance of mankind; all the rest is vain."

He was born a great man. . . . It meant nothing to him that he inherited a dukedom. . . . his tendencies were of a productive nature. . . . just a century more, how much he could have furthered his time in such a position.

Goethe saw Karl August's life as a truly royal existence and penetrated deeper into its inner meaning when he attributed his ability to rule to three outstanding faculties: he had a discriminating judgment of men, he possessed an active energy of love, and he was firm in his inner independence. His judgment enabled him to put everyone in the position in which he could perform his greatest service. His love engendered love; "much of the divine was in him." His inner firmness made it difficult for him "to commit anything unprincely." Here was the image of the perfect ruler of an organic society into which, fifty-three years after his arrival at Weimar, Goethe's picture of Karl August merged.

The measures for which the duke availed himself of Goethe's assistance were conceived in the spirit of the en-

lightened welfare-state of the eighteenth century. Rulers
such as Friedrich the Great and Karl Friedrich of Baden
were, in this respect, the models of Karl August. The practical sense and the human understanding of Justus Möser
had left their impression on both Goethe and his sovereign.
Each of Goethe's activities in internal administration was
connected with a constructive communal end. His chair-
manship of the commission on the building of roads was
devoted to breaking routine resistance against facilities
drawing the west-east German traffic through Weimar
territory. As commissioner of war he tried to save on military expenses and succeeded in convincing the duke of
the futility of his playing with the "military macaroni,"
the soldiery of the small duchy.[16] He undertook the economic restoration of the Ilmenau region through the reopening of the mines and their organization as a co-operative enterprise.

When Goethe took over the presidency of the ducal
chamber—that is, the administration of the crown property—it was near bankruptcy; when he left it it was re-
organized and the budget was balanced. It was his aim to
divert as many funds as the economic situation permitted
to the cultural institutions of the duchy. Not without some
measure of justified satisfaction he began the memorandum
on the institutions of higher learning, written in 1806 for
Napoleon's marshal, Berthier, by reaffirming the judgment,
common in Germany and abroad, that for more than
thirty years the sciences and arts had been cultivated in the
duchy of Weimar with quite extraordinary care.[17]

When Goethe entered the administration of the duchy
the modern rational organization of its institutions was still
in conflict with older feudal traditions. Convinced of the
necessity of adapting administration to the concrete demands of existing problems, he tried to insure better results
in his branches of service by improving their organization.
At the same time he encouraged consideration of the per-

sonal element in relations between the bureaucracy and the citizen. His interest in social conditions at times made him ironical even about his own poetic achievements. "The king of Tauris has to speak as though no hosier in Apolda went hungry,"[18] he wrote to Charlotte von Stein when the misery he observed made it difficult for him to "climb to his old castle of poetry."

His human interest in the restoration of an individual's "usefulness," which caused him to spend considerable of his own means for the support of friends in distress, was also his guiding principle in the personnel problems of his administration. In such matters, he decided on the basis of the degree of usefulness in the community which could be expected from the person under debate, be it in the case of an appointment or of a pardon. In eighteenth-century usage the term "a useful subject" had a meaning similar to that which the expression "a good citizen" has today. Goethe's conviction as to the importance of the service rendered by the individual to the community of his fellow men—a conviction basic to his image of the ideal society— dates back to his first experiences in government. In his recommendations in matters of personnel, especially in regard to supporting the education of the children of deserving fathers, Goethe also considered family traditions. It was a part of his organic conception of society that not only the individual but also the family to which he belongs must be considered for the sake of the whole.[19]

Goethe's experience in government is reflected throughout his literary work. Not only his own independence of thought but the freedom which, at times, was possible at Weimar is evident from the comedy The Birds, in which Goethe paraphrased Aristophanes for the court.[20] He pokes fun at every aspect of governmental conceit; for instance, in his satirical portrayal of Rome, from whose eagle, from whose "mayors or city-sergeants," the heroes of all times derived their dignity and insignia. He ridicules the crosses in the buttonholes that constitute the "honor" of princes and their subjects, patronage and its effects on character, the bohemian's dream of an earthly paradise, and the bureaucracy and red tape of the mercantilist state. The "strange but truthful story" pursues the aim of all irony: to lift the veil of conceit from the values of life. Its striking effect was the greater since Goethe himself liked to play the role of the human hero *Treufreund*, "Faithful Friend," whose longing for another and better country brings him into the company of the birds and their malcontent leaders, the parrot and the owl. The irony of this play spares neither small nor great. Its simply human intention is the same as that which twice in *Faust II* prompts Goethe to ridicule the emperor's court and war. There, however, the broader dimensions and deeper significance of the parody reveal a pessimism alien to *The Birds*. Although after his return from Italy Goethe's views continued in the direction they had taken during his first decade at Weimar, the French Revolution and the age of Napoleon had deepened his awareness of the demonic element of history.

Goethe had taken an active part in Karl August's efforts to prepare, in face of the centralizing tendencies of Emperor Joseph II, a federation of the smaller German states, the *Fürstenbund*. These efforts came to a climax with the death of Friedrich the Great and ended with the failure of the duke's hopes in 1788. This bitter experience was soon followed by the revolutionary events. After his return from Italy Goethe assumed supervision of the institutions of higher learning and other, temporary, assignments. When in 1792 the crown took over the management of its own theater, he became its first director. His primary concern with politics, however, shifted from administration to the repercussions of world affairs. The experiences of his first decade at Weimar had taken away from him any illusions about the nature of political action with which he might have arrived. He had learned of the invincible self-ishness of man, which he considered equally destructive in art and in politics; he had realized the incongruity between ideas and actions, aggravated, in this period, by the enthusiasm of feeling that gave the initial impetus to his own revolutionary course in the field of letters. When the French Revolution broke out, which was to bring about a thorough transformation of Europe's political and social institutions, Goethe had already drawn firm conclusions from his past experience. He felt that an ordered society was the precondition of human freedom. He expected a constructive future from the education of man and community rather than from the overthrow of existing institutions. He conceived of his own task as that of forming, over and above the confusion and uncertainties of his day, the symbols of the sound ways of living which are preformed and latent in the nature of man.

A deep awareness of change and of the sickness of his time never left him. It was aggravated by the immediate contact with the weakness of leadership in the campaign of 1792 in France.[21] For a short while the brilliance of Napoleon's military and administrative genius kindled his hope for the restoration of lasting peace on the European continent. The results of the peace settlement and the antagonism between revolutionary nationalism and anti-patriotic reaction following the wars of liberation, confirmed him in the conviction that only a renewal of the inner bases of man's life held the possibility of a constructive future. As for himself, he had resolved while in Italy to seek a renewal of these lasting values.

The things of this world are transitory. I wish to concern myself with the conditions that last and thus to give eternity to my mind in accord with the teachings of [Spinoza].[22]

From this inner distance he lived through the age of the

Revolution. In restrospect, he summed up his view of it to Eckermann:

It is true that I could not be a friend of the French Revolution, for its atrocities were too close and aroused me day after day, whereas its beneficial results could not yet be recognized. Furthermore, the intention artificially to bring about in Germany scenes like those which had been the consequence of necessity in France, could not be insignificant for me.

Just as little, however, was I a friend of arbitrary rule. I was thoroughly convinced that it is never the people who are responsible for a great revolution; it is the government. Revolutions are impossible as long as governments are continually just and continually watchful, in order that they may forestall revolutions through timely improvements, rather than resist until what is necessary is finally enforced from below.

Because I hated revolutions, I was called a friend of the existing status. This, however, is an ambiguous title which I decline. If everything existing were excellent, good, and just I should have no objection. But since there exists much that is bad, unjust, and imperfect, along with many good things, a "friend of the existing order" often does not mean much more than a friend of things outdated and bad.

Time, however, is in continuous flux, and human affairs take another form every fifty years, so that an institution which was perfect in 1800 may perhaps be a disease in 1850.

Moreover, only that is good for a nation which has emerged from its own core and out of its own general need without aping others. What may be wholesome food for one nation at a certain age level, may prove poison for another.[23]

Goethe's balanced judgment discloses the level from which he observed history, not only in retrospect but as it passed before him—with a detachment and an *amor fati* which made it possible for him to achieve an independent view and, if necessary, to take independent action. It is self-evident that such independence kept him above party opinions and made him appear ambiguous and undecided to their protagonists of whatever political shade. Intent upon "a heightened intuition of the immense events in world affairs," Goethe sought their significance in the light of human existence in general, rather than in their relationship to a particular and therefore subordinate entity. The nation was not an end in itself either when, in 1772, he reviewed Sonnenfels' book on patriotism or when, two-score years later, he discussed with the historian Luden the national problems of the German lands after the Napoleonic wars.[24]

As a man and a citizen the poet will love his fatherland, but the fatherland of his poetic powers and his poetic activity is the good, the noble, the beautiful, which is the property of no particular province and no particular land. This he seizes upon and forms wherever he finds it.[25]

Goethe's criterion is the culture which a nation is able to attain and to hold. Rather than a particular state or nation, the human community as such came to be the object of his thought. Since each people gives to its culture traits that belong to its own particular individuality, the morphological conception of the individual applies also, in a metaphorical sense, to peoples; what is desirable is different from what is desired.

In our language we need a word to express the relation between the idea and the reality of the people, as childhood is related to the child; the educator must listen to childhood rather than to the child, the legislator and governor to the "peoplehood" rather than to the people. The one always expresses the same thing, is reasonable, consistent, pure, and true; the other, for all its willing, never knows what it wants.[26]

When forming a judgment on political events or on concepts, Goethe's invariable tendency was to proceed from their particular and momentary character to their universal context. Writings commenting on a local or historical moment often, therefore, express significant views of society, leading to the original phenomenon of social order. Both the "Pageant" of 1798 and the "Prelude" of 1807 celebrate the moment of the restoration of peace by interpreting peace as an animating power which restores the possibility of "pure" activity.[27] The activity which Goethe calls pure is precisely the endeavor of man to mediate between the eternal and the temporal. Goethe's social thought is conceived in view of this fundamental function of human existence. Such "pure activity" is the only fulfillment which fate has in store for Eugenie in the drama *The Natural Daughter*. She had to be deprived of her social prerogatives, she had to be expelled and humiliated, in order to grow, according to the plan of the trilogy, toward the moment when her pure human nature, *reine Menschlichkeit*, would reconcile the antagonistic forces of society.

At the center of Goethe's ideas of government we find the distinction between the expedient and the desirable. His moderate formulation bears the mark of practical experience. Acting according to expediency means betraying the statesman's ethical responsibility. Acting on the basis of preconceived notions disregards psychological and sociological realities and is bound to fail. Instead of speaking of desires, Goethe speaks of the desirable as an impersonal and objective standard. Into this concept of "the desirable," the possible is already integrated. The governor's task of mediating between what is and what is desirable, requires wisdom. While clever opinions are easily obtained, unselfishness is necessary to that wisdom from which alone fruitful action stems. The wisdom to find the desirable, to remain aware of it, and to translate it into reality is the task of the ruler.

Sometimes Goethe apparently despairs altogether of man's capacity for attaining wisdom; it seems denied to man by the gods. In such moments, he comes close to Prometheus' skepticism in *Pandora*, which is, however, not without an element of hope. Instruction and example,

he says, are of little use. From day to day men try their
way with the thoughtlessness of children. He wishes that
they might learn from the past and make the present their
own by exhausting the moment and giving significant
form to it.

> . . . *Lehr und Rede,*
> *Selbst ein Beispiel, wenig will es frommen.*
> *Also schreiten sie mit Kinderleichtsinn*
> *Und mit rohem Tasten in den Tag hin.*
> *Möchten sie Vergangnes mehr beherz'gen,*
> *Gegenwärtges, formend, mehr sich eignen,*
> *Wär es gut für alle; solches wünscht ich.*[28]

The median position which the desirable takes between
what is and what ought to be, corresponds to Goethe's
conception of society as a part of dynamic nature. It
allows us to support the development of society's inherent
entelechy rather than to shape society by imposing an
abstract ideal. Moreover, thought and experience correct
each other; a clear consciousness is needed of the reasons
why "the ideal" cannot be reached. The attempt to im-
prove what cannot be improved, produces adverse consequences. Therefore Goethe resolves "to accept as given,
whatever cannot be improved upon, and then to try to
counterbalance it."[29] He is perfectly aware of the elusive
character of man's action. Tyche, chance, follows its own
laws. It may change man's intentions to the opposite, even
on the way to realization, and yet it may produce an indispensable good out of obvious errors, "as though a
genius would often obscure our *hegemonikon,* our guiding
spirit, so that we err to the advantage of ourselves and
others."[30]

True to his so-called realism, Goethe considers recognition of the general limitations of man as basic to political
action. In politics as in the arts, he directs his criticism
primarily against the self-centeredness of the individual

which tempts him to act according to expediency or solely
for the sake of his personal advantage. Moreover, Goethe
criticizes shrewdness in government because it tends to
undermine trust. Such criticism presupposes that both administrator and subject are capable of realizing the objective significance of governmental measures, that they can
think in terms of the organic whole they serve. In contrast
to the predominant tendency of modern political thought
to eliminate ethics from its calculations as an imponderable
factor, Goethe makes this factor the very center of his
thought. If there are any remedies at all for the ills of
society, they will be found in the ethical resources of man.
The self-resignation of the individual which guides the
wanderers in *Wilhelm Meister* is the ultimate source of
any constructive communal action, and it is required in
particular in the ruler. At the time of his closest co-
operation with Karl August, Goethe wrote in his diary:
"No one who fails to renounce himself entirely is either
worthy or capable of ruling."[31]

Antonio in *Tasso* represents the self-control and prudence the man of affairs needs. Jarno-Montan in *Wilhelm
Meister* is a similar figure. This clearsighted nobleman is
versed in the affairs of state and court. Baron Jarno later
becomes the geologist Montan. His sharp observation penetrates the vanity and fallacies of man and society and
causes him at last to turn to the miners, among whom he
works before joining the Abbé's group of emigrants. His
taciturnity is itself a criticism of society, and so is his love
for the mineral world, in which he recognizes a symbol
of order that leads beyond all self-delusion. He approaches
nature by studying its geological bases, society by exercising a fundamental craft, and his own life by returning to
the profession of which he is master because he grew up
in it.

The attraction which this figure exercised upon
Goethe's mind is indicative of his seriousness in penetrat-

ing to the solid fundamentals of social life. The way in
which Jarno conceives of geology and mining reflects
Goethe's own predilection. Like Jarno he searched for the
gifts of nature hidden in the earth and combined the philosophic aspect of this activity with its communal usefulness. Goethe had "nursed" the mining industry at Ilmenau to "its virile strength." The speech which he gave
at the festival of 1784 anticipates the simple social conceptions of the wanderers in *Wilhelm Meister*.[32] It calls
for co-operative good will in protecting the common enterprise "by removing obstacles, clearing up misunderstandings, suppressing obnoxious passions, and thereby
contributing to the commonweal." The image of an "organic society," fundamental to Goethe's social philosophy
in general, governs also his activity in establishing this one
particular enterprise, which must necessarily reflect the
general law. His social common sense kept him close to
the thought and personality of Justus Möser. In 1781 he
wrote Möser's daughter, the editor of her father's writings:

I am striving day by day to educate myself according to the
best of tradition and the truth of nature which is always in
operation, so that, from experiment to experiment, I am guided
in my effort to come closer, by acting, writing, and reading, to
that which stands highest before the soul of each of us,
although we have never seen it and cannot name it.[33]

From his practical experience, made on a religious
ground, there resulted Goethe's organic conception of
the human community. As an idea or original phenomenon it belonged to the orbit of the desirable and was
detached from the surface of the historical realm. To
bring the desirable down to the level of the actual and
concrete, as nineteenth-century "realism" was inclined to
do, was to misunderstand Goethe's conception of evolution and inevitably led to a determinism alien to him.

Goethe knew that state and society are subject to time

although related to the timeless. Like poetic creation, political action tends to survive, to earn the gratitude and "the blessings of posterity." But no calculation, not even the most brilliant historical philosophy, can tell the statesman how long his work will last. He cannot be sure of its survival at all because it is inevitably involved in the flow of history. The normative image, which should govern man's effort in establishing the just society, is, however, independent of time. The order of the human community results from a striving toward fulfillment of the norm inherent in the nature of man. The same law governs nature and spirit, and their manifestations are to be conceived as metaphors of the "original light." The mediating function of man is basic to the well-ordered community, in which life is healthy and thriving. To reconcile the eternal and the temporal, however, is the privilege of all:

> *Nicht der König*
> *Hat das Vorrecht; allen ists verliehen.*
> *Wer das Rechte kann, der soll es wollen;*
> *Wer das Rechte will, der sollt' es können,*
> *Und ein jeder kanns, der sich bescheidet,*
> *Schöpfer seines Glücks zu sein im Kleinen.*
>
> . . . .
>
> *So im Kleinen ewig wie im Grossen*
> *Wirkt Natur, wirkt Menschengeist, und beide*
> *Sind ein Abglanz jenes Urlichts droben,*
> *Das unsichtbar alle Welt erleuchtet.*[34]

The universalistic and organic character of Goethe's view of the human community is evident from the decisive place it assigns to the concepts of man and mankind. The comprehensive, synoptic faculty of Goethe's mind did not prevent him from the most "realistic" criticism of this or that nation (including his own), of personalities, events, and opinions. Neither did it preclude love for his people. As he was in some cases disgusted with individuals, so he was at times disgusted with the Germans in general.[35] He suffered on account of them, and he complained bitterly about their miserable conduct in political matters. His love, however, was greater than his criticism. But the object of his love was man rather than the physical whole of those who spoke his language. He loved them for the promise inherent in them, as a branch of mankind, called to share in the realization of the best there is in man. The love of one's people is justified if the order of one's own values is sound. Then one cannot love the false object and one's love cannot become exclusive.

The structure of Goethe's image of society gives to it a place apart from the political theory of his time. He deviated from the tendency of the absolute state toward regimentation by the degree of initiative which he was ready to grant the individual. He was not a radical liberal either in the political or in the economic sense, because he held that wise supervision by competent authority was indispensable. Some of his practical suggestions tended toward co-operative organization. He was averse to the French idéologues, such as Helvétius,[36] because he saw them dealing in a mechanistic and uniform fashion with an object which was organic and manifold. He considered violence, both from above and from below, as directed against life and as demonic by nature. He was deeply aware of the problem of power, since he was close to the affairs of the world and yet, by destiny and resolution, inwardly distant from them. He expected good government from the self-mastery which man should develop through his mediating thought and action. There was no doubt in his mind that nature wanted man to be free. But he was too conscious of the difficulties inherent in this task of mankind to trust formulas or organizations. The demonic can use many a mask. Thus his attitude in

regard to the pre-eminent political issues of his later life—
revolution, the new order of Europe, constitution—was
historical in the sense that it was based upon the concrete
situation as he saw it rather than upon ideological partisanship. But his judgment of good government he summed
up in the unequivocal maxim: "Which government is the
best? The one that teaches us to govern ourselves."[37]

Toward the end of his life Goethe gave to his vision
of the "original" human community the form of his social
utopia. Written in the cryptic and yet readable style of
his old age, this image is detached and concrete at the
same time. With a light hand Goethe gives to the attentive reader the hints of its symbolic language. And yet the
roots of this image should be sought in the practical concern of the young Goethe with the secret of the human
community. Like his views of religion and art, so also his
conception of government arose from the unprejudiced
meeting of his personality with the concreteness of life.
His political thought, like his philosophy of religion and
his aesthetics, bears the marks of the independence of his
procedure. The statesman is a lawgiver, as is the artist
or the philosopher. The material in which he works, however, is the unruly stuff of history. It disturbs him by
showing drastically the ephemeral side of his effort; it
exposes him to the temptations of power, vanity, and
self-delusion; it demands resignation and self-mastery
without reward. The political man is, like the artist, referred to a transcendental significance of his actions. The
most oppressing darkness of history does not leave man
without hope because he can always advance to the inner
meaning of things. With his inner sense he can elevate
himself to the idea of justice.

The author of *Götz von Berlichingen*, the drama of the
passionate and courageous fighter for justice, still held, in
the wisdom of his old age, that man's capacity to think
what is right is the source and condition of his greatness

and beauty. As the symbol of man's calling to lift his thought and himself to the level of right, Goethe once interpreted the figure of a genius soaring over the globe and pointing down to the earth with one hand, upward to the stars with the other.

Und wenn mich am Tag die Ferne
Luftiger Berge sehnlich zieht,
Nachts das Übermass der Sterne
Prächtig mir zu Häupten glüht—

Alle Tag' und alle Nächte
Rühm' ich so des Menschen Los;
Denkt er ewig sich ins Rechte,
Ist er ewig schön und gross.[38]

When man lifts his thought to the level of right, his mind moves toward the "original phenomenon." He divines the eternal through its temporal metaphor and recognizes his calling.

5

Growth and Achievement

The Rhythm of Thought and Action—Consolidation:
Iphigenie, *Tasso*, *Egmont*—Responsibility
for Culture: Schiller—The Detachment of Wisdom
Friends and Enemies—The Old Truth

THE RHYTHM OF thought and action which Goethe considered the quintessence of the art of living and which he increasingly mastered gave the convincing character of a testimony to the fruits of his life and work. Personality and idea were interwoven in his literary and scientific production as well as in his conversations and letters. He never separated his thought from concrete experience. Never satisfied with personal impressions, he sought their impersonal meaning. The characteristic form of his image of man and society, its combination of concreteness and symbolical significance, was possible because of this remarkable capacity to withdraw from contacts with men and affairs into the isolation of productive work and to return to "the world" with undiminished intensity. "What I did not live through, I did not write or say"[1]—these words to Eckermann suggest how the encounter of inner and outer experience, of *Gemüt* and *Welt*, were for Goethe the source of poetry and wisdom. The extension within the finite leads man toward the infinite:

Willst du ins Unendliche schreiten,
Geh nur im Endlichen nach allen Seiten.[2]

The cycle *Gott, Gemüt und Welt* reflects this productive art of living, which made lyrical poetry and geological studies, administrative action and intimate communication with friends equally intrinsic parts of the personality.

Thus Goethe understands the mission of the poet from his exposure to and acceptance of a particular way of living rather than through his medium of production. It is this conception which Wilhelm expresses in the *Apprenticeship:*

The sensitive soul of the poet, easily moved, proceeds like the circling sun from night to day, and his harp is tuned with gentle transitions to joy and pain. Out of the ground of his heart, the beautiful flower of wisdom grows. Others dream while awake and are frightened out of their senses by immense imaginations. He lives the dream of life as an awakened one, and the rarest events are to him at the same time past and future. Thus the poet is also the teacher, prophet, and friend of gods and men.[3]

When Goethe was distressed about the discrepancy between his potentialities and their realization, when he complained about his "failures and omissions," he found new strength in the resolution to continue objectifying his capabilities, namely, in the urge to form which inspired his youth as a tempestuous force and enlivened his old age as a reliable flow of productive energy. Thus he himself regarded his life as the organic development of an entelechy, obedient in spite of all contingencies to an inherent law and, like a tree, adding ever widening rings of growth through a succession of metamorphoses. More than once his fidelity to the mission of the poet compelled him to separate from his own past. He suffered under the curse of this compulsion to wander as much as those from whom he parted. He sought and found the means of overcoming such separations in the regenerative power of work and in his faithfulness to the significant moments of experience.

The serenity and firmness in mastering the rhythm of life characteristic of his later years were a conscious and central part of his ethics, and brought his growth to conclusion. Goethe's long-drawn-out development evidently was inevitable for a personality of his artistic independence and universality. From the dramatic fragments of his *Sturm und Drang* it is apparent how he conceived of his own experience in terms of its generally human meaning. Consequently the consolidation of his personal life could be achieved only simultaneously with the crystallization of his convictions. This consolidation took place in his fifth decade, after his return from Italy in 1788. In solving for himself the problem of human freedom, Goethe also laid the foundation for his view of the desirable form of communal existence. In regard to both individual and society, he strove toward the reconciliation of independence and necessity by a productive balance of freedom and order.

The era of *Sturm und Drang* had made Goethe aware of his potentialities and had sown the seed for his most significant productions—*Faust, Pandora,* and in a sense *Meister.* When Goethe resolved to give order and form to his productivity by disciplining his life and work, he succeeded in overcoming the restless inwardness of the *Sturm und Drang* and in penetrating to the normative core of human existence. Especially during the first five years of this central phase of his life, Charlotte von Stein had an essential function in the consolidation of his personality. Goethe's relation to her was decisive for the crystallization of his ethical consciousness, his literary form, and his firmness in affairs of the world. She was for him the immovable pole toward which he gravitated "in the midst of the noisy movement of life." He felt a preordained unity of souls between him and this sympathetic individual who, it seemed to him, must be the "sister or wife" of a previous existence.[4] Again through his letters we learn of his happiness over the certainty of her love, of his feeling that his life was "renewed" through her, of his suffering under the resignation he had to impose upon himself.

Goethe's communion with Charlotte enabled him to

overcome the longing for a "recovery from life,"[5] of which
the figure and the songs of Mignon are poetic crystallizations. Through Charlotte the transcendent nature of love,
the tension between the male and female principles of the
creation and with it the power of the "eternally feminine"
to draw man upward, came to be a vital experience for him.
His deep friendship for her was indispensable to his realization of the mediating role of the poet, as the poem "Zueignung" explains. Her moderating influence, the sense of form
and measure which she strengthened in him, the urge toward
fulfillment of life which she supported, the shelter she gave
him—each of these aspects of Goethe's bond with Charlotte
was an integral element of his growth. Around her personality he crystallized an image of a human being capable of an
active and self-restraining life with others and symbolizing
at the same time the potential reconciliation between the antagonistic forces of existence. Reminiscent of a courtship of
the age of chivalry, Goethe's relation to Charlotte provided
the productive tension out of which the first version of
Meister and the dramas *Iphigenie, Tasso,* and *Egmont* could
grow.

These dramatic works reflect Goethe's transition from
predominant subjectivity to productive acceptance of man's
function within society. In them Goethe gave to his convictions about man, society, and culture the first classical formulation. Iphigenie, the incarnation of a pure and beautiful
ethical being, breaks through the vicious circle of guilt and
curse by healing the conflicts of violence through the peaceful power accessible to her higher self:

> *Gewalt und List, der Männer höchster Ruhm,*
> *Wird durch die Wahrheit dieser hohen Seele*
> *Beschämt, und reines kindliches Vertrauen*
> *Zu einem edlen Manne wird belohnt.*[6]

This "astonishingly modern and un-Greek" play, as Schiller
called it,[7] epitomizes "pure humanity" by giving it the deci-

sive role in the solution which is to establish a redeemed life. It symbolizes the this-worldly realization of a chiliastic impulse. Goethe remained faithful to this striving for the fulfillment within the process of life of man's higher potentialities. In his later works, however, he laid the accent upon the transitoriness of the moment of fulfillment and upon the element of grace which brings it about. Eugenie in *The Natural Daughter* is akin to Iphigenie. In both these dramas reconciliation is possible because of the "pure humanity" and inner truthfulness of their heroines.

Torquato Tasso, the drama of conflict between the impatient and suspicious subjectivity of genius and the prudent firmness of men able to rule themselves and society, reaches for an image of the ethical foundation of a cultured life. A tension within Goethe himself is reflected by the contrast between the poet Tasso and the statesman Antonio. Their ultimate union symbolizes the reconciliation of the longing for the realm of love and beauty with the mastery of social reality in the resignation to the desirable. When Tasso, in the end, clings to the rock of Antonio's character, he accepts the order which alone grants the possibility of realization to the gift of genius. It is a Medicean ideal of state which the Duke of Ferrara follows in holding Tasso at his court and in protecting a talent that needs protection though it may not know it. The golden age for which everyone longs is not to be won by unbridled liberty but by devoted service:

> *Der Mensch ist nicht geboren, frei zu sein,*
> *Und für den Edlen ist kein schöner Glück,*
> *Als einem Fürsten, den er ehrt, zu dienen.*[8]

Men of good will will be able to enjoy the beautiful world if kindred hearts unite in renouncing selfishness. The golden age is neither past nor future but can arise here and now through a community in which order and freedom find reconciliation in the spirit of friendship.

Mein Freund, die goldne Zeit ist wohl vorbei,
Allein die Guten bringen sie zurück.
Und soll ich dir gestehen, wie ich denke:
Die goldne Zeit, womit der Dichter uns
Zu schmeicheln pflegt, die schöne Zeit, sie war,
So scheint es mir, so wenig, als sie ist;
Und war sie je, so war sie nur gewiss,
Wie sie uns immer wieder werden kann.
Noch treffen sich verwandte Herzen an
Und teilen den Genuss der schönen Welt.[9]

This image of the good life which the princess conveys to the poet is part of the lasting foundation of Goethe's social thought. Decades afterwards, in reply to the University of Jena's recognition of the fiftieth anniversary of his arrival at Weimar, he formulated it in the words:

Only inner intentions of mutual good will and trust can promote what is insistently demanded as the most indispensable good in the City of God and of ethical conduct.[10]

The tragedy of Egmont, who dies "for the freedom for which he lived and fought," develops the issue between freedom and order on the political plane. The hero, courageously trusting higher guiding powers, is the incarnation of the constructive good intentions of noble humanity. Alba suspiciously believes only in control through unconditional authority. To prevent the destruction of the ancient liberties of the Netherlands, which the Spanish conqueror threatens, Egmont presents to Alba his people's demand for preservation of their freedom by recounting those elements in their character which justify trust.

They are men worthy to tread God's earth, each complete in himself like a small king, firm, active, capable, faithful, loyal to old customs. It is difficult to win their confidence, but it is easy to hold it. Firm and solid! They can be oppressed but they cannot be subdued.[11]

Egmont's appeal fails. The cold representative of the *raison d'état* cannot be converted to the reason of good government. Egmont is made aware of the decision taken concerning his people and himself—a decision which "no prince should ever take."

In order to govern them more easily, he intends to weaken, to suppress, to destroy the energy of his people, their spirit and the idea they have of themselves. He wants to corrupt the inner-most core of their individuality.[12]

Through *Egmont* Goethe evoked the ancient Germanic freedoms as Justus Möser had made them understandable to his time. These liberties rest upon the honor and self-respect of the individual and are the essence of Goethe's organic conception of the state. In contrast to the arbitrariness of absolute government, the ethical ruler has the duty to help man toward the realization of his potentiality for self-government.

In each of these dramas the force of human purity is in conflict with the demonic in man and society. In *Iphigenie* this tension is solved by the triumph of the spirit of reconciliation, in *Tasso* by the community between poet and statesman; in *Egmont* the tragic end is mitigated by the apotheosis of the hero which is indispensable to the expression of Goethe's basic idea. If Goethe was to convey the results of his experience of social existence, none of these plays could follow a conventional dramatic pattern. Their form and meaning are determined by Goethe's faith in the reality of a "higher" energy accessible to man. This energy leads Egmont to martyrdom, forces Tasso to subject himself to prudence, and inspires Iphigenie in the crucial moment of decision. The integration of this "human purity" into concrete existence is the problem common to these plays, in which Goethe presents his constructive answer to the abysmal chaos latent in human existence. Goethe took these works with him on his "flight" to Italy, to give them their ultimate form. His concentration on them gives a hint as to the reason why he resolved to reach out for a "new beginning."

This decision had been foreshadowed for many years and was taken at a juncture when the branches of administration entrusted to him did not require his presence and when Karl August had succeeded in his project of the *Fürstenbund*. Then finally Goethe "thought of himself," as he expressed it to the duke, who indeed had often encouraged him to do so. Although there is no sufficient account of the personal events immediately preceding Goethe's seemingly abrupt departure, it is impossible to doubt that it meant to him both "rebirth" and continuation. The renewal he sought and found resulted in a healing of his Northern inclination to separate the real and the phenomenal, the physical and the intellectual. When he "put everything at stake" he meant to be alone with his *daimon*, to be once more a personality rather than a figure in society, to be free to choose his own future, his companions, his way of living.[13] An invincible compulsion led him south to a people on whose faces, as he said a few years after his return, the hand of God is more legible than on those of the Germans.[14] It was not so much the Italian scene which he sought as the unity and soundness of living, the joy over the day in the sun granted to man, a confirmation of the constructive attitude toward life which his own nature seemed to intend. The formation of the idea in the spiritual-physical reality of life, the growth and modification of the living being into an "image" of the idea, the whole voluntary and involuntary activity connected with Goethe's use of the word *Bildung* was the goal he set himself on the Italian journey.

This step which demanded a withdrawal to the very basis of his existence required at the same time the review and completion of works begun in the past—in *Egmont*, for instance, of a conception dating back to the *Sturm und Drang*. The faithfulness to himself for the sake of which he left for Italy,

included a continued relationship to his friends. His letters
to Karl August and Herder demonstrate a continuously active effort to keep alive a friendship with which whatever he
did in Italy was deeply connected. Those to Charlotte reveal
a tenacious struggle against losing her. He confessed to her
that for her sake alone he would return. If nevertheless he
lost this love, the reason must be sought in the very consolidation which his life in Italy brought about, and in which
Charlotte was unable to follow him.

Ready now to crystallize in himself an image of man
which he could envision as the intention of the creation, he
wholeheartedly seized upon the moment granted to him in
"the realm of color and form" in the midday sun of which
the "Sturmlied" speaks—the moment in which he could experience "harmony and totality" in contrast to the unsatis-
fied "Faustian" search in man's self.

> O, wie fühl ich in Rom mich so froh! Gedenk, ich
> der Zeiten,
> Da mich ein graulicher Tag hinten im Norden
> umfing,
> Trübe der Himmel und schwer auf meinen Scheitel
> sich senkte,
> Farb- und gestaltlos die Welt um den Ermatteten
> lag,
> Und ich über mein Ich, des unbefriedigten Geistes
> Düstre Wege zu spähn, still in Betrachtung ver-
> sank.[15]

The ultimate certainty he attained about the normative intention inherent in existence came about simultaneously
with his discovery of the *Urpflanze*, his productive encounter with the art of antiquity and the Renaissance, his
unceasing effort to grasp the visible form through the observing eye of the designer, and his theoretical concern
about the significance of art. He lived in the midst of a circle
of friends: the artists Tischbein, Hackert, Angelika Kauff-

mann, Raphael Mengs; he devoted sympathy and care to Karl Philipp Moritz, whose inner development, recounted in the novel *Anton Reiser*, reminded him of his own inner conflicts of growth. Only toward the end of his journey did he lift the incognito which protected him from social contacts other than those he chose. He did not know which form his life might take after his return and kept open the avenues of art, poetry and politics. He tasted to the full the freedom which had been curtailed in the Weimar years. When he finally left Rome he did so resolved to work for the growth of a sound life in the North.

The inner certainty which he had attained was, it seems, the main reason for the isolated position in which he found himself during the first six years after the Italian journey. The consolidation of his own personality and thought affected his relation to Charlotte when he returned, a changed man firmly grounded in himself. Outer and inner circumstances compelled him to center his energies on his work in poetry and science. His journey had helped to establish resignation as the principle of his ethical convictions, and resignation now became his own bitter experience. His relationship with Charlotte Vulpius began shortly after his return. It developed into a marriage of conscience almost two decades before Goethe gave it legal sanction. In spite of the touching tenderness and care he had for her, he was conscious of having renounced a "perfect union" such as is represented in his picture of the love of Wilhelm and Natalie.[16] With misgivings he had seen the duke accept a position in the Prussian army while Weimar still required his full devotion; now he accompanied Karl August on his campaigns, but from his return from Italy onward his center of gravitation was the domain of his own productivity.

In retrospect, the years after Italy which Goethe devoted to further studies of nature and art, and in the course of which he wrote the "Essay on the Metamorphosis of Plants" and "Simple Imitation of Nature, Mannerism, and Style," appear as preparatory to the subsequent decade of his collaboration with Schiller. It was during these years of comparative isolation that he established his purposes in every field; his yearning for the South as it had found expression in Mignon's songs, was stilled, and his turn toward objectification is reflected by his command of the classical verse form which he uses in the *Roman Elegies*, in the *Achilleïs*, and in *Hermann and Dorothea*. When Heinrich Meyer, the Swiss painter and art critic whom Goethe had met in Rome, came to Weimar, the group of collaborators and helpers began to form which participated in Goethe's studies with unceasing devotion. From such modest and faithful helpers as Riemer, Chancellor Mueller, Eckermann, and even Soret, who in Goethe's last decade became an educator at the court, we have invaluable accounts of the ways in which Goethe animated the circle around him.

It was Schiller, however, who encouraged Goethe to resume work on *Faust* and *Meister* and to share publicly in the responsibility for standards of culture in a moment when all aspects of the European situation seemed to point to disintegration. After years of coolness and suspicion, Schiller's noble and inquisitive mind was able to reconstruct, in his own terms, the unity of Goethe's personality and pursuits, and thus to give him a response which was both a continual stimulant and a sympathetic competition.

The friendship with Schiller is reflected in the exchange of letters which Goethe published. It gives a day-by-day account of the thought, production, and mutual criticism of both poets from 1794 to Schiller's death in 1805. *Hermann and Dorothea*, the *Parable*, *The Natural Daughter*, and *Achilleïs* are among Goethe's works of this period. From it date his conception of the *Novelle* and his contribution to *Winckelmann and His Century*. It was during these years also that he founded the journal *Propylaea* to serve the appreciation, theory, and practice of art in a classical sense. Through their own publications, through the theater, and through their journals, Goethe and Schiller joined in a common effort of a normative and critical nature. Their common polemics in the epigrams of the *Xenien* constitutes the eristic side of their work in establishing literary, aesthetic, and educational standards. They resolved to impart to the German-speaking world an awareness of, and a sense of responsibility for, aesthetic form as an organ of ethical culture and conduct.

In the history of German thought, this outstanding activity of two personalities of rank meant an attempt to consolidate national culture on a high level of universal significance. In western Europe the rise of national consciousness followed the emergence of the modern nation-state which, in the age of absolutism, supplanted and progressively destroyed the feudal structure that had prevailed throughout the Occident during the Middle Ages. This development had by-passed both Italy and the German countries. Only in Goethe's time did the last remnants of the supernational medieval Empire fall under the blows of the Napoleonic reconstruction of Europe. In his youth Schiller had staked everything on the rebellion in the name of human dignity and freedom against the narrow arbitrariness of small-state absolutism. Through Kant's philosophy of ethics he was led to understand the ethical significance of beauty. With Schiller, Goethe maintained that what is decisive for man is the universal end of human existence rather than attachment to any particular phenomenon, be it the individual, the state, or the political nation.

To Goethe the community with Schiller meant the fulfillment of a wish, the significance of which reached far beyond the decade of their co-operation. This friendship was the first instance of a communion of minds that could endure in spite of deep-seated divergencies. Neither Herder nor Jacobi had been able to accept Goethe's readiness to co-operate in spite of differences of conviction. Both Herder and his irritable and eccentric wife were motivated in their attitude toward Goethe by subjective, and frequently imaginary, misgivings. Jacobi never lost hope of ultimately converting Goethe to his own views and refused, in the end, to recognize the spirit of mutual respect which is essential to friendship. Schiller, on the other hand, did his utmost to lend Goethe his helpful criticism, which was acceptable precisely because it was built upon an understanding reconstruction of Goethe's inner necessities. The image which Goethe had formed in "Die Geheimnisse" came close to realization when one man, of a thoroughly different fiber, could join him for the sake of a common aim. Never again did Goethe find so productive a relationship, even though a similar spirit of friendship was at the basis of his relations with the composer Zelter, with Wilhelm von Humboldt, and with Count Reinhard.

French literature and thought had for about two centuries benefited from the discipline imposed by the Académie Française. The development in Germany of literary standards, as well as of philosophic thought, could not rely on the support of a national institution. The manifold mental world of the German-speaking countries was, in a way, as anarchic as the political status of the Germanies had been since the High Middle Ages. Goethe and Schiller did not intend to encourage uniformity and, even had they wanted to, would probably not have succeeded. But as authors and critics they felt a responsibility for raising and clarifying the standards of the spoken and written word. Where their classical conceptions met with resistance—from Jean Paul, for instance, and from most of the Romanticists—they indirectly exercised a challenging influence through their firmness. In response to the uncertainties of their time they conscientiously attempted to shape the mental world of their contemporaries, for they were convinced that the mediating realm of literature was a decisive factor in the formation of life, and that the humanism on which their position rested was an indispensable agent in defending the dignity of culture against partisanship and political domination. That politics should not become destiny, as Napoleon put it,[17] was the practical aim of Goethe and Schiller. This principal tenet made their attitude toward the political realm a liberal one in the sense of subordinating the political and technical means of public affairs to the conception of the "good life."

Both poets lived in close contact with European affairs, and Goethe especially, by virtue of his position, was fully informed about the course taken by the Revolution and its subsequent imperialistic expansion. His clarity of judgment, which was so evident at the battle of Valmy, the decisive moment of the campaign in France in 1792, never left him. Through the revolutionary and Napoleonic eras he lived from day to day in full awareness of the uncertainty that accompanied each phase of these twenty-five years of crisis and war. Even the calmness of the later Restoration Period did not deceive Goethe; he was aware of its inconclusive and preliminary character. Schiller, through his drama written for the people's theater, intended to create a firm vision of human dignity in the inescapably tragic course of life. Goethe dealt directly with the political problem of the revolutionary era when he tried to unmask the self-delusion of the revolutionary dilettante in *The Citizen General*, or to oppose doctrinaire and ideological conceit by sound reason and genuinely social understanding in *The Uprooted Ones*. A reflection of the age more congenial to his art was the symbolism employed in his preludes and in *The Natural Daughter*. The epitome of the image of life by which he opposed the spirit of disintegration he saw in the French Revolution, was the epic *Hermann and Dorothea*.

The confirmation and expansion of high-minded and responsible conduct were the ethical ends of Goethe's and Schiller's "educational liberalism." There was certainly some inclination toward cultured living, *höhere Bildung*, among the Germans of their time, which encouraged Goethe and Schiller in the hope that "those possessing it might group

themselves, by and by, around them."[18] The consequences
of their venture to uphold the realm of the mind against the
threatening chaos are immeasurable. Undoubtedly the immediate repercussions of their action are far outweighed by
the lasting effect of the works it engendered, which ever and
again call for the liberation of man from the all-engulfing
threat of the destructive and unruly demonism of political
events. As he came to know Goethe's personality and to
realize the unity of his pursuits, Schiller enthusiastically recognized that here was a man who was impervious to the
social and intellectual discrepancies of the modern world, a
man healthy in a Homeric fashion, the fulfillment of an idea.
Because of Goethe he felt infinitely strengthened in his own
endeavor to promote, over and above "the political turmoil,"
"the quiet building of better concepts, purer principles, and
nobler ways of living, upon which, in the end, all improve-
ment of the social situation depends."

The more the restricted interest of our days imparts their
tension to the individual's feelings, confines and subjugates them,
the more urgent the desire becomes to liberate them again
through a general and higher interest in that which is *purely
human* and which lasts above all influence of the times, to re-
unite the politically divided world under the banner of truth
and beauty.[19]

On the eve of nineteenth-century nationalism, to which Napoleon's suppression of freedom contributed more than any
other single factor, the German-speaking world was called
upon by the formative energy of Goethe and Schiller to
center its striving on the formation of man in the spirit of
pure humanity; *reine Menschlichkeit* was to be the foundation of a reunion of men divided against each other.[20]

In the midst of the breakdown of the last vestiges of central Europe's ancient institutions, Goethe became seriously
ill and did not expect to live. At this very moment, Schiller
died unexpectedly. "I thought I would lose myself, and
now I lose a friend and, with him, half of my existence,"

Goethe wrote to Zelter.[21] Thereupon he entered that critical period with which his "old age" began. With Schiller's death and the French invasion that soon followed, the immediate past seemed to belong irretrievably to history. Goethe was uncertain whether he would recover his poetic creativity at all. He turned at first to science and began to complete his theory of color. His work on its history interpreted the development of a particular branch of cognition as a significant part of man's intellectual evolution. He thereby initiated a new type of historical analysis. Soon after, he began to write his autobiography, in a moment which hardly justified the expectation of twenty-five more years of life and of new forms of creative action.

Goethe's poetical productivity re-emerged when his power to love reasserted itself, when a passion arose in him which he re-created in his sonnets.[22] It carried him to the level of the dramatic lyrics of *Pandora* and to the ethical clarity of *The Elective Affinities*. The era of a new and final tone began, in which the fluid richness of the young Goethe seems to merge with the moderating law and the sculptural preciseness of his classical verse. He seems to live and write as though remote from time. The Promethean and Epimethean realms, between which the poet is bound to move, are further separated from each other; Goethe's symbolism now tends to convey the reality of the transcendental by lifting its characters to a higher plane. Pandora is a heavenly figure; Ottilie's self-inflicted martyrdom ends with her transfiguration; the *Divan* poetry is conceived as a mirror of life, not merely in the forms of a far-distant people but also in the feeling it conveys of having been written on another star.

A word about the *Divan*, written in May, 1822, to Zelter, speaks of the universal significance of his relation to Near-Eastern thought:

This Mohammedan religion, mythology, customs, lend themselves to a kind of poetry fitting my age: Unconditional accept-

ance of the unfathomable will of God, serene survey of the
affairs of earthly life which ever and again moves in circles and
spirals, love and inclination swinging between two worlds,
everything concrete being purified and dissolving symbolically.[23]

In the simple forms of the *Divan* poetry or the "Zahme
Xenien"[24] the old Goethe gave to his religious and philosophic wisdom an ultimate lucidity. A human miracle joined
the passion of a youth to the mastership of a septuagenarian
in the "Marienbader Elegie" of 1823. With an inexhaustible
command of the poetic word, Goethe crystallized the totality of his view of the universe in the images and rhythms of
"Selige Sehnsucht," "Eins and Alles," "Vermächtnis," and
the cycle *Gott und Welt*. In this realm, distant from and yet
connected by a thousand threads with the life of his time,
the old Goethe had the center of his existence.

In the beginning of this era, Bettina von Arnim's unre-
quited love made Goethe the object and helper of her own
poetic work in spite of the resignation he had to impose
upon her. The *Divan* poetry, however, was born of a
spiritual communion with Marianne von Willemer, the one
poetess of rank who ever shared fully Goethe's poetical
world and responded with her own being to its tone and
atmosphere. Some of her poems were included in the *Divan*.
The whole work echoes her intangible and responsive
presence. Even though the serene beauty of the *Divan*
constitutes a universe sufficient unto itself, it could not be
imagined without the participation of another soul. A
"surprising power" had initiated a new era of Goethe's
life. Once more this fate acted through a most personal
impulse, once more it imposed upon the poet resignation
for the sake of his work.

A new balance between transcendence and immanence
had announced itself in *Pandora*. It is the work of the
gods, "the higher powers," to grant the desirable at the
proper time. Epimetheus, faithfully living on in the fullness that once had been his, bears more of the author's

traits than the ruler Prometheus. His figure mirrors the distance which Goethe inwardly took from his time and its affairs. This distance enabled him to actualize a realm wholly of his own creation, and it also strengthened the timeless quality of his latest works. Of a many-sided symbolism, they seemed to be sealed—as was literally the case with the second part of *Faust*—until later individuals or generations could disclose the treasure of their secrets.

As in Goethe's conception of human existence, so in his own life, friendship was an intrinsic part of productivity. His art of initiating and cultivating relations of friendship surrounded him with an atmosphere of understanding and trust. In his youth, he had learned from the noble attitude by which Wieland reacted to the attack of the satire *Gods, Heroes, and Wieland*, that "man does not easily obtain a greater advantage than awareness of the inner merits of his opponents."[25] In this instance, Goethe felt defeated and his irony turned into friendship. "One knows what one is only when one finds oneself in others."[26] Goethe even called this discovery of oneself in another human being "metempsychosis," the passing of the soul into another body.

Goethe's friendship, which had been impulsive and passionate in his youth, became more responsible with the increase in his own firmness. The exchanges of his old age reveal the art of objectifying the love for the friend, although his genuine human warmth invariably breaks through his devotion to the productive results of each relationship. He learned, as his Aristipp says in the ironical dialogue between the philosophers and the questioning people, "Die Weisen und die Leute," to "live and let live" within the limits of that which is possible in view of the common ends of society.

> *Den rechten Lebensfaden*
> *Spinnt einer, der lebt und leben lässt;*

Er drille zu, er zwirne fest,
Der liebe Gott wird weisen.[27]

Goethe was inclined to praise rather than to blame; he considered the art of enjoyment as an inward inventiveness which supports the objectification of the inward richness of human existence. In so far as his life was a work of art, its unity resulted from an ever renewed effort at the constructive formation of hours and days and years. He succeeded because of his skill, diligently acquired, in balancing spontaneity by the conscious formation of his talents and in sensing the vital potentialities of human relationships. He felt fully alive only when others participated with him in good will and kindly feelings.

The correspondence of Goethe with his friends (only the exchanges after 1800 have been carefully preserved) reveals another dimension of his productivity. His influence upon the mental formation of the men and women of his time can scarcely be gauged. The replies to his letters and the documents telling of personal contacts with him express absolute confidence in his sympathy and respect for his personality and judgment. In his old age his letters are sometimes like messages conveying his position on political, religious, and literary problems. In similar fashion he availed himself of Eckermann, Riemer, and Chancellor von Mueller, who were not only collaborators but at the same time witnesses and depositories of his thinking. It was thus that Goethe remained in close contact with the sciences and the arts in Germany and abroad. Among his correspondents were Fichte, Hegel, Schelling, and Schopenhauer; the historians Niebuhr, Johannes von Mueller, and Ranke; Savigny and the brothers Grimm; Lord Byron, Carlyle, and Walter Scott; Manzoni and Madame de Staël; the Dane Ohlenschläger, the Americans Cogswell and Everett—to mention only a few names which indicate that the actual experience of a worldwide interrelation of thought was the basis on which Goethe conceived of an epoch of universal exchanges:

the union of groups of good mental standards which hitherto had little contact with each other, the recognition of one common purpose, the conviction of the necessity to keep informed about the current course of world events, in the real and the ideal sense.[28]

The universality of Goethe's thought united, in his later years, with the vitality of his human relations to create the vision of an active responsibility for "the world" assumed by men of foresight and good intention. The figure of the Abbé in *Wilhelm Meister's Travels* reflects this conception of *Weltfrömmigkeit* and translates it into his world-association of wanderers.

Even friends and well-meaning visitors had, however, to overcome a certain stiffness on Goethe's part before they could elicit the warmth and freedom in which his personality came to the fore. The Harvard scientist Cogswell, who expected "the most repulsive reception" and experienced the opposite, ascribed his surprise partly to Goethe's modesty, partly to their common interest in mineralogy:

His exterior was in every respect different from the conceptions I had formed. A grand and graceful form, worthy of a knight of the days of chivalry, with a dignity of manners that marked the court rather than the closet that belongs to Goethe, are not often the external characteristics of a man of letters. Soon after being introduced to him, with the politeness of a real gentleman, he turned the conversation to America, and spoke of its hopes and promises, in a manner that showed it had been the subject of his inquiries, and made juster and more rational observations upon its literary pretensions and character than I ever heard from any man in Europe.[29]

When the intangible element of understanding and good will was for some reason lacking, or when Goethe's judgment prompted him to refuse to a visitor or correspondent that recognition which he was ready to give to the smallest talent if he could approve of its basic tendency—then he became truly inaccessible or even hostile. His verdicts about Kleist's *Penthesilea* and Immermann's "philosophic-phantastical nonsense" are but examples of such a resolute withdrawal into his own productive pursuits. Inevitably those who remained strangers saw him in a distorted light. Heinrich Heine, after his visit in 1824, explained the discrepancy between his and Goethe's nature by contrasting the egotist Goethe, bent upon the enjoyment of life, with the enthusiast Heine, ready to sacrifice himself for the idea. When the revolutionary journalist Börne launched his bitter attacks on Goethe, he acted as a partisan against a man who refused to subscribe to the "party spirit" because of his conception of measure and independence. Goethe's judgment about his critic Menzel, who became Börne's nationalistic opponent, pertains as much to Börne himself:

He is a talent which avails itself of the party hatred as an ally and which would not have had any effect without it. One frequently finds examples in literature where hatred takes the place of genius and where small talents appear significant because they present themselves as agents of a party. Likewise one finds in life many persons who have not enough character to stand alone; they attach themselves to a party, feel that they are thereby strengthened and that they represent something.[30]

The strife which, in political thought and in literature, was characteristic of the German situation in Goethe's last decades, had to appear as "useless" from his universal and detached standpoint. In 1830, after saying: "a German writer, a German martyr," and adding that in England and France, with Molière, Rousseau, Voltaire, and Byron it was no different, he remarked to Eckermann:

And if it were alone the stupid masses who persecute higher beings! No, the one gifted person and the one talent persecute the other. Platen scandalizes Heine and Heine Platen, and each of them tries to run down the other and to cause him to be hated, whereas the world is large enough for peaceful living and producing, and everyone has in his own talent an enemy who gives him enough to do.[31]

Although the poetic production of the old Goethe was achieved with the unperturbed certainty of the Ephesian goldsmith, the time itself was demonic enough to keep him constantly reminded of the dangerous and ambivalent character of the human situation. It demanded and received his attention, not only in decisive moments of political history but in the course taken, in this era, by literature, art, and education. A second activity accompanied Goethe's poetic and scientific work in his last decades, and in it his will to influence his contemporaries through criticism and encouragement seemed at times to be as resolute as in the years of his friendship with Schiller. The horizon of his attention, which had always included the heritage of antiquity, was widened once more, through his travels to the Rhein and the Main, by a new appreciation of the Gothic Middle Ages. While the flow of reproductions and originals continued to keep him in the center of the rising historical consciousness of art, his suggestions and his criticism, sometimes polemically pointing at dangerous aberrations, were directed to the efforts of contemporary artists.[32] Not only German but also Italian, French, English, and Slavic literature and historiography found in him a reviewer.[33] In this role he continued to further his "healthy Hellenic-patriotic" convictions, not without leniency toward minor talents, but with clear antagonism or merciless silence where a "false direction" threatened the standards he felt called upon to defend. Hardly one of Goethe's days seemed to pass without being truly lived, in sorrow and joy, in work and in the free flow of thought, on the remotest level of the universal conception of *Faust* or in immediate contact with the events of the hour.

It was in his last years that Goethe arrived at the ultimate conclusions to be drawn from the premises on which
his life and work had grown. Goethe incorporated the
result of his experience in the image of the healthy society
toward which Wilhelm Meister is educated and into which
he is finally received. This community is to bridle the
demonic elements through the resolute insight into their
existence and the equally resolute struggle against their
temptations. Aware of the dynamic character of the universe and of man's function within it, Goethe presented
this image as the epitome of the desirable, of those objective
norms and convictions which alone, he felt, would render
fruitful the communal existence of man.

The light of Goethe's mind was strong enough to attract
to him kindred minds among all the nations. At the very
moment when modern nationalism set out on its course,
Goethe's morphological vision anticipated an ecumenical
culture. He saw a world literature emerging from the thriving beginnings in his era, in which accelerated communication announced the coming end of national isolation. In
Goethe's sense, the function of literature and of the man
of letters consists of a supreme guardianship over the self-
understanding of man and of his support on the road to a
life worthy to be lived. The community of minds which
he required from those striving for good ends should also
serve this generally human rather than any particular purpose. Again, Goethe's conception of world literature is
not meant to threaten the right to existence of the manifold forms rising along the path of mankind, nor did he
overlook the possible frictions which might emerge along
with this facility and readiness for better mutual acquaintance. He knew that all national literatures have in common
the concern with the nature and destiny of man; the deeper
their works are rooted in the universals fundamental to
human existence, the readier public consciousness will
become for mutual understanding and enrichment, the

stronger will grow a common spirit among those responsible in the world of the mind.[34]

Even Goethe's concern about world literature, however, was subordinated to his ultimate confidence in the unfathomable order of the universe. It was because of this belief that he did not lose hope. Such confidence is an act of faith, underivable and indestructible. Over and above the cycle of birth and death, to which everything temporal is subjected, Goethe believed in the regenerating power of the spirit, participation in which is the ennobling potentiality bestowed upon man. His convictions about the relations of man to the universe were the foundation on which the architecture of his work and life was built.

In the poem "Vermächtnis," "Legacy," Goethe created, at the age of eighty, an epitome of this view of life. He refers man to the enduring norms of being that govern and preserve the living universe and embody the wisdom of God, "the sage who ordained the motion of the earth around the sun." The conscience alive in man is "the sun of his days"; his life in and with the wealth of the outer world, balanced by reason and tempered by prudence, permits him to realize that "the moment is eternity"; he will be productive in obeying the universal guiding power, *das allgemeine Walten*. It is the old truth, discovered long ago, that Goethe advises man to grasp as the lasting bond among noble minds:

> *Das Wahre war schon längst gefunden,*
> *Hat edle Geisterschaft verbunden:*
> *Das alte Wahre, fass es an!*
> *Verdank es, Erden-Sohn, dem Weisen,*
> *Der ihr, die Sonne zu umkreisen,*
> *Und dem Geschwister wies die Bahn.*

A small group of men is united in this spirit throughout the ages. They "anticipate, reflect, and prepare each other."[35] The quiet work of love, as poets and philosophers create it, will arise from serene and active resignation to the order of existence; it will call forth and help to renew the noble impulses of man.

> *Und wie von alters her, im stillen,*
> *Ein Liebewerk nach eignem Willen*
> *Der Philosoph, der Dichter schuf,*
> *So wirst du schönste Gunst erzielen:*
> *Denn edlen Seelen vorzufühlen*
> *Ist wünschenswertester Beruf.*

THE UNIVERSE AND MAN

In the mind of man and in the universe as well there is no above or below; everything has equal claim upon a common center that manifests its invisible presence by the very harmony of all the parts with reference to it. All the quarrels of older and newer schools down to our own day spring from our separating of that which God brought forth as a unity in his creation of nature.

Review of Stiedenroth's Psychology, 1824

6

Cosmology and Cognition

Goethe and Philosophy—A Spiritualist Cosmology
Morphology and Intuition—The Organic
Conception of Nature—Polarity and Intensification
Nature and Man

THE METAPHYSICAL CHARACTER of Goethe's thinking and
the control which he exercised upon his methods justify
us in considering him as a philosopher. The genesis of his
philosophic thought is closely related to his personality and
its growth; his view of the universe was conclusive and
encompassing; it had an inherent structure, and his metaphysical poetry, his study of nature, his criticism of knowledge, and his aphoristic wisdom emanated as organic parts
from his philosophic thought. His philosophic anthropology and his conception of society, history, and culture
have a definite and logical place within the unity of his
thought.

When Goethe broke through the shell of the philosophic
and methodological doctrines prevalent in his youth to embark upon his own search, he acted as he did in creating his
poetry: An imperative urge compelled him to bring into
harmony the experience of his inner existence with that of
the outer world. His feeling of nature and his experience
of personality united in a view of the universe and man
which is consistent within itself and revives the nature

philosophy of Renaissance spiritualism. Goethe developed
it through his studies of nature and, from the end of the
century, through his close contact with the philosophic
thought of his time. Against the mechanistic conception
of nature he set his own organic interpretation. He found
a method appropriate to his ends in his morphological procedure, and formulated a view of the prime Being which
reconciled his religious experience with his philosophic
and scholarly cognition. The center of this cosmology is
the symbol of the creative spirit. In the realm of nature
this spirit manifests itself as organic life and in the realm
of thought as an intensification of this organic life. Goethe
applied the same morphological approach to the realms
of both nature and man and used the same basic concepts
in his metaphysical poetry and in his study of nature.

The spirit as such is ineffable and can be approached
only through its manifestations. From this insight Goethe
derived a sober and detailed awareness of the limitations
of cognition.[1] It balanced his reverence for the spirit of life,
which he felt at work in himself as a part of nature and
culture. "Truth is similar to God; it does not appear directly but we must divine it from its manifestations."[2]
These manifestations in nature and culture mutually illuminate each other: As on each level of nature one species
serves to clarify the others, so on the level of man one
religion serves to throw light on others; the comparative
study of art clarifies the particular phenomena of art and,
at the same time, the structure and function of art as such;
in novel and drama one character is clarified by his reflection in others. Even if taken as wholes, the realms of nature
and of man throw light upon each other especially since
man is a part of organic nature. Goethe's morphological
intuition made apparent to him the universal mutual reflection of all created phenomena, and led him to the reconstruction of the universal whole from its constituent parts.[3]

The results of Goethe's philosophic thought are integrated into the rhapsodic beauty of his metaphysical poetry; his investigations of nature are interrelated by a comprehensive philosophic quest; his conception of evolution has a metaphysical character: by inquiring into the forms of metamorphosis Goethe studied the flow of energy which engenders these forms throughout the universe.

It was the totality of Goethe's studies and thoughts which made him able to draw the manifold of nature and culture into one image, as in the eight lines of the poem "Wenn im Unendlichen dasselbe." His experience of the energy of life in himself was fundamental to his philosophic thought. This experience was of a religious character in that Goethe regarded life as a gift and man as a being to whom is granted the consciousness of all individuation as a manifestation of the creative spirit. If we regard this religious foundation of Goethe's thought as mystic, Goethe was one of those mystics who returned to the phenomenal world with their experience of the numinous to testify to it, to strengthen it through the exposure to doubt, and to embody it in their work.

The strength of Goethe's own philosophic impulse determined his relations to the philosophic movement of his time.[4] They varied from neglect and aversion to the serious study of its methods, the recognition of its indispensable service and, in relation to Schelling, the warmest participation. Goethe regarded the academic tradition of Western philosophy as a part of culture, as one of the various ways in which man tries to conceive of the universe and himself. He did not think that he was "talented for philosophy proper," but he assumed the right to judge it on the basis of his own philosophic thought. The discursive form of philosophy he saw as arising at a late stage in the historical metamorphoses of the mind; the philosophic epoch precedes the prosaic one. It was with this narrow definition of philosophy in mind that Goethe said of the philosophers that

they can offer only forms of life. It is up to us and to our nature
and capacities how they fit us and whether we are able to give
them the required content. We must examine ourselves and
everything we absorb from without as carefully as we do food;
otherwise we perish from philosophy or philosophy perishes
from us.[5]

Superior to the interpretation of being is life itself.
Goethe subordinates the forms which the philosophers
offer for the understanding of life to our own experience
of being. The living human being remains the judge of
philosophy; in other words, man is able to approach the
divine necessity of the sphere of being and to base his
thinking on participation in it. Goethe presumes a philosophic *Urerlebnis*, a fundamental inner experience of being
through which the particular existence of the individual
touches upon the universal Being, or, rather, the universal
Being partakes in man as his creature. Thinking of this
experience is an act from which evaluation results, and
therefore Goethe is able to demand a criticism of philosophy on the basis of man's own existence. Through this
basic experience there is conveyed to man the positive and
constructive energy which makes it possible for him to
give value to the world as well as to himself. With this
energy in mind Goethe addressed to Schopenhauer the
words,

Willst du dich deines Werts erfreuen,
So musst der Welt du Wert verleihen.[6]

The question remains how Goethe further defined this
fundamental experience of life to which philosophic and
poetical forms are historically relative. The answer is given
by the conception of creative nature in the totality of his
work. His reinterpretation of Spinoza shows how, even to
the system of an admired and carefully studied philosopher,
he gave a significance in accord with his own deeply rooted

convictions.[7] In the conflict between Faust and Mephisto we witness the opposition between nihilism and the recuperative strength of faith.

As we know, Goethe experienced the ultimate depth of despair, but also healing forces capable of carrying him beyond it. What are the healing forces? In his poetry he conceives of them as energies of life; they are at work in nature and appear through grace; among the manifold symbols which he formed for their manifestation we find spirits, angels, and demigods like Ariel and the angels in *Faust*, and Eos and Pandora; we find allegorical figures like Majesty and Peace in the "Prelude" of 1807. Healing forces are demonstrated by characters in Goethe's epic and drama, such as Antonio in *Tasso*, Iphigenie, Natalie in *Wilhelm Meister*. They reflect the regenerative strength of Goethe's own personality; human reason has access to them and resignation is required if they are to do their work. Goethe's experience of these healing forces forms the basis of his philosophic and social convictions and determines his position within the history of thought.

Goethe subordinated the historical course of thought to life. He experienced life within himself as that urge to form which he understood as a part of nature. This same nature can be studied as an organism; out of the cooperation of inner and outer experience Goethe formed his view of an all-comprising dynamic universe. During his lifetime he widened and refined these foundations of his thought through the critical study of past and contemporary philosophy and by the development of his own methodological consciousness.

In poetry and prose the immediate approach and the aphoristic form of Goethe's philosophic thought comes close to that of the pre-Socratics, who also built upon observation and intuition of nature. Goethe's original phenomenon is related to its manifestation as a Platonic idea is related to the phenomenal world. His conception of metamorphosis presupposes the Aristotelian entelechy understood as the formative energy inherent in the manifestations of nature. Plotinus' interpretation of the universe as emanating from the creator serves to support Goethe's explanation of the unity of the creation, the correspondence between macrocosm and microcosm, and the tension in man between his impulse toward living and his love for the realm of ideas which become manifest through life. Faust calls this tension the dualism between the two souls in his breast.

Thus it was in the style of the Neo-Platonic tradition that Goethe formed his relations to the heritage of Western philosophy and religion. He further attained clarity in his own ways of philosophic thinking through his study of the thought of his time.

In a polemical mood he once stated that he never thought about thinking. His essays, schemata, and aphorisms about methods of cognition prove the contrary. The observation of his own mental actions taught him that knowledge results from the co-operation between sense-perception and pre-existent mental forms. Although he tended to interpret Kant's transcendental criticism in terms of his own metaphysics, he felt himself supported by the *Critique of Pure Reason* and understood the synthetic judgment a priori as a corollary of his belief in a pre-existent creative cognition. He felt drawn to Kant's *Critique of Judgment* because in it he saw nature and art explained as productive through an inner urge and as meaningful in themselves. Finally he found in Kant's postulate of an archetypal reason, the *intellectus archetypus*, a statement which seemingly led in the direction of his own thinking, the intuition of the original phenomenon. Goethe realized that by the *intellectus archetypus* Kant hinted at a divine reason inaccessible to man. He took the occasion, however, in his essay "Anschauende Urteilskraft,"[8] to apply Kant's term to his own understanding of the correspondence between the universe and man. We approach the prime Being in the realm of cognition as well as in that of ethics. It is "through the intuition of an ever-creative nature" that we may become worthy of participating spiritually in its productions.

Goethe read Kant at Schiller's suggestion, and it was this contact which prompted him to give an account to himself of the relations between object and subject, experience and science, analysis and synthesis. Invariably, however, he felt compelled either to reject or to reinterpret Kant, whereas in Schelling he recognized a congenial mind.[9] The reconciliation of nature and spirit in Schelling's philosophy of identity coincided with his own fundamental convictions. In defending Schelling against Jacobi's criticism, Goethe defended his own tenets without following the philosopher into the details of his argument. Philosophic analysis requires conceptual formulation, separation, and definition. Goethe's mind tends toward the synthesis of the image and gives to it a precision of its own. He expressed this difference by a comparison between poetic intuition and philosophic hypothesis:

Poetry points at the secrets of nature and tries to solve them through the image. Philosophy points at the secrets of reason and tries to solve them through the word.[10]

In either case we use signs and express "neither the objects nor ourselves completely."

The symbolical image is Goethe's most congenial means of stating his view of the universe. It permits him to mirror the metaphysical through the physical, the natural through the supernatural. Goethe's notes on the cognitive significance of poetry and the nature of symbolism show us the bearing of his methodological studies on his work. Language is anthropomorphic in character and through it a metaphorical realm, a "new world," comes into being.

All phenomena are inexpressible because language is a phenomenon in itself which is only related to the others but cannot identically reproduce them.[11]

Through the conventional use of words, however, the poet's language penetrates into "deeper relationships." In language, "word and image are correlative to each other and seek each other continuously." The word suggests to the mind that it go beyond the verbal sign; in other terms, it challenges the formative energy of intuition. To Goethe, poetry is ultimately a cognitive act related to truth through the person of the poet; it is "prophetic" in character. This is what Goethe means when he has the poet receive "the veil of poetry from the hand of truth" and when he entitles his autobiography *Poetry and Truth*. By adding to the latter the subtitle "Out of My Life" he connected, in his seventh decade, the reflection of his youth with a motto of his existence. The poet lives for the truth and he pursues his search for the truth in his own right.[12]

Goethe's conception of truth has a metaphysical basis. The act of cognition, like the voice of conscience, is to him a response of the subject to the object, in which two parts originating from the same whole co-operate. Goethe could interpret Kant's *Critique of Judgment* metaphysically because he was convinced that a preformed knowledge is latent in man's nature. What Plato called "anamnesis," the reminiscence of things previously seen, he conceived of as "anticipation." "Had I not borne the world in myself by anticipation, I would have remained blind even with eyes that see."[13]

The act of cognition is possible only because of the relationship between microcosm and macrocosm. The human mind refracts the truth and passes it into a different, anthropomorphic medium, but it shares in the truth just as, in Goethe's theory, colors are reflections of the one clear light. Goethe likens to this light the highest guiding power accessible to the human mind, which he calls "spirit." This equation is more than a metaphor for him:

Light and spirit, the one governing the physical, the other the ethical realm, are the highest indivisible energies of which we are able to think.[14]

Both light and spirit ultimately emanate from the same cosmic ground. In contrast to the opaqueness of matter, the prophetic personality is related, through an inner light, to the cosmic light. Makarie, the sibyl of *Wilhelm Meister's Travels*, possesses this gift. Through her Goethe conveys his belief in man's participation in the macrocosm. He conveys it with hesitation, for he is aware of the limits of cognition. In it, nevertheless, culminates his fundamental belief that God manifests himself through nature and therefore through man, who is meaningfully related to him.

It was this view of man's position in the universe which gave Goethe certainty about the healing forces that lift the human being over the abyss of despair. His most intimate experiences as well as each step in his nature studies confirmed him in this certainty. It explained and helped him to accept the reality of life as a creative projection of God, a cosmos in process of giving form to the chaos. It led him to the search for the typical and recurring forms of this manifestation of an ineffable ground. It made him modest in cognition without impairing his energy for study, and it formed the cognitive basis of his religion of reverence. Goethe's cosmology and his analysis and practice of cognition are an integrated unity.

In his autobiography, Goethe tells the cosmogonic myth by which as a youth he formed his first view of the universe.[15] Within the tradition of Renaissance spiritualism which his cosmology follows, Goethe's thinking represents a momentous step. Like Paracelsus and Jacob Böhme, he was driven by inner exigencies toward a universal synthesis, but he demanded of himself methodological clarity in his cognitive procedure and recognition of its limitations. He transformed the spiritualist philosophy of nature by developing his morphology on the basis of the natural sciences of his century. With the aid of the concepts at which he had arrived as a scientist, he gave to the spiritualist theosophy a lucid form and made it accessible to the modern mind through his metaphysical poetry and prose.

In Goethe's cosmological interpretation the creation is the self-explication of a prime Being which is identical with the ground of all existence—Böhme's *Ungrund*. This self-explication results in an antagonism of polar forces which determines all movements within the universe. The task of man in traversing his cycle of life is to reconcile this polarity in himself. Since man, through his cognitive faculties, is destined for freedom, the cosmology has an ethical significance for him.

Faust tries to grasp the secret of the universe, which has neither beginning nor end, through the anthropomorphic metaphor of its inception. He takes this step when interpreting the first sentence of the Fourth Gospel.[16] In his attempt to find in the origin of all things their essence and unity, he interprets the Greek *Logos* at first as the word, then as the meaning, then as the power, and finally as the action. He is dissatisfied with the translation of *logos* into "word," *Wort*, because the word is merely a sign distinct from its meaning. Yet the term "meaning," *Sinn*, does not convey the active element essential to the concept of creation. Therefore he replaces it with "energy," *Kraft*. Again this proves insufficient since it carries the connotation of a potentiality which, as such, can be divorced from the act by which it becomes real. Thus he is led to translate *logos* into "action," *Tat*. His previous solutions are discarded in so far as they are not valid in themselves; at the same time they form qualifying overtones which accompany the word ultimately chosen. By laying accent on action, Goethe concurs with Paracelsus and Böhme, who understand the explication of the original Being as the act of God's fiat.

Goethe's formulation in *Faust* is repeated in a poem of the *Divan:*

> *Und er sprach das Wort: Es werde!*
> *Da erklang ein schmerzlich Ach!*
> *Als das All mit Machtgebärde*
> *In die Wirklichkeiten brach.*[17]

The fiat is accompanied by pain, for the individuation which it causes creates distance from the origin and the pain of selfhood. The pains of birth are the first pains; they announce that along with life there is that separation from the divine ground which creates life by contraction. The power of contraction is, however, accompanied by its polar opposite, the power of expansion, which tends to overcome the narrowness of individuation by breaking through it in the direction of the universe. The expansive power tends toward reconciliation and reunion. Love is its primary manifestation. As Eos, the dawn which precedes the new day, it appears in *Pandora*. The dawn, Jacob Böhme's *Aurora*, is the symbol of reconciliation in the same *Divan* poem which describes the painful fiat of the creation. What was separated through the act of creation is now able to love: Light was divorced from darkness and without longing and sound the elements dispersed into infinite barren space; everything was mute and God was alone; then he created the dawn which developed the realm of colors from the polarity of light and darkness, the reflection of life in color and sound which reunites the particular with the universal.

> *Stumm war alles, still und öde,*
> *Einsam Gott zum erstenmal!*
> *Da erschuf er Morgenröte,*
> *Die erbarmte sich der Qual,*

Sie entwickelte dem Trüben
Ein erklingend Farbenspiel,
Und nun konnte wieder lieben
Was erst auseinanderfiel.

In the eighth book of *Poetry and Truth* we find the same explanation of the universe as the process of emanation and return. The trinity first created itself and then, through the principle of contraction, the realm of living matter. Lucifer, however, the highest of these creatures, "forgot his higher origin and believed he could find it in himself; from his first ingratitude originated whatever does not seem to comply with the meaning or intention of the divinity." The divinities thereupon gave to the infinite being the opposite tendency—the capacity to expand back to the origin. The contracting power which causes all individuation alienates all things from their origin, the expansive power tends toward return. The universe is motion, governed by the universal rhythmical law of contraction and expansion, systole and diastole. This "rhythm of the world spirit" is embodied on the human plane in the contrast between Prometheus, the incarnation of contraction, and Epimetheus, the epitome of man's aspiration beyond himself. The cycle of life is a threefold movement from alienation, through living in the polarity of existence, toward return to the origin. In the poems "Mahomet's Gesang" and "Gesang der Geister über den Wassern"[18] it is man's soul which follows this rhythm like the water that descends to rise again:

Vom Himmel kommt es,
Zum Himmel steigt es,
Und wieder nieder
Zur Erde muss es,
Ewig wechselnd.

In terms of this universal rhythm, manifest in nature, man may understand the experience of his own self.

By a sequence of images Goethe's poem "Weltseele" embraces this dynamic universe from its inception to the rise of the human world. Enthusiastic creative forces are called upon to leave their "holy" unity and to spread through all realms, to take on the form of ideas, luminous as the stars, to seize upon yet unformed stellar bodies, to govern the atmosphere, and to prescribe their formation to the stones. They separate as water and earth, as night and day, and reappear as a multitude of living figures in the light, to become manifest, finally, in the male-female polarity of human life. This praise of the emanation culminates in a celebration of the reconciling power of love and ends with the demand of gratitude for the gift of life, which is to be given back to the universe whence it came.

Weltseele

Verteilet euch nach allen Regionen
Von diesem heilgen Schmaus!
Begeistert reisst euch durch die nächsten Zonen
Ins All und füllt es aus!

Schon schwebet ihr in ungemessnen Fernen
Den selgen Göttertraum,
Und leuchtet neu, gesellig, unter Sternen
Im lichtbesäten Raum.

Dann treibt ihr euch, gewaltige Kometen,
Ins Weit und Weitr' hinan;
Das Labyrinth der Sonnen und Planeten
Durchschneidet eure Bahn.

Ihr greifet rasch nach ungeformten Erden
Und wirket schöpfrisch jung,
Dass sie belebt und stets belebter werden
Im abgemessnen Schwung.

Und kreisend führt ihr in bewegten Lüften
Den wandelbaren Flor

Und schreibt dem Stein in allen seinen Grüften
Die festen Formen vor.

Nun alles sich mit göttlichem Erkühnen
Zu übertreffen strebt;
Das Wasser will, das unfruchtbare, grünen
Und jedes Stäubchen lebt.

Und so verdrängt mit liebevollem Streiten
Der feuchten Qualme Nacht!
Nun glühen schon des Paradieses Weiten
In überbunter Pracht.

Wie regt sich bald, ein holdes Licht zu schauen,
Gestaltenreiche Schar,
Und ihr erstaunt, auf den beglückten Auen,
Nun als das erste Paar,

Und bald verlischt ein unbegrenztes Streben
Im selgen Wechselblick.
Und so empfangt mit Dank das schönste Leben
Vom All ins All zurück.[19]

It was through his own existence that Goethe became aware of the correspondence between inner and outer experience. Schelling's philosophy of identity confirmed his conviction that a pre-established harmony unites the phenomena of nature and those of the mind, and that on all levels of the dynamic universe the same fundamental polarity is at work:

It is the life of nature to separate what is united and to unite what is separated; this is the everlasting systole and diastole, the continuous syncrisis and diacrisis, the rhythm of inhalation and exhalation of the world in which we live and move and have our being.[20]

Schelling's deduction of the dynamic process corresponded to the premises and results of Goethe's morphological intuition; therefore he feels "definitely drawn" to Schelling's doctrine, studies the *System of Transcendental Idealism*, and desires a thorough union of their views. The ultimate unity of the creation which Goethe expressed in the poem "Weltseele," the spiritual creativity of the prime Being, the dialectic relation of potencies which engender intensification in the process of life—these were convictions Goethe held in common with Schelling.

The manifestation of God through the organic process of nature is the secret which Goethe calls "the patent secret."[21] His faith and his knowledge join in the certainty about God-in-Nature. Cautious even in naming the ultimate Being and skeptical of theological speculation as exposed to anthropomorphism, Goethe conceived of faith as a "holy vessel" into which everyone puts his best.[22] To him the "best" was the revelation of the functional unity of nature and spirit; he experienced it as an inner strength and he recognized in it the principle explaining the universe. Thus he was aware of the ineffable "otherness" of the creator, but could also see the "otherness" balanced by man's kinship with the created universe. His religious experience of life was the source of his constructive acceptance of life and his cosmological cognition supported him in his faith.

From the religious core of spiritualist thought, Goethe developed his study of the phenomenal world. In the course of this study he worked out the morphological logic essential to his science and his poetry. We find his first significant concern with this logic in his interest in physiognomy.[23] To some degree the Renaissance philosophy of nature used a physiognomic method. The "signatures" of things, important to Böhme and Paracelsus, were a clue to their essence. When interpreting man's face and figure as representing an inner reality, the physiognomist studies simultaneously nature and mind. Aware of the limitation of physiognomy as of any mode of cognition, Goethe defended his tentative effort by saying that "judgments have their physiognomy as much as things," a statement which hints, as early as 1775, at his conception of the responsive character of knowledge.[24]

Goethe's physiognomical interest marks the beginning of his studies in nature in contrast to his earlier enthusiasm for nature. He gave to physiognomy a place within a comprehensive scheme of morphology extending throughout the organic world. The discipline of morphology in its turn formed a part of the universal comparative science for which again, in the field of organic life, he drafted a plan. The predominant purpose of this attempt was to oppose the utilitarian viewpoint, which explains each level of nature according to the service it renders to the next higher one, and, likewise, the pragmatist viewpoint, which explains the form of the living being as determined by its outer environment. Goethe believed that each type of nature's creation has a life in its own right. He saw the typical forms of the manifold as growing from within and, at the same time, as exposed to influence from without. This is true of the highest level of organic nature, human existence.

When studying physiognomy, Goethe had to combine three approaches. Simultaneously he investigated nature, he reproduced it as an artist, and he interpreted his inner and outer observations in regard to its universal significance. The insight at which he aimed was philosophical in intention and intuitive in procedure. The study of nature, beginning, in the case of physiognomy, with anatomy, demands scholarly accuracy. Reproduction of the significant traits requires the artistic faculty of distinguishing the essential from the accidental characteristics. The interpretation of physiognomy with the aid of nonphysiognomical evidence leads toward further definition of typical contours. In Goethe's physiognomical intuition his general way of morphological cognition was preformed: The physiognomist tries to grasp the lasting traits of the personality, together with their psychological significance; he then ascends to man as a type and may consider him within the sequence of organic creatures; that is, he proceeds from the particular to the typical.

This ascending movement of intuition forms the core of Goethe's morphological logic. In his morphology he described four levels of thought.[25] The mind works on the lowest one as long as man is content with the useful application of practical knowledge. The next higher one attracts those who are unselfishly curious and requires the calm eye and clear intellect necessary for accuracy while remaining within the given material. The third level is that of intuition, which knowledge, by intensifying itself, postulates and into which it is transmuted. The highest level is that of the "embracing ones whom, in a prouder sense, one might call creative":

They act productively in the highest degree; in that they proceed from ideas, they pronounce the unity of the whole and it is, so to speak, up to nature to fit afterwards into this idea. . . . In all scholarly pursuits one must become aware that one will move in these four regions. One must remain conscious of the region in which one tarries at the moment.

This sequence of levels ascends to the creativity of genius or inspiration. Man reaches the highest level of cognition through his inner correspondence with the universe. To this prophetic knowledge intuition is subordinated. Intuition is a step beyond disinterested and accurate knowledge; in spite of its tending toward the universal it is still concerned with the particular. Skeptical about rational analysis and the ensuing abstract conclusions, Goethe demands the continuous correction of conceptual formulations by intuition. Intuition requires the sympathetic understanding and reconstruction of that object the inner meaning of which it attempts to grasp. In science as in art, it approaches the typical, the original phenomenon which Goethe later also termed "idea."

The intuition of the typical discloses the organization underlying the manifold of the concrete world of objects.
When investigating the metamorphosis of plants, Goethe arrived at the idea of the "original plant" which revealed to
him the principle of the leaf's unfolding as governing the
whole of the vegetable kingdom. The metamorphosis of
animals suggests to him

an anatomical type, a general image, containing possibly the
forms of all animals and permitting, therefore, the description
of each animal according to a certain order. From the general
notion of a type it already follows that no single animal as such
can be set up as a standard of comparison; nothing particular
can be the model of the whole.[26]

On each level of nature there is a definite relationship between freedom and necessity. No member of a species can
transpose himself into another one. The metamorphoses of
the species are predetermined and variation is admitted only
within these definite limits. Thus Goethe interprets the anatomy of seals as indicating that outer conditions may cause an
adaptation to the outer form while leaving the inner form
untouched.[27]

The levels of Goethe's morphological cognition illustrate
his intention of conceiving the individual phenomenon by
means of the type of which it is a specimen. This is the basis
of his concept of *Humanität:* The entelechy inherent in man
is that of the type; its development was the intention of nature in man's creation. The universe as such remains inaccessible to finite cognition. The manifestations of the universal
spirit, however, which for Goethe comprise the visible
world, lead to the conception of this spirit as the universal
archetype in which all types participate and which partici-
pates in all types. Through anticipation it is possible to conceive symbolically of the universal unity. Of this highest
"embracing" knowledge it is again Makarie who is the
symbol.

Scholarship requires the distinction between idea and experience. The act of self-discipline by which the scholar masters the polar tension between them constitutes the "objectivity" of knowledge. Intuition mediates between the anticipation of the whole and the observation of the particular. It also forms the link between Goethe's nature studies and his metaphysics. Thus Goethe is capable of viewing "man as a part of the universe, the mountain as a part of the geological whole, the limbs as a part of the organism, and it is, to be sure, always intuition which states the metaphysical connection."[28]

In Goethe's method, which, some years after his arrival in Weimar, he regretted having applied previously in so half-hearted a fashion, we recognize once more his tendency to strive for the "inner meaning" of things. For him, morphological intuition reconciled the dualism between faith and science. By understanding man as an integral part of an organic whole, and as related to it as microcosm is to macrocosm, he overcame the difficulty caused by the mediate and relative character of knowledge. He distinguished sharply between the postulative and the ascertainable results of thought. His consciousness of the procedure of intuition guarded him against giving to man and his position within the universe a man-centered interpretation.

When, in "Wald und Höhle," Faust expresses his satisfaction with the intuition of the creator which is granted him through the manifestations in nature as well as through man's own inner self, he shows that he has grown beyond his earlier restless intention of forcibly imposing himself upon nature by penetrating to the innermost source of all things. His development parallels Goethe's own. Goethe contented himself with his morphological intuition precisely because he considered it the only way of approaching the secret of existence. Thus his concept of evolution, always connected with the search for the original phenomenon, was a means of recognizing the intention of organic nature, or in other words, of ascertaining the norm inherent in the phenomenon. In contradistinction to later theories of evolution, its transcendental basis is fundamental to Goethe's theory.

Goethe's view of nature as a living organism continued the spiritualist cosmologies of such Renaissance thinkers as Pico della Mirandola and Giordano Bruno, Paracelsus and Jacob Böhme. Their cosmological thought stands in contrast to the concept of nature as mechanism, which also developed during the Renaissance era and culminated in Newton. The organic cosmologist sees in creative nature an immanent force producing the continuous flux which we observe together with its regularities. The mechanistic interpretation of nature searches for mathematically measurable laws governing the processes which we recognize in nature. It postulates the universal validity of these laws on the ground of the thesis that a uniformity of substance can ultimately be presumed. In both cases the demiurge is bound to the forms he engendered and the laws he created. As a final consequence of the mechanistic interpretation, however, he becomes a prime mover, as in the philosophies of deism, whereas in the organic interpretation he is immanent in his creations as an energy of life in both a physical and a psychical sense. The two contrasting types of thought must result in equally contrasting attitudes toward nature and its cognition.

The mechanistic mind trains its cognitive faculties so that they may be dominated by the analytical power, and it searches for results which can be mathematically formulated and ascertained by experiment. The organic school tries to balance the cognitive faculties, admits intuition as a legitimate element of them, and is interested in the quality and typology of the products of nature. As regards man's relations to nature, for the mechanistic mind the accent is on man's potential mastery of nature, whereas for the organic school it is on reverence for nature, in which the divine is immanent. The discursive form of mechanistic thought makes it possible to separate faith and science, or even to oppose them to each other. For organic thought, to which the inner experience of man's self is of cognitive value, faith and science are inseparable.

As an organic thinker, Goethe was bound to come into conflict with the mechanistic method and its results. His implacable opposition to Newton's theory of color was symptomatic of his antagonism to the mechanistic view. Conflict was inevitable between the two methods of inquiry into nature—the one regarding nature as a mechanism and aiming to express its motions by measurable quantities, the other investigating nature as a living organism and discerning qualitative manifestations of a force which animates and directs the life process.[29]

Like Leibniz and Schelling, Goethe was convinced of the "identity" of outer and inner experience. The particular reflects the whole; what is inward is also outward:

> Müsset im Naturbetrachten
> Immer eins wie alles achten!
> Nichts ist drinnen, nichts ist draussen:
> Denn was innen, das ist aussen.
> So ergreifet ohne Säumnis
> Heilig öffentlich Geheimnis.[30]

The sensation of color results from the co-operation of the object with the physiological organization of the eye; it is a classic example of the convergence of inward and outward and suggests the consideration of the scales of colors and tones as an a priori experience. For Goethe, however, all cognition was responsive. He was interested in these responses rather than in the Kantian "thing as such" and felt justified in this concentration by the philosophy of identity, which corresponded to his metaphysics. He considered the experience of color to be the result of the dualism between light and darkness, in which terms he conceived also of the dualism inherent in the emanation of the universe as a whole. He used the word *trübe*—troubled, turbid—to point out reduced transparency and the resulting confusion in nature as well as in human life: the *turba* in *Pandora* hints at such a stage of disorder before the new covenant is established. A reduction of transparency is on the one hand a decrease of light, on the other an increase of darkness. The mediating character of color, refracting light through darkness, gave to Goethe's conception of color the universal significance which it had for him.[31]

In consequence, the physiological act of the retina was as important to Goethe as were the rays of light on which the physicists concentrated their efforts to the disregard of the physiological and even psychological effects of color upon the observing subject. Goethe's research into nature had an encompassing intention which he found counteracted by Newton's investigation, since that was restricted to the quantitatively measurable. The metaphysical implication of Goethe's conception of light as an original phenomenon compelled him to oppose Newton's interpretation of light as composed of the scale of colors. Without denying to mathematical and atomistic investigation its proper function, Goethe tended toward a synthesis, which was unthinkable for him without a qualitative and dynamic interpretation. He wished to bring out the philosophic significance of the theory of color and therefore demanded of the physicist that he arrive at understanding of the original phenomenon.[32] Goethe's struggle against Newton and his school was a reaction against the one-sidedness of the mechanistic natural sciences. Their methods and results were opposed to his organic view of the dynamic universe.

The Italian journey had suggested to Goethe the study of the problem of color. His return to Weimar was followed by an integration of his personal experience, his study of nature, art, and history, and his literary work into a unity which implemented his cosmology. The fragment on Nature which was written down by Tobler in 1782, and the epilogue appended to it by Goethe himself in 1828, indicate both the lasting foundations of his thought about nature and his progression, through his morphological studies, to the conception of formative laws governing the life process.[33]

Nature is understood as an artist incessantly engaged in the process of creation. Life is

Nature's loveliest intention and Death is her device for insuring plenitude of life. . . . Pondering and meditation are perpetual to her; but it is not as humanity but as nature that she muses. She has no speech or language, but she creates tongues and hearts through which she feels and utters. Her ultimate perfection is Love; it is only through love that she can be approached.

Goethe's poetic image of nature stresses the otherness of the creative power by presenting it as an artist of a universal imaginative capacity. It conceals from its creatures the direction and meaning of the course it has set for them. Love is the culmination of the creative process and the essential cognitive clue to its inner meaning. Goethe adds that we do not know whether nature sees the drama which she herself plays. We are the ones who witness it, although "from our particular and restricted point of perception."

When he read the essay again almost fifty years later, Goethe considered the view he had held in his youth as "a comparative tending toward a superlative not yet attained." He defined what was missing in the essay as "the intuition of the two great moving forces of nature, polarity and intensification." Goethe's enduring conviction that the universe was a dynamic organism had been expressed in the fragment. The old Goethe, however, emphasized the gain his studies had meanwhile brought him; namely, a grasp of the law constitutive for the universal movement, which lends itself to cognition through morphological analysis and synthesis.

As a morphological philosopher, Goethe pursued the manifestations of the demiurge throughout nature. His studies were accompanied by poetical crystallizations or projects which may have been intended as parts of a philosophic epic on Nature. By it he hoped to renew his "beloved Lucretius" in his own fashion. At the time of his closest cooperation with Schelling, between 1798 and 1805, Goethe felt encouraged to strengthen the "inborn method" by which he approached nature, art, and life. He admired Lucretius as a synthesis of "man, Roman, poet, and philosopher of nature."[34]

In the poem on Nature Goethe intended to combine the description of its typical phenomena, the intuition of its inherent law, and its cosmological interpretation as an organic unity through the realms of its manifestations. This epic was to serve as a guide to the universal synthesis which he sought. It was to comprise the totality of his studies, from astronomy and the formation of the earth to the levels of organic life and the nature of man. The formulation of the two principles governing the universe which Goethe mentioned in the epilogue to the essay on Nature dates from this era.

Intensification as the result of polarity suggests the metaphor of the spiral. The opposites ascend to a higher level at which they are integrated. It is not a simple fusion which brings about this intensification. "But the union can occur in a higher sense, in that the separated parts at first intensify themselves and then through the union of the intensified parts they produce a third thing which is new, higher and unexpected."[35] Goethe observed this spiral tendency on each level of nature. He did not apply it to the evolution of history as a whole but he recognized it as the ethical chance of individuals and even of communities.

The evolution of Wilhelm Meister is a process of intensification in which the same basic forces of personality ascend from level to level. The solution of Iphigenie's problem is presented as a higher synthesis. The unexpected metamorphosis with which the *Novelle* comes to its conclusion is an intensifying reconciliation of forces. The course of Faust mirrors the same intensifying tendency, which continues even after his death in the ascent of his immortal part.

In the realm of man, the polarity out of which intensification is to arise is evident from the functional relation between inward and outward, reason and emotion, selfhood and love. Goethe sees the tension kindled and revealed by love as a potential force of intensification which "draws man upward." In the case of man, the choice between simple fusion and intensifying synthesis is left to the individual, and therefore, on the human level, the law of polarity and intensification takes on an ethical significance. The tension between the contracting and the expanding powers in his nature is given him as a chance for intensification. Goethe's admiration for Greek culture, for the Greek achievement of "harmony and totality," is directly related to his understanding of the law of polarity. The reconciliation of the dynamics within the human microcosm he saw as a reflection of the law inherent in the macrocosm. The revelation which classical art represented for him corresponded with this dynamic view of the universe.

With the intensification which nature brings about from level to level, the boundaries of necessity widen. The process of crystallization already indicated a limited degree of individual formation. The organic life of the plant involves an element of action toward the outer world. Once more the range of freedom is increased in the animal kingdom. Man is potentially the freest of all creatures. He has intellect, reason, and spirit. His versatility is wider than that of all lower levels of nature. He can approach the universe by way of thought and he can relate his own position to it. He is able to connect with his knowledge the meaning he attaches to his life, and to impart to his life a cultural form.[36]

Renaissance thinkers defined man as moving between the animals and the angels. The recognition of the ambivalent situation of man expressed by Pico, Giordano Bruno, and Paracelsus was also the basis of Goethe's anthropology. Goe-

the characteristically transformed it by applying morphological methods of observation to the human being and by
cautiously refraining from unwarranted conclusions with
respect to man's position within the universe. He included
the investigation of man in a proposal which he made for a
new discipline of knowledge in the "Prolegomena for a
Morphology." He defined it as "Zoonomy."[37] In it the study
of organic nature and the study of the mind are combined.

Zoonomy falls into two parts, the physical and the spiritual. They are the two points of view from which the problem should be approached. Goethe thereby implicitly
proposed the study of the mental phenomena of animals by
comparing them with those of man. In the same fashion, he
compared man's anatomy with that of the animals. Whereas
Renaissance philosophers placed man in the center of the
universe, as Pico did in his oration on the dignity of man,
Goethe granted man the distinctive capacity of giving form
to the spirit through language and art. He left open the
question of what significance the existence and cognitive
capacity of man might have within the universe.

Goethe's universe is dynamic, it is a living organism, and
it is infinite. It has history and its future is unpredictable.
"The result of recent research shows that the universe itself
is not complete." Nature is still inventive.

I hold nature capable of still producing precious stones of a
kind unknown to us today. Who can tell what is possible even
today for the immense mountainous stretches covered by the
sea? I do not even like to deny to the dried and continuous continent a similar, although lesser, productive power.[38]

Nature is an infinity in motion. It is incessantly productive,
it adds new typical creations to the old ones, it has organization, but its system is not closed. "It is life and succession
from an unknown center towards an unrecognizable limit."[39]

Goethe's integration of each of his pursuits into the whole
of his morphological philosophy is, as an attempt at syn-

thesis, more important today than any of his particular discoveries and observations. He anticipated a reconciliation between the tenets of science, art, religion and philosophy. In his own work, he applied the same method to the sciences of nature and to those of the mind. He saw in scholarly research a support for, rather than a hindrance to, his search for the normative.

Modern natural scientists are, in contrast to most of their nineteenth-century predecessors, no longer convinced of the exclusive validity of the mechanistic procedure; they are more intent upon synthesis, and more receptive to attempts at synthesis such as Goethe's.[40] If the conflict between Goethe's and Newton's theories of color dissolves when one recognizes that they "deal with two entirely different levels of reality," if the modern scientist is aware of the need for, and the justification of, a balance between the realm of outer reality and that of inner structure, between quantitative and qualitative analysis and judgment, Goethe's thought on nature attains a significance which is more than historical. It is even more significant where modern scholarship has been tempted to introduce the quantitative methods of the mechanistic natural sciences into fields of knowledge, such as the humanities and the social sciences, which have the human world as their object and require a different approach.

Schiller expressed the very essence of Goethe's striving for synthesis in the letter which precipitated their friendship:

Your observation which rests upon things with so much calmness and purity never exposes you to the danger of the bypath on which the speculative mind and the arbitrary and merely self-reliant imagination so easily go astray. Everything that analysis seeks with great pains is contained in your correct intuition—and much more completely; only because as a whole it is in yourself, your own wealth is concealed to yourself; unfortunately we know only what we divide. Minds of your kind therefore rarely know how far they have advanced and how little they have to borrow from philosophy, which can only learn from them. Philosophy can only dissect what is given to it; giving itself, however, is not the task of the analytical mind, but of the mind of genius, which unites under the dark but certain influence of pure reason according to objective laws.

For a long time, although from a certain distance, I have watched with ever-increasing admiration the way of your mind and the procedure which you set for yourself. You seek the necessity of nature, but you seek it on the most difficult way, from which any weaker energy would cautiously refrain. You take together the whole of nature in order to be enlightened about the particular; you seek the explanation of the individual in the totality of the forms by which nature manifests itself. You ascend step by step from the simple organization to the more complex one, in order to reconstruct finally in a genetic fashion from the materials of the whole edifice of nature the most complex of all of nature's organizations, the human being.[41]

The cosmological quest from which Goethe's work arose explains the unity of the manifold aspects which this work offers. Each of the levels of nature revealed to him the one all-embracing process. Thus he found himself in one and the same world whether he studied the solid and immutable ground on which organic life is borne, or the fluctuating productivity of organic nature, or the human realm of art and thought. After a momentous exchange of ideas about the fundamental characteristics of world history, during which his personality took on "something solemn and, so to speak, prophetical," Goethe broke out with the words: "Children, let me now go alone to my stones down there; for, after such a conversation, the proper thing for old Merlin to do is to reconclude a friendship with the original elements."[42]

In the poem "Wenn im Unendlichen dasselbe" Goethe gave to his view of the universe the most succinct form. In the Creator alone there is eternal calm. Within the infinite, the same recurring forces, breathing the lust of living in their antagonistic striving, build a thousandfold dome through a flux without rest or end, as parts of the organic architecture of the whole.

Wenn im Unendlichen dasselbe
Sich wiederholend ewig fliesst,
Das tausendfältige Gewölbe
Sich kräftig ineinander schliesst,
Strömt Lebenslust aus allen Dingen,
Dem kleinsten wie dem grössten Stern,
Und alles Drängen, alles Ringen,
Ist ewige Ruh in Gott dem Herrn.[43]

The demiurge of this whole remains unfathomable and man's cognition is limited. A demonic element, surprising and incommensurable, is at work in the universe. Its very creativeness manifests itself as a tension between cosmos and chaos. Man is related to both these aspects of the creation and he finds them both in himself. If he faces the situation into which he is thrown, he will learn the art of admiration and astonishment which Plato called the mother of everything beautiful and good. Like Plato, Goethe regarded admiration and awe as the foundation of cognition. Through this creative response he is given the chance to support the cosmos against the chaos within himself and his world. This potentiality is his dignity.

Understanding friends recognized Goethe as a man who had attained this almost prophetic dignity when, in moments of unhindered communication of his deeper self, he spoke of his cosmological convictions, struck by admiration and awe, and responding to the numinous by the clarity of his intuitive reason. In such moments his friends saw him "as a mediator between God and men."[44]

7

The Nature of Man

The Polarities of Human Existence—Faust:
Striving and Redemption—Love,
Cognition, and Growth—The Hierarchy of
Mental Faculties

MAN FORMS A PART of the everlasting movement of the universe. His thinking is finite but it reaches beyond time and space. He is given the consciousness that his existence is governed by the polarity of dynamic creation. The function of his life consists in the reconciliation of the manifestations which this polarity assumes within his own nature. As an individual he is separated from the whole; as a personality he longs for reunion with the whole. The archetypal polarity which Goethe understands as the manifestation of the one primal Being is repeated in the human microcosm. Man's life "drawn together into one" is a trial of the freedom which is given him.

To Goethe there is no greater gain in life than the revelation of the "patent secret of nature." An infinitude of thoughts arises in an ever-renewed ascent of forms out of the creative ground of God-Nature. Goethe understood with reverence man's function within this cosmic process of becoming of which he is a part. In the poem which he wrote on contemplating Schiller's skull, he praises the works of nature and of man, the spiritualization of matter, and the preservation of the spirit's creations:

Was kann der Mensch im Leben mehr gewinnen,
Als dass sich Gott-Natur ihm offenbare?
Wie sie das Feste lässt zu Geist verrinnen,
Wie sie das Geisterzeugte fest bewahre.[1]

The individuation of man is not an apostasy. In Goethe's cosmogony the divinities counteracted Lucifer's opposition by giving to man an urge toward expansion. Man shares with other creatures the power of contraction which is manifested through his individuation. The power of expansion is given to him in a higher degree than to others, through his mind.[2] Here he is distinguished from the merely animal and here his personality reaches beyond what is merely individual.

Nature as a whole Goethe regards as a manifestation of spirit. The Earth spirit in *Faust* is a symbol comprising the inner meaning and creative unity of the earth: the spirit weaves "the garment of the Godhead." In man, nature reaches a higher level of intensification because man has spirit within him. As the force of higher guidance, spirit is the center of Goethe's image of man. His conception of spirit explains the role he assigned to emotion in human life, it clarifies his understanding of the levels of human cognition, and it is the key to his ideal of a sound fulfillment of life.

The spirit is man's immortal part. So strongly did Goethe feel the entelechy of his own "monad" that, in his old age, he returned to the belief in palingenesis which he had held in his youth. He could even consider it nature's "duty" to assign to a great entelechy another form of existence. Individual immortality, however, was for him a postulate rather than a certainty; man harbors the assurance of it in himself alone. But spirit as such is "the life of life." It is indestructible.

Our spirit is a being of wholly indestructible nature; it continues to work from eternity; it is similar to the sun, which seems to set only to our earthly eyes, and in fact never sets but unceasingly continues to shine.[3]

But man's share in the spirit, by which he is distinguished from the rest of nature, is given him as potentiality rather than as fulfillment. Goethe's demiurge is a god of becoming. The cosmic order is to arise from the chaotic and conflicting world of individuation. The urge to form which Goethe considered the basis of his own personality is a hint of man's position in the midst of this tension between cosmos and chaos. The urge as such is a part of organic matter; but connected with the intention to form, it reaches beyond matter. The urge to form is given to man together with the freedom to form. He is to rule his cognitive, his emotional, and his volitional self by subordinating it to the guiding power of the spirit. As a creature, man is subject to his nature. As a free creature, he is able to search for the universal intention inherent in his nature, to formulate it, and to shape himself.

This ambivalent situation of man, who belongs to organic nature and yet is given spirit, forms the central theme of *Faust*. Out of the historical Faust legend Goethe developed his tragedy in terms of the history of Occidental civilization. Its Hellenic, medieval, and modern elements join in a synthesis centered upon the quest for the cosmic position of man. *Faust* is "the drama of human existence," and its hero is a symbol of the human situation rather than a model for human conduct.[4]

As a scholar, the restless Faust strives for comprehension of the universe, of the law that rules it, of the bond that holds it together. He is not allowed to penetrate to the source of life—which means that it is denied him to impose himself upon nature. When he resigns himself to the feeling of his own unity with nature and to reverence for the ineffable divinity manifesting itself through nature, then he is given a moment of union with the universe. In "Wald und Höhle" he rejoices in the sense of universal sympathy with nature and his contemplation gives him calmness; but he is driven back to the dynamic of life as a lover.

He feels the passion of love to be a divine element within

him, and he recognizes a divine significance in the object of this love. He resolves not to disturb Gretchen in her innocent and restricted life. But stimulated by Mephisto, his desire becomes overwhelming. Gretchen's ruin is an epitome of the human tragedy, in which the most innocent impulse may lead to disaster. Faust's feeling of guilt is a symbol of man's suffering under his individuation; he is unable to overcome this suffering by entrusting himself to the spiritual guidance latent within him.

On a higher level of spiritualization, in the Helena tragedy, Faust relives the experience of love and beauty, the conflict of life accompanying it, and its temporality. By then he has grown enough in mental strength to hold on to the image which Helena leaves behind. It does not dissolve, but in his mind it undergoes another intensification and draws forth the best of his inner self.

> *Wie Seelenschönheit steigert sich die holde Form,*
> *Löst sich nicht auf, erhebt sich in den Äther hin*
> *Und zieht das Beste meines Innern mit sich fort.*[5]

By entering the realm of power, Faust encounters the anarchy and lawlessness of a society ruled by the elements rather than by reason. He undertakes to found a free community for a free people, and once more is involved in guilt. When Care blinds him, the light of his inward self continues to shine. He reaffirms his acceptance of life, its pain and its happiness. Faust dies without seeing his promised land. Not his urge toward cognition, nor his love, nor his political action gave him ultimate satisfaction. His striving was the meaning of his life. Since he never ceased to strive he can be redeemed. Through his failures he has grown, and his spirit ascends to higher activities.[6]

The bond which connects the expansive power of Faust with the universe is lacking in Mephisto. He represents a potentiality within man which draws him toward the subhuman. He encourages in Faust whatever may serve to sepa-

rate him from his universal relationship by attaching him to
the moment through Faust's passion or will to power. By
demonstrating to him that the universe is merely a meaningless up-and-down of formation and transformation, he tries
to draw Faust away from the "right path."

What Werther expresses pathetically, Mephisto treats
ironically. What constitutes Werther's tragedy is Mephisto's function: neither one has the creative faculty to grasp
the meaning of life as a task. The suffering Werther despairs
because his spirit lacks the power of detachment which
would evolve from an act of thought, such as Goethe himself performed, lifting him above his despair. Mephisto, the
"principle of negation," is cynically detached because he
denies meaning and sees only contingencies but no universal
significance. He is admitted within the universe as an opposi-
tional element which involuntarily supports the good by virtue of negation of it. His power of negation amounts to the
self-emancipation of a lower function of the mind which
Goethe terms "intellect." In serving Faust, Mephisto de-
ludes himself about Faust's genuine relations to the universe.
Therefore, in the end, he loses him.

Spiritualization, then, is the aim of man's exposure to the
polarities inherent in his existence. The dialectic course of
life challenges the spirit which is carried by the urge of living matter but tends beyond it. Since man's life is necessarily
burdened with "an earthly remnant, painful to bear," the
action of the spirit is one of striving. The spirit's captivity
within human finiteness makes itself felt by its restlessness.
Human life has an antithetic structure in that man belongs
to "two worlds." Goethe often expressed the dialectic of
this polarity in images familiar from Renaissance theosophy,
such as the contrast of light and darkness or light and fire.
Jacob Böhme saw the fire principle as opposed to the light
principle, the process of life then appearing as a sequence of
action and experience which should serve to transform fire
into light, an elemental energy into a spiritual energy. This

spiritualization cannot be brought about by a withdrawal
from matter, but only by accepting matter and forming it.
Human history presents a continuous effort "to spiritualize
the material and to embody the spiritual."[7]

The distinction and the difficulty of human existence are
bound up with man's cognitive faculty. Because he has the
capacity to know he has the chance for freedom. In order to
know he must live a life in which, by necessity, his vitality
and his wisdom are in continual conflict. Even the genesis of
his thought is connected with emotion. Without the urge to
form, there is no form. This urge, as a part of individual existence, is accompanied by sensitivity.

The Prometheus of Goethe's fragment speaks first of the
affective life of his creatures. Faust feels passion for the
image of beauty before he takes the magic potion in the
witch's kitchen. He had, however, concluded the pact with
Mephisto with a spiritual aim rather than for the sake of passion. He faces life with the full urge toward truth. "Man
knows himself only in so far as he knows the world; of the
world he becomes aware only in himself, and of himself
only in the world."[8] Without feeling, the full experience of
life is impossible and thought remains empty; without
thought, emotion remains meaningless. The tension between
reason and emotion is essential to the nature and the task of
human life. By solving this tension man attains freedom.
Goethe was in agreement throughout with Schiller's classical
formulation of this polarity and its ethical bearing:

Man can be opposed to himself in a twofold manner: either
as a savage, when his feelings rule over his principles; or as a
barbarian, when his principles destroy his feelings. . . . When
nature strives to maintain her manifold character in the moral
structure of society, this must not create any break in moral
unity; the victorious form is equally remote from uniformity
and from confusion. Therefore *totality* of character must be
found in the people which is capable and worthy to exchange
the state of necessity for that of freedom.[9]

To suppress emotion means, for Goethe, to overestimate the intellect; to abandon one's self to emotion means to forego spiritualization. Goethe emphasized spiritualization when he called poetry the transformation of the past into an image and when, characterizing it as a confession, he stressed its personal basis. He insisted that the totality of man's faculties must co-operate in art and in science as well as in life.

Goethe's aphorisms contain rudiments of a theory of emotion which attempts to explain the bearing of different feelings upon the same mental faculty.[10] Thus sagacity is restricted to the surface if it is accompanied by envy and hatred; if united, however, "with good will and love, it penetrates the world and man; it may even hope to ascend to the highest level." Emotion is to art what life is to nature. "Organic nature: alive to the smallest part; art: perceived to the smallest part by the organs of sensation."

Goethe distinguishes passive, centripetal, and active, centrifugal, emotions. The passive ones such as fear can be conceived without object; the active ones sometimes manifest themselves only with the aid of their object. Goethe's personality tended toward the active side of emotions, which he emphasized in his aphorisms. They indicate the relation between emotion and the urge to form. The active emotion accompanies the expansive force of man and the passive emotion follows the contracting one. On the passive side we find, besides fear, deep boredom and sorrow without object; on the active side, longing and conscience, but also the emotion related to hope and to anticipation of the future.

The action of the mind is so closely interwoven with feeling that Goethe even presents the challenge to survey one's own life as an active emotion. In the letter to Christian Schlosser, he related the expanding and the contracting tendency of emotions to the major and minor modes of music.

As the major tone arises from the expansion of the monad, it

causes the same impact on human nature by impelling it toward
the object, toward activity, . . . similarly the minor tone; since
it arises from the contraction of the monad, it also contracts,
concentrates, drives back to the subject, and finds there the
last places of refuge in which the loveliest melancholy is
pleased to hide.[11]

Goethe is true to the constructive principle that man
should not only accept life but should devote himself to the
expansive power inherent in himself. By placing the emphasis on the active side of emotions, the mind can focus upon
those which are constructive and which relate man to the
universe. Even in music the composer exercises an ethical
responsibility. There is an order in the world of emotions
which connects it profoundly with the meaning of human
existence. Emotions are agents of man's growth toward
truth. The sequence of repentance, confession, absolution,
and renewed action developed in Goethe's own nature. He
regarded it as inherent in the rhythm of human existence.

This sequence is reflected in Faust. Toward the end of the
first part of the drama he realizes his failure; he repents and
confesses but tries in vain, with the aid of Mephisto, to reverse Gretchen's fate. In the beginning of the second part
the spirits, led by Ariel, free him from the horror through
which he has lived; the pulse of life is renewed in him and
together with it his awareness of the cosmos to which he belongs He greets the rising sun, the "eternal light," and he
understands life through the symbol of the rainbow, whose
many colors reflect the one light.

Am farbigen Abglanz haben wir das Leben.[12]

Now he is able to return to life. But the forces which give
him back to the "holy light" are not at his command. They
can move him because he has a noble mind, which is capable
of understanding and conceiving resolutely. As in Faust's
redemption, grace intervenes in his renewal after the

Gretchen tragedy. In spite of his striving, Faust must have the support of higher forces.

Love, the most powerful of emotions, offers guidance to the evaluating mind. Goethe regards love as an expansive power which leads man to reunion with his universal origin. The universal tendency of Faust's love for Gretchen brings him into conflict with Mephistopheles, who knows only lust. As the antagonist of the cosmic order he must deny the cosmic significance of love and thus regards it as mere passion. Mephisto, the incarnation of the shrewd intellect in the service of Faust, arranges for Gretchen's rescue. In her plight and in his own, Faust relives the depth of human suffering while he sees Mephisto "gloat and grin over the fate of thousands." The further Faust proceeds in spiritualizing the most personal of emotions, the less Mephisto is able to follow him, and the last step of spiritualization occurs when Mephisto is defeated by the angels' intervention and Faust's immortal part joins in the ascent of the spirits. There to the "higest ruler of the world," the *mater gloriosa*, the Doctor Marianus devotes his prayer. His love has become holy.

> *Höchste Herrscherin der Welt!*
> *Lasse mich im blauen,*
> *Ausgespannten Himmelszelt*
> *Dein Geheimnis schauen.*
> *Billige, was des Mannes Brust*
> *Ernst und zart beweget*
> *Und mit heiliger Liebeslust*
> *Dir entgegen träget.*[13]

It is up to man himself how far he will ascend the ladder of love. Goethe's love ascends like the Platonic eros in the *Symposium*. The emotional and cognitive elements co-operating in the fact of ascending are inseparable. Love and spirit appear as two aspects of the same power. Just as intensification is the end toward which polarity tends throughout nature, it is the end toward which the polarity in which love is actualized is to lead. The attractive power of the "eternally feminine," *das Ewig-Weibliche*, draws us upward. The tone with which *Faust* concludes suggests the metaphysical poetry of the *Divan*; the "Marienbader Elegie" recalls, by its religious name, the feeling which culminates in the presence of the beloved one.

> *In unseres Busens Reine wogt ein Streben,*
> *Sich einem höhern, Reinen, Unbekannten*
> *Aus Dankbarkeit freiwillig hinzugeben,*
> *Enträtselnd sich den ewig Ungenannten;*
> *Wir heissens: fromm sein! Solcher seligen Höhe*
> *Fühl ich mich teilhaft, wenn ich vor ihr stehe.*[14]

Epimetheus, to whom Pandora had once appeared in the form of feminine youthfulness, had then experienced a moment of bliss and was ever afterwards bound by the beauty which had granted it. Goethe saw the supreme power of beauty manifesting itself in a thousand forms. In the "Marienbader Elegie" the beloved transforms herself within the lover's heart into a thousand forms and is ever more beloved. The urge of love prompts the mind to transcend the concrete object of love and to seize upon its inner meaning. The actual event of love joins the life of matter to the power transcending the boundaries of personality, and it not only lifts man's feelings, it also elevates his cognition. In the paradise of the *Divan*, the eternal cycles are described as penetrated "by the pure and lively tone of God's word, through which the souls, prompted by ardent desire, lose themselves in the intuition of eternal love."[15] Love is the uniting bond between the lower and the higher, between the human and the divine. On its highest level man's *amor dei* and the radiance of the "all-loving Father" may meet, as they do in Faust's ascension.

Goethe was aware that he conceived of "the idea in feminine form or in the form of woman."[16] He distinguished between the original phenomenon which he experienced and the concrete individual through whom he experienced it. "Women are like silver bowls into which we put golden apples." The polar constitution of the universe manifests itself throughout organic life as a male-female polarity. Man discovers himself to be only a half. "It does not matter whether afterwards he turns to a woman or to a world in order to constitute himself a whole."

The inner consequence of Goethe's conception of the universe comes close at this point to the ideas of Renaissance spiritualism. There the male-female tension is fundamental to the movement of the universe through a continuous rhythm of unfolding and return. The creative divinity brings forth the spirit of wisdom, Sophia, in which all-pervading love takes the first step toward manifestation. "The spirit of Jesus and the spirit of wisdom are not two different spirits but one inseparable being."[17] The tension of love between man and Sophia is the stimulant to man's ascent. The spiritualist's transfiguration of the feminine into a cosmic principle is identical with that of Goethe, who, by inner necessity, brings his conception of the meaning of love to a climax in the image of the Virgin Mary, the "highest ruler of the world."

Man's position between contraction and expansion, light and darkness, cosmos and chaos, is reflected in the hierarchy of his mental faculties. Goethe calls spirit the highest, deepest, and noblest part of man, the organ by which he is connected with the infinite spirit. He calls reason that part of man's cognitive faculty which is directed toward becoming and which, consequently, operates morphologically. It stands in contrast to the intellect, which is directed toward the given product of becoming and consequently views the material subject to it from the standpoint of its possible use. This secondary level of the human mind is clearly subordinate to reason. When left to itself it produces anarchy, as does the exclusive education of the intellect. Reason, however, may confirm the intellect in the practical realm where it belongs. The intellect does not reach into the sphere of judgment; it is confined to the realm of means and, when left to itself, becomes Mephistophelian. Abandoning man to the mere intellect means depriving him of his higher responsibility. "Whatever frees our mind without giving us mastery of ourselves is pernicious."[18] On the other hand, there is a religious element inherent in reason. By tending toward becoming, this element is attentive to the entelechy and aware of the universe to which it belongs and from which it arises.

Man must be capable of lifting himself to the highest reason in order to touch upon the Godhead which reveals itself through original phenomena, physical and ethical, behind which it remains and which emanate from it. The Godhead, however, works in the living rather than in the dead; it dwells not in the frozen and static, but in that which is becoming, and thus transforms itself.[19]

This conception of reason has a central significance in Goethe's thought. It extends through the cognition of nature, man, and society. Man needs intuition, in the sense of an agent of reason which Goethe gives it, to establish a productive relation to life. The works of the mind, be they art, philosophy, or statesmanship, emerge from reason rather than from the intellect. The extent to which reason shares in man's pursuits decides the quality of the doings of individuals, peoples, and epochs. Whenever Goethe speaks of reason, he distinguishes it sharply from any discursive interpretation of the term and preserves for it a religious connotation. Reason is the organ which, within the limits of human potentialities, makes synthesis possible and thereby supports the mediating responsibility of man.

The reason inherent in man shows him the way toward a sound life. The German *gesunder Menschenverstand* and the French *bon sens* express more clearly than the English "common sense" the connection between man's innate reason and the healthy way of life which nature intends for him. Goethe did not confuse reason with the sum-total of popular opinion, nor did he understand it as a goodness inherent in man, which only needs to be freed from the fetters of civilization. He saw it rather as a part of nature in ourselves, which tends to manifest itself through the conflicts of life. Reason, devoted to becoming, serves the entelechy of man. By training our mind to see the original phenomena, we are able to grasp the idea or intention which nature is developing in its products. Thus we can distinguish the perfect norm from its imperfect realization, nature's tendency toward health from its creatures' confusion and sickness.

It is at this juncture that the conscious intuition and reasoning of the scholar meet with common sense. Inherent in the human mind is the notion of health. When "the genius of sound human reasoning secretly whispers into the ear of every newborn being"[20] the law which leads him on the right path—namely, the rhythm of thinking and action—this genius intends health. Sickness and error are a challenge which man, in so far as his limitations allow, must turn into that which is fruitful. Goethe could not be discouraged in this conviction either by the ineffable character of the universe which, he realized, might at any time defy anthropomorphic notions, or by the demonic upheavals of history. With a thousand tongues nature conveyed to him, inwardly and outwardly, the validity of the normative core of his phenomenology of man and nature.

Goethe's conception of health as inherent in the human entelechy had inevitable consequences in regard to his understanding of art, science, and ethics. In spite of the tragic aspect of human life represented by the drama of Faust, Goethe regarded human existence as capable of fufillment. Man's insight into the polarity of his life will help him to find a solution to the riddle he constitutes for himself. In this solution his religious sense is reconciled with his understanding of beauty and with his search for truth. By resigning

himself to "the desirable" he arrives at peace with himself
and with others. Day by day he can bring into a unity the
dispersing parts of his self to form the functional whole to
which they belong.

Wilhelm Meister is an image of the possibility and conditions of such healthful fulfillment. Man is not healthy if he
either refuses to face the world or cuts himself off from the
religious ground of his existence. The religion of reverence
practiced in the Pedagogic Province teaches man how to
live in accordance with this conception. Natalie, the leading feminine figure of the novel, is the model of the human
norm as Goethe saw it. The canoness, *die Schöne Seele*, is
one-sided because she tends too exclusively toward the life
of the spirit. Therese, level-headed and efficient, is one-
sided because she is denied the gift of the highest reason.
"Precisely because Natalie is holy and human at the same
time, she appears as an angel, whereas the canoness is only
a saint, Therese only a perfect earthly being."[21]

When Schiller, in a letter to Goethe, thus described the
three figures, he called Natalie "the only aesthetic person."
In her, emotion and reason, matter and spirit, were reconciled. True to his conception of aesthetics, Schiller saw
her physical appearance as a testimony to the harmony
which her personality had attained. Beauty has a religious
function in that, as an original phenomenon, it serves the
universal purpose.

There are only two true religions: that which acknowledges
and prays to the holy dwelling in us and around us, without
form; and that which does so in the most beautiful form. What
lies between is idolatry.[22]

Religion is not in need of art, for it rests upon its own seriousness. But "art is built upon a kind of religious sense,
upon a deep and unshakable seriousness; it is for this reason that it so often tends to join religion."[23] As an intensi-

fication of nature in the human realm, the sublime expressed in art cannot contradict the entelechy of man.

Faith in the *creator spiritus* was the foundation of Goethe's own religion and of his understanding of the nature of man. Therefore he could seek the "firm religious anchorage"[24] of his faith in the potentialities bestowed upon man by the creator. He came to consider the education of these potentialities as indispensable. He saw as many dangers in clerical formalism and otherworldliness as in the negation of the spiritual dimension. To him religious forms were historical, faith was timeless. When he says that he who does not possess science and art *ought to have* religion, he is by no means employing a Voltairean irony. On the contrary, both scholarship and art depend on the recognition of the numinous and are impossible without it. Faith does not stand in contrast to science but is its basis.[25]

The old Goethe came to regard the churches as "beneficial mediators," for he held that "the light of the untroubled divine revelation is much too pure and radiant to be appropriate and tolerable for the poor, weak human creature."[26] As for himself, he upheld the "point of view of an original religion, the point of view of pure nature and reason which are of divine descent." Living in spiritual communion with those "wise and good to the highest degree," he understood that the greatness through which the human entelechy reached its historical culmination was the work of the divinity rather than the product of merely human forces. In his last conversation with Eckermann, he mentioned as witnesses to the working spirit the names of Mozart, Raphael, and Shakespeare.[27]

8

The Response to Life

Suffering and Serenity—Truth and the Art of
Living—The Ethic of Friendship
The Demonic—Original Virtue—*Novelle*

THE UNIVERSAL POLARITY as it manifests itself in human
nature tends toward an ultimate reconciliation. Man's
longing for reconciliation is ineradicable, whether it be
expressed as Ganymede's desire for union with the divinities, or as Faust's urge to comprehend the universe, or as
Epimetheus' hope for Pandora's return. On the level of
resignation—that is, under the impact of the resolution to
spiritualize human existence *sub specie aeternitatis*—reconciliation occurs in moments when the character of man
attains harmony and totality, and it becomes manifest in
the perfect work of art.

In contrast with the Christian interpretation of history,
Goethe divorced his conception of reconciliation from the
notion of time. He interpreted life and history in terms
of their inner dynamics and saw them as a cosmic process
by which matter is spiritualized and spirit embodied. The
universe has no end in time and the end of human history, like its beginning, is hidden. Hence Goethe understood the chiliastic hope of man as the expression of an
indwelling higher force corresponding to the element of
grace, which is beyond his control. When both come together in the proper moment, reconciliation occurs. In

consequence Goethe sees no last judgment but a permanent judgment, no ultimate salvation but a recurring salvation.

Goethe's insistence upon a constructive response to the human situation determined his attitude toward suffering and guilt. Man, on his wandering, does not live and act "in the truth." "If God had purposed that mankind should live and act in the truth, he would have had to arrange things differently."[1] In other words, failure and guilt are necessary ingredients of the human situation. But man is able to transmute them into something good. "There is no situation that cannot be ennobled through action or endurance."[2] In Goethe's ultimately monistic conception of the universe, fire stands in a dialectic relation to light, failure to restoration, despair to hope. Just as he kept silent about his own suffering, he was reluctant, when speaking of Christ, to touch upon the crucifixion and emphasized the resurrection. He was averse to any tendency to dwell on human failure without offering a way to overcome it.

The idea of man contains a normative element and man's nature tends toward the realization of it. Since life is a test and since man is called to mediate between the antagonistic forces within him, there is no radical evil in Goethe's ethics. Each of his negative or critical statements has a positive corollary, expressed or implied. Man is guilty-unguilty; in other words, he is responsible for the extent to which he does or does not bring to realization his own constructive potentialities. He is denied perfection which he can, at best, only approximate. Both perfectionism and nihilism vanish when man faces clearly his situation, its limitations and its possibilities. Wilhelm Meister recoils in horror from the nihilism of the actor Melina, and he is defeated when he meets Lothario, whom he had judged prematurely by standards of moral perfectionism.[3]

Goethe's ethics calls for the overcoming of suffering and guilt. He himself had to win serenity and freedom

anew every day. His poetry leads the reader into that
realm above the adversities of existence which he himself
was able to attain. The poetic production of the young
Goethe had a cathartic and reassuring effect upon him;
the lyrical poetry of the old Goethe mirrors the clear
serenity which he came to understand as a duty. Obedience
to this ethical command, however, cost him continual
struggle. When he said that each separation carries a threat
of insanity, when with the warmest compassion he wrote
to his friend Zelter about the suicide of the composer's son,
when after the death of his own son, August, he withdrew
into silence and solitude and severed relations with a close
friend of his son's who felt justified in intruding upon this
solitude, he betrayed that, in his old age, he was as much
exposed to inner suffering as in his youth, when he spoke
freely about it.

Many a sufferer has passed before me; upon me, however,
was imposed the duty to endure and to bear a sequence of joy
and pain, each single bit of which might in itself have been
fatal.[4]

By speaking of his own duty to endure through joy and
pain, Goethe referred the sculptor Rauch, the recipient
of the moving letter of consolation in which this passage
occurs, to his calling, and he added that work is the first
step "toward restoring one's self, so far as this is given to
man." The energy with which, during and after the deepest physical and psychological crises, Goethe was able to
carry on with his work, his resolution to continue in objectifying himself, proved regenerative. The universalism
of Goethe's thought showed him the way by which he
could win back the calm which was daily threatened.

The guilty-unguilty human being suffers from his ethical
failures. His freedom gives him the choice of a variety of
ways of action, and in each ethical situation it gives him
this choice in a new form. The voice of conscience, in

conflict with other and stronger impulses, is neither unequivocal at all times nor does it develop without experience.
Moreover, conscience is not combined with sufficient foresight to prevent its defeat by the unforeseeable consequences of actions which are at variance with their motives.
In this ambivalent situation man finds support in his relation
to truth and in his capacity for friendship.[5]

Truth, in Goethe's sense, is the object of man's striving.
"The first and last thing required of the man of genius, is
love of truth."[6] "Love of truth becomes manifest in one's
knowledge of how to find and to appreciate the good
everywhere."[7] Both statements could be taken as common-
places, the latter as an equation of two unknowns. Seen
within the whole of Goethe's thought, however, they yield
a more profound meaning. Truth is not the sum-total of
objective conclusions reached by a succession of workers
during the course of intellectual history and completely
dissociated from individual personalities. Truth serves the
constructive and fruitful intention of life and it results from
living the true life. It requires unselfishness based upon
devotion to the idea—the highest and most difficult achievement in self-mastery demanded of the man of genius. He
must subordinate himself to the universal purpose. Man's
relation to truth is ethical in character; he is called upon to
transcend his personality for the sake of truth. Love is his
guide, for, as we have seen, Goethe considered mental
acumen to be productive when allied with love, but stag-
nant when allied with hatred or envy. Man does not live
in the truth but he must strive for it throughout his life.

The pupils in the Pedagogic Province of *Wilhelm
Meister* comply with this ethical demand in the exercise
and esteem of reverence. Goethe assumed that the human
entelechy is equipped with the ability to work out ethical
freedom. He regarded the habits which are imposed by
education as nothing more than a support for the individual
in his self-education. He had faith that there is alive in the

nature of the good man "the dark urge toward the right way." The Lord confirms this when, in the Prologue in Heaven, he allows Mephisto to try Faust:

> *Ein guter Mensch, in seinem dunklen Drange,*
> *Ist sich des rechten Weges wohl bewusst.*[8]

Man shares potentially in the realm of ideas. He approaches it through his life, the results of which emerge from an unselfish fusion of man and work.

Goethe illustrated this road of self-education and maturity by a parable in *Wilhelm Meister*. In the first stage of his travels Wilhelm meets Montan, who helps him by word and example. In a conversation about man's education, Montan points out to Wilhelm a near-by charcoal pile[9] and asks him to describe what is done with it: how the wood is piled up with just enough air coming in, how the fire is kindled and, when in full blaze, is covered with grass and earth to damp the flame, so that the wood will slowly carbonize and be made usable. Montan calls himself "an old coal-basket full of hearty beechen coal." He intends by this metaphor to convey more to Wilhelm than the thought that man is called to serve his fellows in the exercise of a useful profession. The whole man must be consumed in this burning; it is the precondition of his quality; and man ought to consume himself by assembling, protecting, and using his potentialities in an intelligent way so as to bring forth the best possible result.

This ethical way of living is accessible to everyone. The old Goethe, as we have said, was convinced that the particular, closely observed, will open up the perspective of the universal, and that the universal can be approached and appropriated by the human mind only through the particular. Thus the inevitable concentration of a man's energies on a specialty does not in itself prevent him from attaining fulfillment as a personality. The good person, says Montan in the same conversation, "sees in the one thing he does right the symbol of everything that is done right." The qualities of men are different by nature, but to each individual nature has given equal opportunity to work toward the totality of his own personality; and every human being ought to be given this opportunity by society. The balance of man's forces in the sense in which Schiller conceived of it, as the reconciliation of reason and emotion, is an ethical goal which can be attained if man keeps his ethical consciousness alive. The right ethics will reveal itself in the sound rhythm of thought and action of the lived experience.

It is essential for Goethe, however, that a man take what is truly *his* way rather than that of others or of "the times." For "the rudder of man's fragile vessel is given into his own hand so that he may follow the will of his reason rather than the caprice of the waves."[10] Therefore it is necessary that man realize those limitations of his individual capacity within the boundaries of which he can alone be productive. Then "the lowest human being can be complete, . . . but even beautiful qualities are darkened, suspended, or destroyed, if the indispensable balance is lacking."[11] These fundamentals of individual ethics are of far-reaching consequence for Goethe's view of the desirable society, and they are reflected in his social and political judgments.

The old Goethe confessed that in "idea and love" he had found the truth that dominated his art of living and outlasted the joys of youth and the satisfactions of manhood. Idea and love transcend time and space.

Goethe respected mathematical measurement within its proper domain. He was aware, however, of "something which reaches far beyond time and space, and which belongs to all."[12] He considered "idea and love" the presupposition of the achievement even of mathematical procedure. The saying from Makarie's archive which contains the above quotation confirms the recognition of the highest accessible truth as the source of harmony and achievement. Intuition of the typical, that is, penetration to the original phenomenon, leads beyond the results obtainable by quantitative observation. Idea and love, the ultimate and lasting impulses and goals of man in cognition and action, relate man to the realm of timeless Being.

In spite of the fact that this metaphysical dimension is accessible to man, he cannot be spared the experience of despair, error, and guilt. He is, however, given at the same time an innate ethical faculty which can be developed by life itself and appealed to by others. Friendship, reaching to the core of personality, is decisive for the growth of the ethical organ. Lost between the radiant heavens and "night and death and hell," man finds himself in the midst of uncertainty:

> *Ein Wunder ist der arme Mensch geboren,*
> *In Wundern ist der irre Mensch verloren;*
> *Nach welcher dunklen, schwer entdeckten Schwelle*
> *Durchtappen pfadlos ungewisse Schritte?*
> *Dann in lebendigem Himmelsglanz und-Mitte*
> *Gewahr, empfind ich Nacht und Tod und Hölle.*[13]

The exposed situation of man could not be presented more drastically than in this poem, included in *Wilhelm Meister's Travels*. That it was written in Goethe's old age and with a clarity of insight not in the least inferior to that evident in the poems of his youth, gives proof of his lasting concern with this situation. But Goethe also gives a constructive answer. Man should not content himself with realizing his situation; he must also find the inner strength to respond productively to it.

> *Bist noch so tief in Schmerz und Qual verloren,*
> *So bleibst Du doch zum Jugendglück geboren;*
> *Ermanne Dich zu rasch gesundem Schritte!*

Komm in der Freundschaft Himmelsglanz und Helle,
Empfinde dich in treuer Guten Mitte!
Da spriesse Dir des Lebens heitre Quelle.

The tone of the early poem "Edel sei der Mensch" still betrays an endeavor to reach firm ground in the shifting inner and outer world. The answer of the later poem in *Wilhelm Meister's Travels* emerges from an inner certainty. The dialogue in it reveals that the solitude of Prometheus has been lifted, that the community of friendship is real; in the midst of it flows "the serene source of life." The human problem has a solution—not one which can last forever, but one which is offered as peace is offered to the individual, day by day and year by year. Goethe intended with his utopia to create an image of this solution. Even under the pressure of cumulative human failure he refused to deny man his justified hope. He found in man's inner resources and in his capacity for communion with others the potentialities of a constructive answer to his situation. Man is bound to err but he is capable of approaching the truth.

Friendship is an appeal to man's innate ethical faculty because, through the eyes of love, he is seen as *Gestalt*, as an entelechy in the state of becoming. Friendship creates a ground of confidence from which man can break through his isolation, find his way toward communion with others, and thus obtain the strength to objectify himself. Wilhelm Meister's relation to the friends of the Tower attains this constructive character. Like hope, confidence is a power which releases confidence in the one to whom it is offered. It quickens the ethical faculty to which it appeals. This faculty is felt as an inner intention which Goethe calls *Gesinnung* and which he sharply distinguishes from opinion.[14]

In his relationship with Fritz Jacobi, for example, we have seen how Goethe maintained the community of their inner intentions over and above the divergence of their opinions. The inner intentions are productive in that thought and action emerge out of them. They develop within the range of "the person, his nearest relationships and demands," and often they are determined by the narrow conditions to which man's experience of life is confined. Goethe intends to free man from these effects of contraction. He believes in *gute Gesinnung*, a good ethical disposition, as a reality which is basic for a productive life. He believes this in a wholly unsentimental fashion and thereby surprises us of today, who are little inclined to accept good intentions as an unequivocal reality. However, the parallelism of immanence and transcendence, which is essential to Goethe's conception of man, must have as its corollary the acceptance of this belief in an innate ethical disposition which is the counterpart of selfhood.

Goethe's ethical thought anticipates the distinction between *Gemeinschaft*, a form of human relations which is based on mutual confidence, and *Gesellschaft*, a form of association which is built upon contractual relationships on the assumption that good intentions cannot be trusted. Goethe built his image of the ideal community upon this spirit of *Gemeinschaft*. This principle is contained in the answer which the erring youth receives in the poem quoted above from *Wilhelm Meister's Travels*: the creative atmosphere of friendship shall receive him. To what extent Goethe's views are relevant for us today is a problem that centers around the issue of whether man should still consider himself capable of communication and of living in a community based upon inner intention, or whether he should feel wholly restricted to living in a contractual organization based upon technical exigencies and collective opinions, or even whether he must live in the Leviathan's hell for which the only valid phrase is: *homo homini lupus*.

The opportunity open to man for a positive solution to his ethical problems has its counterpart in an aspect of

human existence which seems beyond the control of reason.
Goethe called it "the demonic." It operates within the
individual and within history. It appears as an invincible
element of man's individuality and as a form of destiny.
Eckermann, in the last years of Goethe's life, elicited a
series of statements about it.[15] The demonic has, in common with the *daimon* of man's personality, an unalterable
quality. The demonic is conceived of as an interfering
force which comes from the realm of the unknown, but
it is not wholly destructive. Usually Goethe speaks of it
as a neuter, but he also refers to "demons " The demonol-
ogy of the Renaissance spiritualists, which included both
bad and good spirits, is not merely a figure of speech with
which to grasp the inner meaning of things when other
forms of approach can no longer help us. Goethe believed
in this intermediary realm, although he discouraged any
search into it.

Goethe did not consider himself a demonic personality,
but he admitted that he was subject to such personalities.
He called Karl August demonic "to the highest degree."
"The Greeks considered demonic creatures of this kind
to belong among the demigods." "But," Goethe added a
few days later, "it would have done him [Karl August]
good had he been able to grasp my ideas and higher interests. For when the demonic spirit left him and the merely
human remained, he did not know what to do with himself and was badly off."[16] In this case the demonic presents
itself as a charisma, irresistible to its bearer and attractive
to others, yet unreliable because it comes and goes. It tends
to choose somewhat dark and troubled ages: "In a clear
and prosaic city such as Berlin it would hardly find one
single occasion to manifest itself."[17] Nor is Mephistopheles
demonic, because he is much too negative.

The inner antagonism of Goethe's dynamic universe
uses ways which are impenetrable. The universal movement has an architectural unity which, however, contains

demonic forces that cannot be understood. We can do nothing with the demonic except to name it. The demons may endanger reason as much as they further it. Goethe felt that something demonic was at work when he found a friend in Schiller. He entitled an essay about the beginning of their relationship "Fortunate Event"—"Glückliches Ereignis."[18] The sudden transformation of their cool and critical relations into a productive friendship could not have been foreseen; the contrary was more likely, as Schiller's letters prior to the event make evident. The fact that both he and Schiller had arrived at a stage of development which made them ready for this union does not satisfy Goethe; that they could respond to each other at precisely the moment when their meeting could become most productive for both of them, still gives evidence of some unfathomable factor at work. Goethe had a sense for the truly historical character of things which ultimately escapes philosophic and sociological explanation.

Egmont's *daimon* shows many traits of the young Goethe himself. Egmont could not be a statesman like Oranien nor could he look at the world in Oranien's way. The demon of his goodhearted and trusting spontaneity elevates him and ruins him. This is also the case with Götz von Berlichingen. His noble inner intention toward justice is of overpowering strength. It is the central element of his character and brings about his tragedy. In so far as the writing of these plays had remedial value for Goethe in the struggle with himself, they testify to his inner experience with the demonic. Mignon has an "abnormal" longing for home. She looks backward longingly to a pure origin and is unwilling to accept life, which is strange, meaningless, and inadequate to her inner self. Her longing is unconquerable, and at the moment when the fragile thread connecting her with the world through Wilhelm and Felix is threatened, she perishes. When Goethe said that the whole novel was written for the sake of Mignon, he gave a hint of the general significance of this demonic character: its purity and beauty harbor the germ of destruction because the demon denies to her unprotected soul the means for metamorphosis—in other words, for the full course of life. Mignon is the incarnation of an inwardness which tempted Goethe himself. But the novel bears the name of Wilhelm Meister, it centers around his figure, and one of its main aspects is Wilhelm's development beyond Mignon toward the life of resignation. Mignon dies when he is already a part of the Abbé's community. He has become strong enough to hear and to follow the message with which Mignon's burial culminates—the call to return to life.[19]

The demonic appears as a crosscurrent within the dynamic universe. Faust insists upon the removal of Philemon and Baucis. When they refuse to leave, he seeks a compromise with his bad conscience by a reconciling act of magnanimity. He commands that they be brought to another place to live. But his intentions are thwarted by the course of events and he becomes guilty of the death of three innocent people. His injustice, a concomitant of power, is aggravated when the action he had ordered takes a demonic turn. Events elude man's planning and counteract his wishes. A demonic power seemed to elevate Napoleon to an invulnerable position; the same power ruined him. Napoleon's downfall is reflected in the book "Timur" of the *Divan*.[20] The elemental demons conspire against the "tyrant of injustice": Timur is destroyed by the winter ice. Against the strongest titan a stronger adversary will rise.

In 1812, Goethe may have hoped that a poetical expression of the wish for peace might have some influence. He addressed it indirectly to Napoleon: "He who is able to will everything wills also peace."[21] But it was not given to Napoleon to bring about the peace of Europe, the *Pax Romana* which Goethe had in mind. In the introduction to *Epimenides' Awakening* Goethe retracts this hope and explains:

> *Den Frieden kann das Wollen nicht bereiten:*
> *Wer alles will, will sich vor allen mächtig;*
> *Indem er siegt, lehrt er die andern streiten,*
> *Bedenkend macht er seinen Feind bedächtig;*
> *So wachsen Kraft und List nach allen Seiten,*
> *Der Weltkreis liegt von Ungeheuern trächtig,*
> *Und der Geburten zahlenlose Plage*
> *Droht jeden Tag als mit dem jüngsten Tage.*[22]

Mankind threatens itself with annihilation. The demonism of power calls forth an adversary of equal strength. The demonic belongs to the continuous process of contraction and birth, which is accompanied by pain. When the Promethean independence of man approaches the titanic, it calls forth its own destruction. Goethe recognized the demonic as an undeniable element in the "affairs of the world." But even in this point he did not remain merely cognitive. His realism was not without hope nor without recourse to remedial potentialities.

Goethe's conception of the demonic reveals a negative aspect of his thought—an aspect to which, for obvious reasons, our century is more attentive than were our forebears. It illustrates the degree to which Goethe was aware of the limitations of man. He had experienced them himself. His departure for Weimar was demonic in the sense that the decision was made *for* him rather than *by* him. The impulse which caused his flight to Italy and his secretiveness about it seem stronger than any of his explanations. He simply had to go. A demonic element surrounds even the other hegira—his first journey to the German southwest at the time of the *Divan* poetry. In each of these cases he felt driven into an unknown realm of existence. And each time, he found a productive answer to the exigencies of the new situation. We may be critical of his inner difficulties during the first Weimar period. We may regret that what he sought in Italy was more essential to him than Italy itself. But Goethe as he was is important to us because the formative energy of his mind accepted the demonic within and about him. He did not permit himself to feel merely exposed to it; he responded to it.

Thus, in the end, even the demonic is a challenge to man's resourcefulness. Because he is aware of the demonic element in life to the extent of recognizing the "monster" latent in man, Goethe is separated from eighteenth- and nineteenth-century optimism. He differs from twentieth-century pessimism because of his conviction that man is not left alone with the monstrous within and around him. The demonic cannot be abolished, but we need not on that account give up the struggle to hold our own in face of it. Man should make the effort "to set the figures in the game astutely."[23] Goethe's conception of the demonic has certain characteristics of the Renaissance concept of *fortuna*. The responding human capacity was *virtu*. The poem "Seefahrt" shows as strongly as the "Symbolum" man's ability to answer the good or bad challenge of *fortuna*. The human being should be confident that he can establish a significant relation to the universe. His trust in genius, in the gods, in God, is the foundation of his strength.

The theory of emanation characteristic of Goethe's concept of the universe prevented him from accepting an orthodox interpretation of original sin. Man is "guilty-unguilty." God not only made man imperfect and separated him from the universe as an individual, he also gave him the power to overcome imperfection.

Viewed from the standpoint of ethics, certain manifestations of human nature force us to ascribe to it a kind of radical evil, an *original sin;* other manifestations require us to grant to it also an original virtue, an inborn charity, righteousness, and, especially, an inclination toward reverence. If this essential source is cultivated in man, if it is brought to active life and public significance, we call it *Pietät*, as did the ancients. . . .[24]

This passage from Goethe's review of Salvandy's historical novel *Don Alonzo, ou l'Espagne*, is in spite of its brevity representative of Goethe's religious ethics. The "noble forebear" Cicero[25] considered this reverence the foundation of all virtues. "*Pietas gravissimum et sanctissimum nomen . . . fundamentum omnium virtutum.*" Goethe recognizes its power in the relations of parents with their children; it is weaker in those of the children with the parents; it pervades all human relationships and those of man with the animals, with nature and culture;

it embraces everything, and since the world belongs to reverence, it devotes its last and best part to heaven; reverence alone keeps egotism in balance; if, through a miracle, it were to emerge instantly in all men, it might save the world from all the evils of which it is at present sick, perhaps without remedy.[26]

The universal significance which Goethe gave to reverence was fundamental to his image of the good society. Goethe felt that Salvandy, the young author of the novel, could have arrived "at the highest result of wisdom" only because "the holy grace of God and nature penetrated him." In fact Salvandy pointed out that dignity, success, and inner happiness can be obtained only at the price of virtuous resignation, which, together with reverence, forms the quintessence of Goethe's ethical thought. "Reverence" expresses in one word Goethe's forward-looking religious attitude, which he also termed *Weltfrömmigkeit*, piety toward the world.[27]

Original virtue is only one aspect of Goethe's ethical view of man. The other aspect is original sin, or, in terms used more often by Goethe, error and guilt. There is no more moving picture of human guilt and, in this case, of a demonic and "innocent" guilt, than that of the harpist

Augustin in *Wilhelm Meister*. There is no possible doubt about Faust's moral guilt, from which he is absolved by grace in response to his striving. Recurring failure, renewed effort, and repeated guilt accompany him to the end. Ottilie, in *The Elective Affinities*, accepts her guilt, which is aggravated by the demonic occurrence of the death of the child, for which she holds herself responsible.[28] Man's imperfection forms a part of the universal process. But imperfection is not the only quality of human existence. By obeying her conscience, which demands that she punish herself, Ottilie's original virtue counteracts her guilt. She makes her own death the object of her urge to form and thus her death becomes that of a saint. Goethe did not deny that man is bound by sin and his own egotism nor that his efforts are fragmentary and temporal, but he emphasized the productive response to the human situation which man is able to give by making a renewed attempt to develop his inborn virtue as the proper answer to failure and guilt.

Man, who must not try to escape the exigencies of his existence, is bound to remain in the sphere of contraction as an individual and to suffer the pressure of it. All religions and philosophies, however, teach that there is an occasion and even a duty to elevate ourselves over and above this depressing condition. We are required

to fulfill the intentions of the Godhead on the one hand by abandoning ourselves in a regular rhythm, since on the other hand we are compelled to reaffirm our selfhood.[29]

The polarity of human existence is reflected in the tension between holding onto one's self and losing one's self, between sin and virtue, the solution of which Goethe considers as man's ethical task, the meaning of the religious conduct which he termed *Weltfrömmigkeit*.

The older Goethe grew, the more he was inclined to view the healing and reconciling forces of life as an impersonal element of genius which can come only at the proper time. In the *Parable*, in *Pandora*, in *Faust*, in *Wilhelm Meister*, the readiness of man is the precondition of the approach of these healing forces, but their actual coming remains an act of cosmic grace. We learn of this grace in Faust's regeneration after the Gretchen tragedy and in his redemption by the angels.

It is found again in the mythical image of Goethe's *Novelle*.[30] There, grace operates through the pure heart of a child. The child, another Daniel, is victorious over the demonic element. The theme of the story belonged to those images which had been developing for decades in Goethe's mind. He formed it into a tender design of translucent symbolism, like a patent secret. Every part of the story is within the range of the possible. And yet Goethe himself compared the culmination of this tale with the unexpected and miraculous metamorphosis of a plant when it puts forth its blossom. In accord with the monistic structure of his thought, Goethe considered the miraculous to be both natural and supernatural at the same time.

In the *Novelle* we are introduced to the happy life of a small principality. We see the prince taking leave of the princess for a few days of hunting and we are given some hints of the organic co-operation which enlivens the whole community and is reflected in the way in which prince and princess share their inclinations and activities. On the day of the annual fair the princess rides through the town with her uncle and a knight to visit the old castle in the mountains. The landscape is significantly laid out; only near the old castle has nature overgrown the work man has done in the past. In the peaceful exchange of the fair, the people of the mountains demonstrate their useful and happy co-operation with those of the plains. These scenes of reason and self-contained activity seem to predict only happiness. The uncle alone remains conscious of the uncertainty of all things human. He knows that government is subject to change in spite of care and wisdom, and a fire through which he had once lived during the fair makes him constantly aware of the unbridled elements which are always ready to invade the zone of fruitful order.

And suddenly this time, too, a fire breaks out in the fair, and this catastrophe is immediately followed by the threat of a second. The wild animals of the show break loose—and the tiger comes up the mountain and threatens the princess. The uncle's fearful recollection now appears to be almost a foreboding. The knight kills the tiger, but his courage and devotion are vain, because the tiger was tame for those who knew how to handle him. Face to face with the tiger's owner, who appeals to the knight's humanity to save the lion, the knight's chivalric pride vanishes.

The child, like Daniel, tames the tyrant of the forests. By pulling a sharp thorn out of his paw he proves himself the lion's friend, and then quiets the animal with his song. "God and art, piety and good fortune must do the rest." The purity of heart and the courage of the child prove superior. The lion is not fettered, but he is tamed again. He has his honor and his freedom. At the end of this tale, whose symbolism hints at his faith in the purely human, Goethe describes his Daniel: "Truly, the child in his transfiguration looked like a powerful victor. The lion was not like one defeated, his strength remained hidden within him. He was rather like one tamed who has been entrusted to his own powerful will."

9

The Archetype of Society

The Purely Human—*Pandora:* Self-Sufficiency
and Catholicity of Existence
Freedom, War, and Peace—The Energy of Hope

THE LYRICAL CONCLUSION of the *Novelle* hints, in its utter
simplicity, at "the ideal which comes from the heart of
the poet."[1] This ideal represents Goethe's final criterion
also in matters social and political. Goethe's social thought
may appear nonpolitical in that the element of power is
invariably subordinated to forces of a higher nature.
Goethe thinks of the human community in its totality and
therefore denies to the political world laws of its own
which govern a sphere separate from the ultimate ends of
man. Detached from the foreground of the political realm,
Goethe sought the original phenomenon and the normative
character of society. His goal was freedom, and the way
to it is striving for the realization of the "pure humanity"
which dwells in the human being. To understand this
"purely human" is to understand Goethe's judgments on
the political theories and movements of his time.

In a conversation with a Russian nobleman, in which
he abandoned his habitual reticence, Goethe summed up
the significance of his life and work as "the triumph of
the purely human."[2] This potentiality of human existence
stands in conflict with the *merely* human part of man's
nature. The goal of the trial of life is the victory of the

purely human. The purity of Iphigenie's feeling and thought brings about the peripety of the drama. The purity of the child Daniel is akin to the purity of heart which Wilhelm Meister desires to obtain from God. The strength of the conflict between this purity and the contingencies of life is evident in the most impressive form from Goethe's conception of "the pure Christ." Goethe saw the returning Christ as a living criticism of mankind, including the Christians. The life of man is not pure but perturbed. The returning Christ is destined for a second crucifixion. Living through this conflict between the purely human and the exigencies of the temporal sphere constitutes the task of man and predicates the mission of the poet Goethe.

This tension between the purely human and man's existence arose by necessity. In the world of plants Goethe had recognized and learned to love a process of metamorphoses in accord with an inherent law. In the tranquillity of this vegetative world he had sought refuge. Man, however, is given the choice between good and evil, affirmation and negation. He is exposed to demonic forces and to his own uncertain judgment. His affairs are shaped by continuous perturbations:

Within the immense life of the universe, that is, within the realization of God's ideas in which the true reality consists, a special result arises for our personality: the power to affirm and to negate prejudice and apprehension, hatred and love; therein the temporal has its existence, and God has counted on this perturbation and, so to speak, lets us have our way with it.[3]

Were it otherwise, the role of man as a mediating agent and of life as a trial would not make sense. Because perturbation is a corollary of human existence, the purely human has a transcending quality. Conversely, when regarded from the level of the purely human, the world of affairs takes on an inferior aspect. The evaluation inherent in Goethe's synthesis forbids him to base his view of society on the individual or on the state or on society as such. His social thought refers to the entelechy of man and its cosmic significance. Thus the poetic images by which he illuminated the purely human have a metaphysical basis.

The festival play, *Pandora*, touches these foundations of human existence. It arose out of a renewal of Goethe's creative capacity and confidence, and it gave a response to the disturbing world situation of the Napoleonic era. The first act was written in the fall of 1807 immediately after the "Prelude" for the reopening of the Weimar Theater by which Goethe celebrated the restoration of peace. A continuation of the play dates from May, 1808. This scheme permits us to reconstruct the whole unequivocally enough to justify, for our purposes, the consideration of the two parts as a unity. *Pandora* presents the mythical image of the original phenomenon of society.[4]

Archetypal conditions of communal and personal life unfold through the contrast of the brother Titans Prometheus and Epimetheus. As in the fragment of Goethe's youth, the Prometheus of *Pandora* is the lord of his creatures. Epimetheus lives in contemplation of the bliss he experienced through his union with Pandora, and he keeps longing for her return. Epimetheus has with him one of his daughters, Epimeleia, the other, Elpore, being with Pandora. Prometheus, on the other hand, is surrounded by the people whom he governs. It is he who represents the incarnation of foresight and ability, resigned to solid work in the realm of the possible. He no longer protests against the gods; he acts. The mildness with which, in the fragment, he acts toward his daughter, he shows, in the play, to his antipode, Epimetheus. Understanding that he and his brother have chosen wholly different views and destinies, Prometheus holds to his decision to keep away from the "god-sent demons." Epimetheus, in the hope of Pandora's return, devotes to the "demons" all he is and has. Prometheus had rejected Pandora before Epimetheus was united with her and suffered the consequent pain.

The dialogue between the brothers develops to the utmost the two antithetical possible ways of perceiving the sublime: the Epimethean way in which each phase of reconstructing Pandora's image tends toward an inner significance, and the way of Prometheus who turns each word of his brother into an outer observation which, although not without respect, is without devotion. To Prometheus the demonic and the divine are equally dangerous, unreliable, and tempting as the elements which threaten any well-ordered existence. He proves the value and the limitation of his self-restricting and self-sufficient way. It is Prometheus who appears as judge against his own son Phileros, and Prometheus who knows how to ward off the invading enemy and how to extinguish the fire. He had educated the various groups of his people to master the domains of communal life to which they were assigned—the shepherds and the smiths, the tillers of the soil, fishermen, and warriors. He keeps them within the limits which he considers are those of possible happiness, within the limits of human nature, to which it is given "to see the lighted, not the light itself." Prometheus lives for the present, and to him Epimetheus seems lost in the past and the future, only half-living in endless pain, a somnambulist, a prey to irremediable care and hopeless longing. His sympathy and understanding suffice, however, to make him realize that Epimetheus' way is as laudable as his own, for we live by bearing our hardships, be it through suffering or through action.

Prometheus is skeptical about the higher possibilities of human nature. A short memory prevents man from turning past experience to his advantage. His frivolous lust for living in the moment causes him to seize quickly what he finds and to throw it away again without thinking "how he might form it toward higher usefulness." Teaching and example are of little consequence. Although sufficiently equipped for living, the human race does not use its gifts. Man neither gives enough thought to the universal meaning of his own past nor is he resourceful enough to make fully his own what he actually lives through in the present.

It is in accord with such skepticism that Prometheus expects nothing good from Pandora's box, the *Kypsele*, which, in the second part of the play, becomes accessible to men. Its contents seem the highest prize to Epimetheus; to Prometheus they are as dangerous as the donor. His people when confronted with the *Kypsele* act without higher insight; each group offers advice as to what should be done with it from its own narrow viewpoint. Prometheus simply wants it buried and put entirely out of sight. At the end of the first act, Eos, goddess of the approaching dawn, censures him for his self-reliant neglect of the gods. It was not he who saved his son Phileros from death in the water, the punishment he inflicted upon himself in despair. The "indestructible urge of life itself brought him back reborn." Eos, the symbol of reconciliation, when she announces a new day, points out to Prometheus the limits of his thought and action. Men know what to wish for, the gods know what should be given.

> *Fahre wohl, du Menschenvater! Merke:*
> *Was zu wünschen sei, Ihr drunten fühlt es;*
> *Was zu geben sei, die wissens droben.*
> *Gross beginnet Ihr Titanen; aber leiten*
> *Zu dem ewig Guten, ewig Schönen*
> *Ist der Götter Werk; die lasst gewähren!*

The Promethean Titan is pushed farther into the background as reconciliation progresses. Pandora's return breaks through the boundaries which he set for the human community. It is not he but Epimetheus who is united with Pandora and elevated with her, and from whose side—from Epimeleia—comes the interpretation of the *Kypsele*. "Transforming the past into an image. Poetical repent-

ance, Justice"—these are the words by which Goethe outlined Epimeleia's prophetic speech before the *Kypsele* and
the effect of her words. The basic condition of the act of
renewal is the vision of the normative by facing the aberrations of the past. Repentance follows this restoration of
measure and prepares the return of justice. The forces of
life can be purified and heightened precisely in Epimetheus' way; poetic repentance frees man from the burden
of an experience which he had neither understood nor
overcome, and thereby removes a hindrance to the growth
of the good life. The sequence of tragic conflict, interference from on high, firm recognition, repentance, and
renewal gives to the play the character of a sacrificial act
of catharsis.

Following the *Kypsele*, Pandora returns. Her first act is
to paralyze the "violent ones" who, even toward the
Kypsele, prove to have a merely destructive capacity. Fishermen, shepherds, and all who are in continuous contact
with nature come to her side at once. The meaning of
beauty reveals itself in the Arcadian beatitude and fullness
which arise. The piety and calmness of the sabbath day prepare the *moria*, the establishment of a new covenant. The
gift of the gods, the *Kypsele*, can be declined by the individual but not by the people. Thus, in the end, Prometheus
remains alone in his opposition.

When the *Kypsele* opens, it discloses a temple. In it are
demons; they keep to their seats, bridled like the tamed lion
of the *Novelle*. Science and art have their place. A curtain
covers an unapproachable mystery. Phileros and Epimeleia
are the leaders of a priesthood. All join in exchanging
speeches and songs addressed, in the beginning, to Pandora.
With the coming of Helios, the sun, Epimetheus is rejuve-
nated and elevated with Pandora. Then the establishment of
the covenant is consummated by the consecration of the
priests. The acceptance of the *Kypsele* culminates in the
foundation of a community which reconciles the realm of

Epimetheus with that of Prometheus and fulfills the potentiality latent in the communal situation of man.

In this mythical image the moment of fulfillment is short. It extends from the advent of dawn to sunrise, from Phileros' emergence out of the waters and Epimeleia's rescue from the flames to the elevation of Epimetheus and Pandora to a higher sphere. The decisive hour is beyond human will. It comes and it must go again. Dignity and beauty, says Eos, become manifest only to veil themselves anew. The place of man's action is there where he can lay hold of the fleeting moment of reconciliation and embody it in lasting symbols. Therefore the priests are consecrated after the founders' withdrawal. The priesthood is to serve the memory of the moment of foundation and, thereby, the duration of the covenant. The return of Pandora is a free act of divine will, an act of grace made possible by Epimetheus' faithfulness. The laws of communal living, revealed in the act of Pandora's return, are to be kept and cultivated by an institution which is devoted to the duty of maintaining the decisive event of the past, the moment of foundation, as the central spiritual property of the new community.

Both in content and in form *Pandora* was hardly understood in Goethe's time, whereas today no one doubts that in this most classic and lyrical of his plays Goethe's "most mature and conscious mastership embodied the poetical intentions in word and rhythm." The tonal and rhythmical structure of this play anticipates possibilities of the German language which, as has been rightly observed, came to life again only at the turn of the nineteenth century. This culmination of Goethe's symbolical style involves the rediscovery of baroque forms. Pandora as a lawgiving mediator between man and the gods re-creates the unity between the phenomenal and the real. The phenomenal world to which she returns is related through her appearance to the realm of ideal realities; the temporal is a parable of the eternal.

In Goethe's creation of a new, solemn form of mythopoesis, *Pandora* holds the decisive place. "It is the mythical play of eternally human life." Through it Goethe's conception of the poet as rendering a social service by his work, and of the poet's mission as reaching for the normative rather than the pleasurable, becomes fully manifest. Wisdom, artistic consciousness, and emotional productive impulse here attain a perfect balance. In the midst of the Napoleonic wars, the poet of an individualistic era created a symbolical play by presenting the fundamental problems of human community and by doing it in a form chosen to articulate the elusive spiritual elements inherent in the original phenomenon of human society. The form of this work had to follow its own law. Its dialogue comes closest to that of Greek tragedy; its chorus is of a simplicity which anticipates the *Divan* songs; its lyrical passages are among the most musical and architecturally perfect of Goethe's poetic creations.

As a whole, *Pandora* is unique in structure, whereas in tone it has affinities with the Helena act of *Faust II* and with *The Natural Daughter*. *Pandora* forms a world of its own comprising the totality of existence in its basic components. Goethe wrote this play out of a serenity of mind which arose as a new life. Twenty years after his sojourn at Rome his concern about the classical norm produced another metamorphosis in this archetypal image of human society. At the time of writing it was a question whether the Germans would be able to retain their own language at all,[5] and a peace was made which no penetrating mind could believe would be conclusive. Goethe's poetic genius was ready to realize the universal significance of danger and destruction and to give a constructive response which, free from all immediate relations to his time, crystallizes the inner meaning of its events.

Neither the Epimethean nor the Promethean realm is sufficient in itself. Without Pandora's return the world of Epimetheus remains exposed to longing and danger. Not

Prometheus but the rejuvenating power of nature saved his son Phileros. It is Epimetheus' fidelity to Pandora and his faith in the prophecy of her return that makes possible the reconciliation between man and the divine. This union is sealed by the union of Phileros and Epimeleia as the superiors of a priesthood. Together with the shepherds, the craftsmen, the artists, and the scientists, they form a community in which the demonic forces are bridled. The new covenant is governed by the spirit of the original religion. The memory of the revelation is given permanence by a cult, with which a culture is to arise. The insight into the incompleteness of the "merely" human supports freedom and peace. Power is put in its place. It is not suppressed but restored to self-mastery. The warlike parts of the community in the end offer to protect the *Kypsele*.

The role of the spiritual element in Goethe's Pandora myth discloses its significance most clearly in relation to his conception of the mind. Not the practical intellect of Prometheus, not even the Epimethean reason capable of penetrating to the inner meaning of beauty, can bring about the new covenant. The contract is concluded through Pandora's mediation with the gods, to whom she addresses herself before speaking to the "sons of the earth." The time of Pandora's return, like the return itself, is altogether beyond coercion and also, in principle, beyond merit. Pandora creates a bond which was lacking. Epimetheus' first union with her was one of anticipation. Her return brings about fulfillment. Goethe hinted, by the institution of a priesthood, at the idea of the priest as the guardian *clericus* who watches over temporal life to prevent it from closing itself to the timeless.

The solution Goethe gave to the problem of human freedom is the same for the community as for the individual. "To declare oneself free is a great pretension, for that is to declare at the same time one's willingness to master one's self, and who is capable of that?"[6] These words, addressed to young poets in an essay in which Goethe characterizes himself as the liberator rather than the master of German poetry, can be taken to represent his conception of freedom in general. Were it not for the purely human, freedom would be altogether impossible. It involves a task of self-education rather than a right. If man is freed from outward bonds and has to find his norm for himself, he is the more in need of an inward bond. This truth is borne out by the suffering and the elevation of the Titan Epimetheus.

The fundamental tenets of Goethe's original society, which largely explain his attitude toward concrete political problems, are evident from his reaction to the French Revolution, from statements he made on actual occasions of war and peace, and from judgments about current problems expressed in memoranda or conversations. We render justice to his political thought only if we assume the latent unity of his concrete and his utopian thought. On first sight, the latter seems rather distant from the so-called realities, as they are today and even as they were in Goethe's lifetime. But Goethe's capacity to return from the perturbations of affairs to a higher perspective was the nerve center of his productivity and enabled him to seize upon the desirable. The full measure of his creative talent could be exercised only with plots or subjects inviting symbolical treatment.

Consequently *The Uprooted Ones, The Citizen General, The Grand-Kophta* seem to us of today as artificial as they seemed to his contemporaries. They prove, however, that neither to the problems raised by the French Revolution nor to the problem of the impostor Cagliostro did Goethe respond simply by taking one side. In many ways he had anticipated the revolution. The scandal connected with the queen's necklace had revealed to him the hollowness and immorality of a social structure which had dominated two centuries.[7] The Cagliostro case indicated the fragility of social prudence. Supplied, because of his position, with information inaccessible to others and as sensitive to social omens as to those of nature,[8] he came to regard contemporary world events as bringing about an irrevocable and destructive transformation—this at a time when men like Herder, Schiller, and Hölderlin were still enthusiastic about the movement of freedom so in accord with their own hopes.

The world of the past seemed doomed. Between the outbreak of the French Revolution and the Congress of Vienna a quarter of a century passed which, from year to year, jeopardized the certainty of life. Goethe's image of the organic society is lifted above a constantly shifting scene in which successive phases of the revolution follow each other—its eastward expansion, the end of the Holy Roman Empire, the reorganization of the European states under Napoleonic domination, and the resurgence of European independence which led to the precarious though long-lasting settlement of Vienna. In opposition to the threatening chaos, Goethe created, as a product of "pure activity," the poetic symbol of a life and a community worthy of the idea of man. The deeper he penetrated to the primarily dissolving tendencies of his age in the realms of politics, thought, and art, the more he felt the call to oppose arbitrariness by law, sickness by the image of health, libertinism by strictness of standards. Goethe's classicism in art was a response to dangers in himself, which he later understood as forerunners of the dangers of his age. Having overcome his own *Sturm und Drang*, he found it possible to turn to "the old truth," namely, to values that endure beyond change. Their representation he considered the service of "pure activity," *reine Tätigkeit*, which arises from the tension in man between the temporal and the timeless.[9]

In *The Natural Daughter*, Eugenie recognizes and explains the all-embracing universality of the threatening evil:

Diesem Reiche droht
Ein jäher Umsturz. Die zum grossen Leben

Gefugten Elemente wollen sich
Nicht wechselseitig mehr mit Liebeskraft
Zu stets erneuter Einigkeit umfangen.
Sie fliehen sich, und einzeln tritt nun jedes
Kalt in sich selbst zurück.[10]

The inhuman coldness which destroys the bond of reconciliation, the bond of the common spirit, is imparted to all
sides of the conflict. Eugenie, whose purely human personality is her sole resource, is destined to restore unity through
a self-sacrificing act. Goethe expects the result he hoped
for not from a "contract"—that is, from an organization
which stipulates definite rules—but rather from the spirit of
reconciliation. The unity of the whole is to be sought not
among the parts but in a higher, third, element. Conflict is
opposed to the norm. Therefore not war but peace is in
accord with the entelechy of man. War is a part of the
chaotic realm from which man is called to win order and
beauty.

The "Prelude of 1807,"[11] composed for the reopening of
the Weimar Theater after the war, was written shortly before *Pandora*. In it, in two scenes following each other
without transition, the demon of war is opposed by the
genius of peace. A woman in flight is persecuted by the
demon of war and, longing for the shelter of the peaceful
hut which she never valued enough so long as she could
take it for granted, she prays in vain to the saving divinity.
Her despair turns into futile attempts to discover reason
behind the progressing destruction, which she feels the
more deeply through her helpless exposure to it.

The play of the demon with guilty and innocent alike is
followed by the return of Majesty and Peace. The allegorical figure of Majesty represents itself in a monologue
as uniting power with justice and, therefore, commanding
confidence. Majesty pronounces the theory of community
by which man is likened to the architect of the universe,
the state to the organic cosmos of nature and art. The figure

of Majesty embodies the idea of *dikaiosyne,* justice bringing
about the good life. The free and responsible citizen is the
foundation on which the just and peaceful community can
be built. His example will be followed and will have a
strengthening effect on the whole. Serving one's community consists in achieving what is ethical and fruitful within
the realm assigned to each of its members. Measure and
balance are the characteristics, and justice is the calling, of
Majesty. When order is restored and understood as a reflection of the architecture of the universe, the spirit of
peace can return. Justice is the condition rather than the
fulfillment of a sound life. Goethe conceives of peace as one
of the healing forces with which Epimetheus strives to
unite. Its coming and duration are beyond the control of
the individual. The courage to bring to realization the
purely human leads toward peace.

The political community thus is not an end in itself. It
serves the conditions under which men may attain a meaningful existence. Man is politically responsible for keeping
human purity alive within the community. As soon as the
purpose of life, on the part of the individual or of the community, becomes wholly political, false evaluations are
bound to enter and the normative image is obscured. Goethe's views are above any partisan conception and express
a social philosophy. The skeptic may doubt the possibility
of its realization, but he cannot deny its desirability. In
Goethe's normative social order, power is united with justice. This union is fundamental to any body politic whatever its constitutional form. Not the desire for peace, but
rather the understanding of its higher meaning and the art
of bringing it about, is lacking among men. Although we
are inclined to place our confidence in legally defined obligations, we often find that they are of little worth if the
spirit in which they were laid down loses its influence.

It is from spirit and reason that Goethe expected the victory of the cosmos over the chaos in human society. For

him the human being who learns to meet this norm, the cultured personality, is the goal of communal life. His judgments on actual problems of his time were related both to this image and to the actual historical situation. He strives for the calm formation of man into a cultured being by restricting the demonic through creative reason. Hence his emphasis on education for freedom rather than on rights, his distrust of political ideologies and of majority rule, and his skepticism in regard to the exclusive training of the intellect.

When man has attained freedom, the "abrogation of the law" is possible.[12] In conceiving such universal freedom as the intention inherent in human nature, Goethe and Schiller concurred. It was precisely the thoroughness of this understanding of freedom as self-mastery that caused their negative judgment of the French Revolution. So long as laws cannot be abrogated because man is not free, they must be preserved, for laws are "attempts to come nearer the intentions of the moral order of the world within the course of life and affairs." Goethe's respect for law was a consequence of this view. "It is better that you suffer injustice than that the world be without law." "It is better that acts of injustice occur than that they be eliminated by unjust means."[13] Morality cannot be furthered by immoral actions, nor by unlawful conduct in the name of ethics. Goethe judged social change by the intrinsic weight of moral thought, and he considered ethical freedom the precondition of political liberty.

These principles were further accentuated by Goethe's negative judgment concerning the human consequences of the French Revolution and its ideas. Each revolution "tends toward a state of nature without law and shame." Such a development is favored by the introduction of general concepts which take the place of experience and common sense and encourage claims rather than effort. "General concepts and great conceit always lead to horrible mischief."[14] Ignorance may then take over, and "nothing is more terrible than the activity of ignorance."[15] We live in the midst of a time of barbarism, for "wherein else does barbarism consist but in that one no longer acknowledges excellence?"[16]

All these verdicts concern the revolution and its ideological aftermath. They developed in a straight sequence from the time of Goethe's return from Italy to his last years. Goethe could be amazed by the satisfaction men drew "from the empty sound of words: an idea must not be liberal! Let it be vigorous, virtuous, conclusive in itself, in order that it may fulfill the divine command to be productive."[17] Goethe was equally opposed to the nationalistic and to the democratic aspect of the liberal movement after the Napoleonic wars. He saw no other guarantee of justice save the ethical attitude of those in power, whatever the origin of their position might be; no other hope for the realization of the original society save living with the arts and sciences in the religious sense in which he understood it.

These positive values he defended against the political demands of his contemporaries. He could take this position the more easily since the government of which he was a part practiced principles of humanity and culture with a notable consistency within its small range. As an administrator, Goethe was inclined to further initiative and self-government wherever productive results could be expected. Even his proposals for the organization of censorship provided for a co-operative self-control on the part of the intelligentsia which would serve as a safeguard against the abuse of freedom.

Goethe's conservatism "arose from the will to save freedom in the world."[18] His faith in pure humanity was never broken. This very faith gave him a perspective from which he could penetrate the demonic immensity of political events. In responding to the rise of a new era of world history by the myth of Pandora's return, Goethe turned to the

most profound insight of which he considered man capable.
He held up an image of reconciliation before a world which
was involved in war and strife, a world which drew the
realm of thought into the political battle and seemed to be
almost as unable as we are today to break the vicious circle
of evil endlessly engendering evil.

Goethe gave a form to the chiliastic energies of his mind
by creating an archetypal image of human society. He embodied these energies in the most classical of figures and in
the strictest of rhythms, as though he wanted to heighten
the life of his work through the concentration of its architecture. The chiliastic thought of the past had rather trans-
ferred to another world or to a golden age, past or future,
man's longing for peace and reconciliation. Chiliasm often
formed the basis of political movements which themselves
took the path of violence and defeated their ends by their
choice of means. The tragedies of Mahomet and of the
statesman Faust are symbols of this temptation. True to the
faith expressed in his poem on Diana of the Ephesians, Goethe kept his chiliasm as a spiritual energy within the present.
Epimetheus longs for Pandora's return, he puts his faith in
the promise of Elpore speaking to him in his dreams, and
his hope is placed in that inner force to which, in the end,
the divinities respond. When in the poem "Symbolum"
Goethe bids man hope, he appeals to an energy of the human self.[19] The inner force of human purity is a part of
this world. From the strengthening of the purely human
Goethe expected reconciliation of the antagonistic forces,
if only for one blissful and revealing moment He hoped
that man, guided by pure humanity, might some day find
the way to a life of true community.

I O

Culture and the Historical World

Culture and History—Historical Truth—Teleology
in the Historical Process—Personality
and Faith—Art and Science as Historical Phenomena
Greek Antiquity as a Normative Type
The Evaluation of Epochs—Spirit and Time
The *Märchen*, a Universal Parable

THE TITAN PROMETHEUS of Goethe's fragment called time
the master of the gods and of himself. As a maker of things
and as a thinker, the human being is subject to the everlasting flux. Belonging to the realms of both spirit and matter,
he is able to lift his work beyond the moment by giving
it a symbolical form through language and art. Through his
culture, which is also historical, man aims at transforming
the chaos of matter into a cosmos of spirit and matter.
The spirit, however, expressing itself in time, works also
to destroy the forms it has created.[1] Its interest seems to be
not so much in the forms themselves as in producing them.
The law of life, the rhythm of birth and decay, governs
the historical world also. This morphological conviction
determined Goethe's understanding of culture and history.

Man partakes in the spirit and this is his distinctive
quality—the quality which, to Goethe, makes the study of
history valuable. Consequently, he saw history as essentially
cultural history. His interest in it was centered upon the
forms by which man lives and conceives his own existence

nd by which he gives expression to this experience in religion, art, and science. In history Goethe sought and re-
lived the creative function of the indestructible spirit. Our
consciousness of three thousand years of history, which is
only a fragment of lived experience as such, testifies to this
function and deepens insight into human existence. Our
understanding of the historical past is incomplete unless
we reconstruct it creatively. We do not *possess* tradition;
we have to appropriate our inheritance anew. Goethe
sought the intensification, *Steigerung,* of nature in the
quality of the works of the mind rather than by any quantitative evaluation. His historical standards were cultural.
The close kinship between his view of history and Jacob
Burckhardt's is evident. The Swiss historian of culture and
art was equally agnostic in regard to the historical process
as a whole and similarly believed in the recurring and
regenerating power of the "spirit of mankind."[2]

It was with the questions of the morphologist that
Goethe approached the manifestations of the spirit in history. In his biographical study of Winckelmann and in his
autobiography he traced the metamorphoses of the human
entelechy in its contacts with the outside world. The notes
of the *Divan,* written "for its better understanding,"[3] describe the Near-Eastern mind as it shapes beliefs and traditions, literature and customs. Out of the evolution of
Western thought Goethe explained the history of the theory of color. In all these studies Goethe reaches out for the
typical and the normative. His admiration of the Greeks is
explained by his interpretation of their culture as coming
closest to the norm inherent in the human entelechy. His
analysis and evaluation of the faculties of the mind led him
to the concept of an organic sequence of epochs in intellectual history. He did not expect to discover the meaning
of existence from a study of the course of events; rather,
his view of the universe and of man determined the questions he asked of history and aided him in understanding

the cultural forms of the past. His historical findings supported his philosophic anthropology.

As the artist meets his object, so Goethe meets history—with his inner sense.[4] Himself a part of history, the historian, like his subject, is involved in the ceaseless stream of becoming and destruction. Capable of understanding the productions of other men and their meaning, he mirrors them in his mind while he tries to shape the fleeting moment of his own experience. Within these limits, the reconstruction of history is, in the last analysis, an art. History has to be rewritten according to the new questions which arise in each epoch. From new points of view the past can be regarded and judged in a new fashion.

Goethe's own procedure granted, on principle, the proper place to critical and descriptive historiography. He did not deny the contribution of historical studies to knowledge, even if the historian's account of the past is tainted by a prejudiced outlook. Goethe's organic thinking and his conception of culture exercised a notable impact upon German historiography and cultural philosophy. Understood in his own terms, analysis of man through the works of the mind promised to be more accurate and more helpful than the study of political history. Even the most conscientious historical analysis forces us "to be content with it as with a legend, lest everything be dissolved into doubt."[5] One can read with comfort Walter Scott's *Life of Napoleon* only if one is determined to become familiar with "the judgment of an ingrained English mind about this great world phenomenon."[6]

Not so much the possibility of national partisanship as the discrepancy between the faculties of the human mind and the complexity of history makes Goethe critical of the narrative purpose of the political historian. In a conversation with the historian Luden he stressed both the evasive character of historical truth and the injustice done to life by the necessarily mutilating contraction which it suffers at the hands of the historian. "How little does the most detailed historical account contain compared to the life of a people, and how little of this little is true!"[7]

When a decisive step in the direction of historical truth was made, Goethe recognized its importance at once. He gave the highest praise to the truthfulness and simplicity of B. G. Niebuhr's *Roman History*, which he considered a model not only of critical historiography but of criticism in general.

The separation of myth and history is invaluable and neither one is destroyed by it; to the contrary, value and dignity are restored to each of them, and it is infinitely interesting to realize how they flow into one again and influence each other.[8]

In his judgment about the first edition of Niebuhr's work Goethe pointed at the critical method which had a decisive influence upon the discipline of history; he approached the second as the ideal reader by re-creating Niebuhr's subject in his own way. "I foresee that the momentous significance of the whole will develop in my mind with increasing weight." He at once grasped the implications of Niebuhr's prediction, which had grown out of his study of the Roman past—the prediction of the imminence of a new barbaric age.[9]

Goethe's skepticism with regard to the methods of the political historian extended to the possibility of establishing universal history. Ranke ultimately came to believe in the possibility of building an image of world history by the continuous study of the parts of its process. Goethe never hoped to understand the epic of mankind from its history, because "this whole never is a whole."[10] In world affairs "the absurd" rules. He firmly resisted even the least temptation to a teleological interpretation of history. World history, he held, does not constitute "an individual phenomenon."

Goethe's skepticism about history led him to ignore historical teleology altogether, whether conceived from a theological, a philosophical, or a moral standpoint. All these three modes of interpretation are combined in the Augustinian conception of history as predestined by the fall of Adam, the incarnation of Christ, and the Last Judgment. In the Last Judgment the temporal and its eternal significance converge. Goethe's understanding of infinity prevented him from accepting historical teleology or from seeking for such a pattern himself. He saw the teleology of history in the rise and decay of personalities and cultures. The continuity of Western civilization and of its consciousness did not even tempt him to think of a secular teleology. The concepts of judgment and salvation freed from any notion of time are implied in the end of *Faust*. They are timeless events breaking through the veil of temporality.

Like Herder, although with a firmer method, Goethe tried to reconstruct the inner meaning and the forms of historical culture. He recognized the law of polarity as at work in the process of history as well as in all creation. Herder, however, was convinced of a steady progress in the development of humanity and thus came close to Kant, who understood the meaning of history as the realization of man's moral entelechy. Goethe considered these hypotheses problematic and flatly denied the possibility of a moral interpretation of history. Still more alien to Goethe was Hegel's interpretation of the concrete course of history in the light of his philosophy of the dialectic manifestation of the world spirit. Measured by Goethe's conscientious modesty, Hegel's conception went beyond man's cognitive faculties and presupposed a function of the human mind within the world process which might be an anthropomorphic self-delusion.

Goethe did not think of the history of mankind as either an ascending or a declining process. When he speaks of a spiral tendency in history, the term has neither a deterministic nor a progressive connotation. While continually refusing to build generalizing theories beyond the scope of concrete observation, Goethe assumed an "eternal recurrence" of the same constitutive factors of historical life. They repeat themselves under conditions which on the surface are subject to continuous change. The problem of man remains the theme of the drama of mankind which is played on the changing scene of history. Upon its lasting elements Goethe's search into the past was focused. His studies in ideas and methods were concerned with the inner dynamics of history, and especially of the history and norms of the mind.

True to his spiritualistic beliefs, Goethe held that not only the history of political power but equally the history of organized religion is "a mixture of error and violence": until the Last Judgment, Arian and Orthodox will wrestle with each other.[11] Pure humanity finds expression through individuals and through friendship. Or it may dwell for a time in communities, as among the "Hypsistarians" who, hemmed in between pagans, Jews, and Christians, decided to respect and to revere the best and most perfect of religions that came to their knowledge.[12]

It is, however, in the mind that creative and reconciling forces are latent. These forces, at their highest, are prophetic in character and capable of producing symbols in which man conceives his entelechy and through which he shapes his future. Poetry and art are built on the ground of prophetic wisdom and they are productive as far as they retain their original religious impulse. Culture arises from this creative impulse of man's original religiousness. Its inspiring power tends toward life rather than death, toward realization rather than ascetic abstention. The works of culture express the spiritual world latent within man. What counts is "the power to project it outward."[13]

History was meaningful to Goethe in so far as through its study by contemplation and analysis he could rediscover and relive the creativity of man. When we see Goethe's interest in the past in relation to his conception of the spirit, the contradiction dissolves between his skeptical judgment about history as a scholarly discipline and his own historical work. In keeping with his view of the universe, Goethe necessarily regarded the life of peoples, together with the life of the individual man, as the raw material through which the embodiment of the spirit and the spiritualization of the body are brought to pass. The antagonisms of history simultaneously resist and stimulate the activity of the forming mind. Through the contact of spirit with matter, of genius with destiny, the nature of man develops its inherent potentialities. To the highest of their manifestations belongs the necessity which reveals itself in the perfect work of art.[14] Thus Goethe was concerned with man's reaction to time rather than with man's determination by it. He saw a challenge in circumstance; what mattered for him was the quality and strength of the response.

Goethe's biography of the founder of archaeology—his contribution to *Winckelmann and His Century*[15]—describes Winckelmann's growth and his later life as the response of his personality to the challenge it encountered. Discovering himself through contact with the outer world, Winckelmann did not yield to its pressure and thus paved the way toward objectifying what was in him. Goethe shows how Winckelmann carried on an unremitting fight against poverty, insufficient education, diffuse studies, and continually adverse circumstances. His *daimon* won a victory over the outside world.

Goethe had abandoned the plan of a biography of Duke Bernhard of Weimar because it was "difficult, if not impossible, to give to the hero a definite and decent physiognomy."[16] Duke Bernhard was too much buffeted about by circumstance and too little the master of his time to crystallize, in Goethe's mind, into a figure of universal significance. But in Winckelmann's obedience to his personal calling he admired the continued reassertion of a strong faith. He felt that Winckelmann endured like a Greek hero the long period of waiting and preparation before he could get to Rome and find there the antique works of art which Goethe calls "the counterparts responding to his nature." Through this exploration Winckelmann was able to "intensify what was in him toward a complete and distinct unity." With everything that he was, Winckelmann responded to the world of art which he studied. His being shaped his life. As soon as he had obtained his freedom, he lived and worked in the spirit of antiquity. Goethe regarded him as the reincarnation of an ancient Greek, self-confident in a healthy pagan sense, and with a deep-seated inclination toward friendship and beauty. His instinct for the right and his well-formed mind, rather than any definite principles, gave him ethical and aesthetic guidance. God was, to Winckelmann, primarily the source of all beauty. As Goethe says of him:

He sees with the eyes, he grasps with the inner sense indescribable works, and yet he feels the irresistible impulse to speak of them by word and letter. He wants to communicate to the listener and the reader the perfectly sublime, the idea from which this figure sprang, the feeling which was kindled by his intuition. Surveying the arsenal of his abilities, he feels compelled to use whatever are the most vigorous and dignified talents at his command. He must be a poet, whether he chooses or not.

It is the *Gestalt* of Winckelmann, the imperative inner form and indefatigable energy determining the contingencies of his life, which Goethe tries to grasp.[17]

Goethe saw Moses as an equally powerful archetype of creative action. He was inspired by this Old Testament figure when creating his *Faust*. In the notes on Moses appended to the *Divan*, Goethe comments on the controversial problem of the Israelites' journey through the desert. He raises the question: "What is going to remain as the foundation, as the archetypal matter, of the last four books of Moses?" His answer explains how, in his view, the study of history may be of use.

The essential, the only, the most profound topic of the history of the world and of mankind, to which all the others are subordinate, is the conflict between unbelief and faith. All epochs which are dominated by faith in any form are brilliant, and encouraging and productive for contemporaries and posterity. All epochs, however, in which unbelief in whatever form wins a miserable victory, disappear from posterity even though they may pride themselves for a moment on a sham splendor. Nobody chooses to concern himself with the unproductive.[18]

By the same distinction between forward-looking, objective epochs and introspective, subjective epochs Goethe illustrated the contrast between the classical and romantic tendencies of his own time, the contrast between health and sickness. He looked for the qualities in Moses which made him the leader of his people although he had the talents of neither a ruler nor a strategist. He found the source of Moses' power in his personality. "Character rests upon personality rather than upon talents." It seems impossible to Goethe that a man of action who shows the greatest vigor in the struggle between faith and unbelief should hesitate in the desert for forty years, "at the threshold of his great goal." What belongs to "all ethical men"—in other words, Goethe's view of Moses as an archetype—guides him in investigating this phase of Israelite history. From the particular he is led to the typical, and the typical, in turn, explains the particular.

The Moses study in the *Divan* notes is not the only expression of Goethe's interest in this fascinating figure. Herder had shown him the charismatic creativity of the prophet. The mythical figure which the Neo-Platonic, cabalistic, and spiritualist tradition had made of the biblical Moses gave some essential traits to Goethe's Faust.

The angel of the Lord appeared to Moses in a fiery flame;
God spoke to him face to face; he mediated between the
Lord and his people; he led the people to the borders of
the promised land, died without entering it himself, and
was buried by God. By his nature, says Goethe, "he is
driven toward the greatest action. . . . He can be deterred
from his way but not from his idea." Faust's dark impulse
toward the right way, of which the Lord speaks in the
Prologue, mirrors Moses' power of faith; the earth spirit
appears to Faust in a fiery flame; he learns to see God "face
to face" in his manifestations; he dies without seeing his
promised land, yet with his inner light burning; the higher
powers intervene at his burial. The fight between faith and
unbelief is also the theme of Faust's life. The figure of
Moses came to be productive for Goethe in his concern
about the ultimate questions of human life. The lawgiver
Moses who initiates the history of his people by conveying
to it the divine commandment remained in Goethe's mind
from boyhood onward as the archetype of the prophet.[19]

Once more, it was the ineffable power of personality
coping with the riddle of existence which prompted Goethe
to translate and comment upon the autobiography of Benvenuto Cellini.[20] Cellini "responds instantly and with all his
might to anything opposed to his being or will." Goethe
regards that impulse as a general characteristic of man. The
stronger the personality, the deeper, it seems, must it be led
into the contradictions of existence. His powerful faith
makes Cellini able to moderate his passionate nature by an
ethical striving and to calm his inescapable sufferings
through a strengthening religious energy.

Goethe's notes on Cellini are, in a sense, a study of man.
The notes on the history of Florence, which are also in the
appendix to the translation, are a study of the creative community from which he sprang.[21] This brief historical sketch
is focused on the question of how the rise of Florentine
culture became possible. This is the problem on which

most modern studies of the Renaissance since Jacob Burckhardt have concentrated. The rise of the civic spirit in
Florence is Goethe's central theme. He shows how out of
the crafts the arts developed, how they remained connected
with religion and in their turn stimulated the crafts, and
how the developing talent for organization increased the
city's economic activities, while the spirit of art dominated
its life. Goethe praises the civic sense of the Medici in contrast to his verdict against the "monstrous and impure enthusiast" Savonarola. His sympathies are with the fellowship of art, which, over and above the inner antagonisms
and external difficulties of the city, gave it a common spirit.
There was a brief "fulfillment of the most beautiful possibilities," a temporary though significant victory of the
form-giving mind. In the formation of cultural groups as in
that of the individual life, the absurdity which rules the
realm of power is the challenge to which the mind must
respond. The tension between the "ideal" and "real" factors of historical formation, between spirit and matter,
is the subject of cultural history.

The morphological view of historical existence readily
lent itself to the inner biography of individuals or cultural
communities. Greater difficulties arose when Goethe tried
to apply it to the evolution of whole branches of culture,
such as the history of art in Italy and in the Netherlands,
and the history of the theory of color. In all these cases
he had to face the methodological problems basic to any
historical study of the humanities. In his schemata and essays on art, science, and the history of knowledge, and in
the text of the studies themselves, he gave an account of
his solutions.[22]

In each of these investigations Goethe understood the
particular as a part of the whole. For example, he regarded
the history of the theory of color as part of the history of
all natural sciences. This whole is ultimately the totality of
the real and the ideal factors of historical existence.

The way in which a scholar conceives of a particular case can be properly understood only if we know his general way of thinking. This holds, whether the intention be to study the scientific opinions of individuals, of whole schools of thought, or of epochs. Thus the history of the sciences is closely related to the history of philosophy, but it is equally related to the history of the life and character of individuals and peoples.[23]

It was from this comprehensive point of view that Goethe approached his plan of a history of art in Italy. The interrelations between physical and anthropological geography, economic structure, public life, and the style of living were to form the basis of the analysis of Italian art.[24] This plan, which Goethe conceived two generations before Burckhardt's *Civilization of the Renaissance in Italy*, went far beyond Burckhardt in scope. While the scheme itself was abandoned, parts of it were taken over into the *Propylaea*, the periodical on art edited by Goethe. The essays on the theory of art demonstrate Goethe's concern with the bases of art as lying in the necessities of life. Art has its origin in the crafts. In an essay of 1789 he contrasts both arts and crafts with modern mechanical production.[25] The artist should be master of his material rather than its slave.

Thus the architect operates on three levels. As a craftsman he can attain his immediate purpose of building a useful structure. He acts as an artist when he succeeds in satisfying the eye by the proportions of his work. He arrives at the highest level of his art when, having mastered the other requirements, he acts as a poet and arouses astonishment and delight.[26] It is the spiritual necessity of creative action with which Goethe is ultimately concerned.

The question remains whether a necessary and meaningful evolution is inherent in the history of art. Winckelmann, "the first to conceive the idea of a history of art," encouraged Goethe in viewing the evolution of art in terms of an organic process. Winckelmann's *History of Art in*

Antiquity describes a cycle of rise and decay. In the history of Greek art Goethe saw the pure organic logic of evolution,[27] whereas in fields other than art the contingencies of history obscure and deflect the "natural" course. In his search for the origins of art Goethe was led beyond the analysis of styles to consideration of art in its relation to religion. Winckelmann had explained the Greek works of art with the aid of mythology.[28] In the polarity between the religious basis of art and its aesthetic manifestation Goethe found the clue to its history. In its course, "style" indicates a climax in which the religious and aesthetic elements arrive at a perfect reconciliation; "manner" is a manifestation of archaic inwardness; "imitation" is the secularization of art by withdrawal from the idea and the increase of material detail.

Once more it is the search for the normative which guides Goethe's comparative study of art and its evolution. For the history of art, a field to which he contributed by theoretical, analytical, and historical writings, he especially demanded the consciousness of standards as fundamental, for

only upon the highest concept of art can a history of art be built; only if one knows the most excellent that man was capable of producing can the psychological and chronological course which was taken in art as in other fields be presented.[29]

Goethe's quest for an organic logic in the history of art led him to the basic distinctions of his phenomenology of the mind. Men "tend to live up to the demands of art rather than to those of science."[30] Art can be thought of as an organic sequence, but science is possible only with an infinite accumulation of material. "The main difference is determined by the fact that art becomes complete in its individual works; science, however, appears unlimited." To produce a whole in science Goethe demands that we think of it as art; consequently we must avoid excluding any

one of the human faculties from the pursuit of scholarship.[31] The history of the sciences presented Goethe with
further difficulties, because there "the ideal part has a different relationship to the real one than in the rest of world history."[32] The real part of the sciences is the phenomena;
their ideal part, the views of the phenomena. The course of
scholarly knowledge is true history to Goethe in the sense
that it is a given process which cannot be constructed on
the basis of an inherent schematism.

In the history of scholarship there are periods of silent
incubation, the importance of which can be understood
only from their consequences.[33] These periods are com-
parable to the time which, in the life of plants, the seed
spends below the ground. There are impressive times of
which little is known beyond a few remarkable fragments,
individuals, or events. Historical epochs finally appear in
the full light of knowledge, but then the whole tends to be
obscured by the parts. Through the interaction of law and
contingency, the course of knowledge belongs to the "incalculable and incommensurable"[34] in world history. Even
transmission of experience is endangered because of the
changes of meaning which words suffer in the course of
time. Ultimately Goethe reverts to the individual as the
main agent of scholarly synthesis. "It is essentially the conflict of the individual with immediate experience and with
tradition that forms the history of the sciences.[35]

It was in harmony with this general insight that Goethe
drafted his plan for a history of knowledge. This appeared
to him as a "great fugue, in which one after the other the
voices of the peoples make themselves heard."[36] Goethe's
anthropological views formed the basis of his distinction
among fields of knowledge such as philosophy, poetry,
medicine, and mathematics. The chaotic element of history
forms the counterpart of all efforts toward culture. There
are confused and violent epochs when "no one has the
time to form himself in his purity."[37]

In the same way Goethe arranged his materials for the history of the theory of color. It is within the context of the history of the Western mind that he views his special subject. Intended to suggest further studies, the treatise is as rich in general observations as in the details it presents. It contains the residue of Goethe's methodological concern with the possibilities of a history of the mind. In his relations to the past, man oscillates between rebellion and loyalty, like the individual, who opposes authority as a child, escapes it as an adolescent, and reinstates it when, as an adult, he has learned that "without the co-operation of others he can do little."[38] In this dynamism of intellectual history the great individuals produce the momentous changes and the great syntheses. The conservation of the works of Plato and Aristotle determined the history of thought and its conflicts. "It is an advantage of our time that its esteem for both of them is in balance, as it was for Raphael when he thought of both these men and contrasted them with each other in the 'School of Athens'."[39]

The balance between the original service of the individual and his collaboration and interdependence with others extends also to time. When Goethe says that "the human mind does not make leaps,"[40] he recognizes an inner sequence in the history of thought which, at a given moment, restricts the range of possible variations. Thus he was convinced that his own botanical studies, and particularly the intuition of the original identity of all the parts of the plant, of the *Urpflanze*, were possible only at a certain level of knowledge. After this level was attained in the eighteenth century, Goethe could bring his disciplined effort to its culmination in his morphology.

The means by which Goethe organized the ideal factors in the history of knowledge was his differentiation of mental faculties. Analysis of these faculties involved an evaluation, and he clearly distinguished between epochs of becoming governed by reason and peacefully devoted to

the sciences and arts, and epochs whose energies are directed toward the outside, governed by the intellect, and
interested in using existing knowledge for war and tech-
nicalization. The danger of epochs of reason is anarchy
and partisanship; that of epochs of the predominant intellect is tyranny. From the typical structure of the mind
Goethe derived the corresponding forms of society.[41]

In his morphological search for the normative, Goethe
found it most adequately expressed by the science of the
Greeks, although they were lacking in the art of experiment. "For the Greeks, science sprang entirely from
life."[42] It was the totality of Greek existence which in one
or another of its manifestations fascinated Goethe again
and again. "No outward interference diverted them from
their way: a favorable chance which, in modern times, is
rarely granted to individuals and never to nations."[43] Like
Winckelmann, Goethe had studied Greek art as the symbol of perfection. During the few fortunate centuries of
Greek antiquity, culture seemed to develop richer inventiveness and deeper insight than in any other domain accessible to Goethe, including the Persian world of the
Divan. Such a manifestation of nature's highest intention
necessarily called for reverence. In the visible realm it is
revealed through the epitome of beauty which, in turn,
symbolizes the holy.

Goethe's "realism" was strong enough to make him
aware that Greek culture belonged to an irretrievable past.
It was not an imitative Greek revival that he sought even
when his classical leanings were at their height. Greek art
meant to him the result of an art of living which, through
creative acceptance and courageous endurance, had won
the spirit its victory. From the understanding of Greek
forms, Goethe expected a strengthening of man's determination and ingenuity in the formation of his own individuality. He embodied the Greek heritage in his poetical
works, which were built upon a mental structure bearing

the indelible mark of a thousand years of Christian history.

Goethe understood the conditions from which the paradigmatic achievement of Greek art had grown not as an easy happiness, harmonious without effort, but as an incessant and difficult striving for the finding and fulfillment of measures. *Pandora* and the Helena act in *Faust* sufficiently prove his awareness of the elemental chaos out of which spiritual man is lifted by the creative moment granted to the deserving. Then the liberating act of reconciliation is possible—the symbolical formation of the perfect that comes near to the timeless. Goethe's relation to Greek antiquity implemented rather than contradicted his conception of man's position within the universe. His admiration for the Greeks remained in harmony with his understanding of the functional relationship between the bodily and the spiritual. As a symbol of the human entelechy the Greeks took on a mythical dimension in his thought. The grave rhythm of the trimeter in the Helena act, widening into the trochaic tetrameter, evokes a sense of the sublime which yields its meaning when connected with the function of the whole act within the drama. As Aphrodite emerges from the waves, so Helena arises from the chaos and remains over and above the elements. The short moment of her union with Faust signifies the realization of the idea. The idea is lasting and, like it, fidelity is saved from destruction, whereas the rest of the brief moment of culture is swept into oblivion by the returning elements. "Helena is the symbol not of all Greek life but of this highest achievement of the Greeks, this principle of form, of ordered purpose, of self-control and self-mastery."[44] The polarity of existence vibrates through the tension between the "Klassische Walpurgisnacht" and the noble realm of Helena's reign, between the vitality of forces and the victorious form which the spirit gives them. Faust, however, stands for the Western mind rediscovering Greek form.

The relation of nature to man is different according to man's varying conditions. By the poets of antiquity nature was seen as the most beautiful living whole. They gave attention only to the highest point in its life, when it reveals itself in man and through him by passion and action; thus one might well be convinced that everything is contained in Homer, the original world and all that may develop from it.[45]

It was the Greeks' conception of human life as a part of nature, their search for the normative, their formative attitude toward life, that Goethe felt congenial to his deepest intention. The fact that in ancient Greece the immanence of the divine could have led to a life of culture was the source of his astonishment and his love. A comparison, however, between Goethe's *Iphigenie* and Euripides' leaves no doubt as to the distance between the two civilizations. Even the most antique of Goethe's works, the *Achilleïs*, reveals under cover of its Greek theme and its metrical form a modern problem.

The whole group of conflicts between duty and inclination, being and obligation, which the Achilleïs expresses, rests upon a secularized Christianity and presupposes the Christian experiences of sin, grace, guilt, conversion, and repentance.[46]

Goethe applied his distinction between intellect and reason to his study of culture, thus arriving at a differentiation of epochs of intellectual history. By various schemes he tried to clarify the inner logic of the mind which manifests itself in history. It was not the problem of historical periods that prompted him to engage in such studies. He was aware that by "periods" we only distinguish predominant tendencies from each other. By "epochs" he understood the emergence and decay of a style of life and thought with definite and typical contours. His essay "Epochs of the Mind" shows how his view of history is interwoven with this conception of the mind and its functions.[47] Law and form are given to man through the mind.

Through its activity man transcends his limitations and, at the same time, sets the order of his work against the threatening chaos. On this immanent-transcendent creativity rests the dignity of man. The phases of culture correspond to this structure of the mind. They arise from a chaotic beginning, creative though formless, and they end in a chaos of dismemberment, confused and unproductive. At this stage the cultural world sinks back into the elemental. Between beginning and end the epochs of the mind develop in organic sequence.

The mind conveys form to the primary chaos in that "a favored spirit pronounces prophetically what he views as though it were emerging." He seizes upon the "original phenomenon" underlying the world that surrounds him by interpreting it as a moment of becoming. Cosmogony is the spiritual act by which the growing order of a cosmos becomes evident. Thus it may form the basis for the organization of the social cosmos. The cosmogonic myth mirrors the image of the universe which a founding genius was able to form. As with Prometheus, Moses, and Mahomet, the action of the founder is one of finding and giving the law at the same time. This function corresponds to Goethe's basic conviction about reason which, by recognizing the process of becoming, "imitates" the gods without seeing what it imitates. The absolute as such is concealed. The mind is called to the venture of coming as near as possible to the fullness of the hidden truth. Culture does not begin with the rational formulation of principles of law, but grows out of religion. At the beginning of culture, the creative mind produces mythical images. Goethe's approach to the problem of civilization was determined by his conception of God as an artist and of man as created in God's image. The formation of the mental world through which culture is conveyed to man is the gift of the spirit.

In the structure of the mind there is an inherent polarity which determines both the rise and the decay of the spir-

itual realm in which the images of meaningful existence
are woven. The cosmogonic beginning is followed by an
epoch which is essentially poetical. A work of creative
imagination such as Homer's lifts man's conduct to a level
dominated by a free, earnest, and noble use of the senses.
With their aid, man seizes upon the manifold phenomena;
he becomes at home in "his" world, although not without
an awareness of its lasting limitations.

The poetical epoch engenders another epoch, which is
called holy or theological. It arises out of "the noble desire
of man to acknowledge a superior being." It belongs "in
the highest sense to reason." It is opposed to the poetic
epoch because it tends toward the comprehension, in terms
of monotheism, of the unity of creation, and toward the
formulation of its insight by a conclusive dogma. This
latter development is inevitably regarded with doubt from
the standpoint of philosophic thought, which opposes theological dogma by the attempt to explain the universe,
including human existence, according to conceptual principles. For Goethe, the philosophic procedure in the end
brings about "a deteriorating enlightenment." It initiates
the "prosaic epoch" which dissolves the transmitted heritage and "destroys entirely the faith which prompts even
philosophic reason to presume an appreciable structural
connection behind the strange phenomena it wonders
about." The prosaic epoch leads toward the "chaos of the
end." This chaos is "not the first one which has impreg-
nated and given birth, but it dies down, it turns into rot,
and out of it the spirit of God himself could hardly create
a new world worthy of him."

In his analysis of the chaos of the end Goethe makes
unmistakable allusions to nineteenth-century civilization.
A center of confidence and faith is lacking, "poetry is divorced from truth," the unfathomable secret is forcibly
formulated and dogmatically defended; individuals emerge
as self-appointed guides and present "their perfect false-

hood as a perfect whole." This chaos of the end—an epitome of Goethe's antagonism to romantic darkness and formlessness, to ideological arbitrariness and doctrinaire extravagance—is the reverse of his positive evaluation of the mind. The scale of values presented in this essay, "Epochs of the Mind," leaves no doubt about Goethe's mistrust of any merely intellectual development of man's faculties. He evaluates the higher functions of reason by showing its position within the developing faculties of the mind. It is evident from the connection of priesthood with theological monotheism that Goethe's essay was not intended as a contribution to the history of ideas in ancient Greece. Its purpose was to sharpen the sense of values, and he wrote it in support of a healthy and productive attitude toward life among his contemporaries.

The tolerance which underlies Goethe's religious attitude also rules his view of the epochs of the mind up to the point where his judgment turns negative—the point, that is to say, where the intellect emancipates itself. The antagonism of poetic imagination, theological unification, and philosophic interpretation is fruitful so long as a living faith is not lost to any of them. On the other hand, the cosmogonic origin of human culture does not constitute more than a beginning, which no romantic recourse to the depth of its imagery ever can bring back. The cosmogony indicates the religious ground which poetry, philosophy, and theology have in common. Goethe hinted at the structure of a productive mind able to initiate another rise of fruitful thought when he compared Giambattista Vico and Hamann as the patriarchs of their respective literary civilizations. Their epochs preceded the ensuing ascendency "like a kind of Middle Ages."[48]

It was in opposition to the doctrine of progress that Goethe evaluated the various types of mental action and their organic sequence. Auguste Comte saw an ascending line precisely where Goethe saw decay. Buckle's conten-

tion that progress was connected with the development
of the intellect stands in direct opposition to Goethe's
warning against the intellect's emancipation from reason.
Goethe had divorced the decay theory of the spiritualists
from its biblical foundation in original Christianity—that
is, from its historical and determinist elements. The golden
age of reconciliation is for him neither in the past nor in
the future. Like the power of hope it is latently present. It
will come to the fore at the right moment, although only
if man's faith remains actively devoted to it like the faith
of Epimetheus. The spirit, the "higher power of guidance,"
allows the shells in which it has lived in the past to be
destroyed, and then begins to produce new symbols. The
spirit also rules our relation to the past. The highest achievements of the arts and sciences cannot be transmitted; even
the understanding of their ideal part is possible only for
the rejuvenating creative powers themselves.[49]

Goethe is concerned with the past in view of the use
man must make of it for the culture of the present and
the future. When he says that a child could be introduced
to the essentials of the human situation by Tschudi's *Swiss
History* or Aventinus' *Bavarian Chronicle*,[50] when he refers
ever and again to the Bible, Plato, and Aristotle as the lasting sources of human wisdom, when he speaks of "the old
truth" to which man ought to cling, he does not intend
to deter us from exploring further the manifold of nature
and history. He means rather to lead toward basic verities
realized and expressed long ago, which he holds it essential
to rediscover and rethink. Not because of their novelty
but because of their truth do knowledge and wisdom attain
significance. Goethe himself lived in spiritual community
with the great minds of the past, and yet to the end he
continued to exercise his responsibility as a judge called
to accept or to reject, to encourage or to warn.

As we have seen, Goethe lived in an era in which the
norms of the past had lost their binding power. Freed of

them, he sought the normative through his own experience and cognition in the fellowship of a few friends who responded as he did to the creative possibilities granted by their epoch or the plight imposed by it. Goethe experienced the reality of the spirit in its creativeness. The inner form which it took in him allowed him to understand its manifestations in the works of the past. In his view of culture, historical vision and normative intuition are interwoven. Feeling himself "a citizen of the spiritual realm, faith in which we cannot decline or give up,"[51] Goethe saw the spirit integrated over the millenniums in ever-recurring forms within the chaotic flux of the individual conditions of history. The theme of history is the tension between spirit and historical time, or, from the human standpoint, the tension between faith and unbelief.

It is between spirit and time that man leads his life. Time is "the greatest gift of God"[52] and man should use it rather than be its slave. This requires resignation to that way of life in which "the desirable" may become reality, in which man's temporal life becomes a parable of eternity. Here we find the measure inherent in the nature of man, the standard which is the object of his longing.

The spirit breaks through the flux of time in the moment of fulfillment, rare as the moment of inspiration, the hour of the prophet, the moment of union in love, the brief day of a cultured communal life. Even in the realm of nature the moment passes in which the perfect becomes manifest:

The final product of ever-intensified nature is the beautiful human being. Nature can rarely produce him, because many conditions resist her ideas; even to her power it is impossible to remain long with the perfect and to give duration to the beautiful which it has produced. For, strictly speaking, it is only for a moment that the beautiful human being is beautiful.[53]

In the dynamism of Goethe's universe the moment, the *kairos,* is a gift and a challenge. To become aware of the

moment in which the spirit breaks through time, in which
the reconciliation of the antagonistic forces of existence
occurs, to make it enduring and then to mediate between
spirit and time, is the chance given to man.

Goethe's conception of the creative moment breaking
through time is the climax of his view of the universal
polarity as a dynamic process. It explains his conception
of history and illustrates the definite place he gave to his
image of man and society within the morphological entelechy of nature. This view is dominated by a balance of
Greek and Christian motifs as they were united in the
Plotinian tradition. In Goethe himself its development was
supported by the inner experience of genius. His certainty
about the intention of God-in-Nature to grant the moment
of reconciliation was the source of his ever-reviving hope
and his regenerating energy.

The human universe as a whole, which through its polarities tends toward harmony and attains it when the time
has come, is the theme of Goethe's *Märchen* or *Parable*.
The old man with the lamp, its central figure, knows that
the secret of the creative moment is a universal law. This
moment of reconciliation creates a whole out of parts
which could not achieve their full meaning while each was
left to itself. Like Schiller's *Letters on the Aesthetic Education of Man*, the *Parable* was written with an eye to the
French Revolution. The priest of the *Conversations of
German Emigrés* who is the narrator says beforehand that
the *Parable* "reminds one of everything and of nothing."[54]
It is a fairy tale in that its problems are solved miraculously
at the proper time. It is also a riddle, and Goethe refused
to disclose more than he had written, though at the same
time he stimulated every attempt at interpretation. He
forced the reader to face the alternative of either putting
the *Parable* aside altogether or re-creating it in terms of his
own experience. As an "artifact which could hardly succeed for a second time," he once likened it to the Revelation

of St. John in that "everyone feels that something is still hidden within it."[55] By its very form this universal parable expresses Goethe's conviction that not everything can or should be made plain, although the most important secret is called in the tale "the patent secret."

The story is the climax of a sequence of tales told among emigrés who are struck by the resistance to meaningful order offered by life both around and within them. How can the right order intended by the creation be attained or restored when its consummation is left to the life process—this is the theme of the *Parable*. We are introduced to a realm in which nothing has the right place and function. Every figure knows that its proper existence ought to be different from its present existence; each seems to live in expectation of salvation. The old man with the lamp is aware of the element of time in the process of life. His light can shine only when there is already some light. The snake provides this light, for she is able to hold the shining gold which the will-o'-the-wisps collect and give away. Three different types of light are related to each other, the lowest being not useless but ridiculous if left to itself; the intermediate light of the snake makes redemption possible when it meets the highest light, issuing from the lamp in the old man's hand. Then "the time has come."

Three events are needed if the redemption is to occur. The river must be bridged by a solid and lasting structure, whereas now only a solitary ferryman takes travelers across, and only one way. The temple in which the monuments of the kings are waiting must move to the right place. And a young prince must be united with the lily, whom he loves and to whom he devotes all his longing. If these conditions are fulfilled the giant whose threat is ever present will lose his power. As yet we are far from this moment. Whatever the beautiful lily touches must die. In spite of good omens she is still prevented from sharing in the joys of life and is left to grieve over her fate.

Ach! Warum steht der Tempel nicht am Flusse!
Ach! Warum ist die Brücke nicht gebaut!

The snake consoles her: "I heard the mighty voice resound through the temple, announcing that the hour has come." The youth, knowing that death is certain, embraces the lily and sacrifices himself.

In the further course of action we see the old man and the snake take an active attitude toward the moment; the old man leads the whole group over the bridge; the snake resolves to sacrifice herself, in the same instant the youth is revived and the door of the temple is opened; inside, for the third time, the word is spoken: "The time has come." The temple moves with the visitors, "who come from the world," to the right side of the river and to the surface. The insignia of power, beauty, and wisdom are given to the youth by the three kings, whereas the fourth king breaks asunder just after pretentiously affirming that he stands on his own feet. The youth joins the lily, assured that, under the protection of "the holy old man, the three holy statues" are restored to their function. He wishes the power of love to crown the work of reconciliation, whereupon the old man smilingly replies: "Love does not dominate; it cultivates, and that is more." The giant is powerless on the temple grounds. In the moment of fulfillment the hawk soaring in the sky turns the light of the sun caught in his mirror upon the group surrounding the altar.

A sequence of metamorphoses precedes the ultimate solution. The restoration of justice coincides with the redemption of the lily. The three kings, representing majesty, beauty, and wisdom, partake in the new covenant, whereas the fourth king, the only one who thinks of himself, vanishes into nothingness. The old man praises the self-sacrifice of the snake; it is he who calls the hawk.

Truth, identical with the divine, never lends itself to our direct cognition: we view it only in the reflection, in the example, in the symbol, in particular and related phenomena; we become aware of it as incomprehensible life and none the less we cannot renounce the desire to understand it.[56]

Through its allegorical figures the symbolical dream of the *Parable* presents reconciliation as the *kairos*, the moment of fulfillment, in which time and action, cosmic grace and wisdom converge. It is seen as a universal occurrence through which the spirit manifests itself in time. On the way to its climax the *Parable* hints at the significance of sacrifice, at the meaning of wisdom within the order of mental faculties, at the longing of both the temporal and the eternal for the perfection of their union. In revealing the healing powers accessible to man, the *Parable* mirrors the nature of man, the mission of art, and the structure of history. There is the ever-recurring task of taming the immense and demonic by joining the dispersive forces within the creation to organic, self-resigning, and therefore fruitful, correspondence. Then the spirit, able to bring to life what is past, will join the body and, through love, impart the highest life to its counterpart, to which it had hitherto been deadly. The depth of mischief, says the old man, may announce salvation when the time has come. The art of striving for the right order among the universal forces to which man is exposed is his way to culture and freedom.

THE IDEAL COMMONWEALTH

Love does not dominate, it cultivates. And that is more.
Parable.

The Community of the Tower

A Novel of Community—Self-Knowledge
and the Art of Friendship
The Tower and the "Cross in Roses"

GOETHE'S METAPHYSICAL THOUGHT and his insight into the chances and limitations of human cognition formed the basis on which his image of man and society crystallized into epical form in *Wilhelm Meister*. Man as a social being rather than as an individual is the hero of the epic; its problem is the possibility of culture not merely of one person but of the human community. The tale is a transparent web through which Goethe's thought and experience can be seen. His cosmology and his view of history, his conception of the mental faculties and his criticism of the modern age underlie as essential elements the image of life he describes. With all the formative energies of his mind Goethe creates a picture which shows the possible and desirable fulfillment of the entelechy of man.

In *Faust* and *Prometheus* Goethe looked at the problem of man from the borderline of the human situation—man's exposure to temporality and magic, and the contrasting awareness of an unattainable sphere of the divine. Faust, the hero of the "drama of human existence," is a symbol of the human situation rather than a model for human conduct. The ultimate unity of *Faust* is formed by the central religious quest of man. The *Prometheus* theme concentrates on man's relation to the divine. Man's participation in "the systole and diastole of the world spirit" is lucidly presented in *Pandora*. This polarity of life is taken for granted in *Wilhelm Meister;* it is felt in the concrete problems which arise in the course of life. But here Goethe places the emphasis upon the solution rather than upon the problem. Aside from characters in the novel who merely serve to clarify the human situation, he created models of the art of living the "good life" as it develops out of friendship.

Goethe's novel *Wilhelm Meister* tells of group of people apparently in possession of mature wisdom. In the first part, *Wilhelm Meister's Apprenticeship*, and in the second, *Wilhelm Meister's Travels*, the leading figure among them is a middle-aged man who, to judge from his dress, is a priest and therefore is called simply Abbé. The Abbé and his friends take a secret interest in Wilhelm Meister, the youth whose name the novel bears. In fact, already in the first book of the *Apprenticeship* one of them crosses Wilhelm's path. Slowly the young man learns to understand their personalities and their intentions. At the proper time he is admitted to the tower of Lothario's castle, where are kept the biographies of the adolescents who grew up under the common care of these friends.

One after the other of them is presented to us in the course of the novel: Jarno, the man of action who later works in the mountains as a geologist; Lothario, a young landowner and soldier; his brother, Friedrich, and his sisters, Natalie and the countess, all of them pupils of the Abbé. We learn that the "Beautiful Soul," the *Schöne Seele*, whose autobiography is contained in the sixth book of the novel, was the aunt of these children, and we visit the castle of their uncle, who respected her without agreeing with whatever religious influence she might exercise upon the younger generation. In *Wilhelm Meister's Travels* the figures of Lothario's family are mirrored in that of Lenardo, as though their author intended to emphasize that they are by no

means unique. Although there is a deep concern with personalities, Goethe's *Wilhelm Meister*, regarded as a whole,
has as its theme the inception and growth of an ideal community rather than the development and education of an
individual. Wilhelm's road to maturity is completed only
within the group of friends by whom he is received toward
the end of his apprenticeship.

Rousseau had set forth his conception of the education of
a free man in the story of Émile's youth. His *Contrat Social*
tried to show, in terms of theory, the way toward a free
society. Goethe combined both these ends in one work. It
is through self-knowledge and resignation rather than
through uncontrolled spontaneity that Wilhelm integrates
his personality; he learns to do so only through the experience of his errors and the support of his friends. Goethe
presented not the theoretical foundation of an ideal society,
but a picture of the good life as it grows out of a common
spirit; the persons who live it themselves embody its principles. The "Pedagogic Province" reflects these principles
through the "religion of reverence," which forms the center
of its pedagogy. Toward the end of the novel, the widening
community of the Tower prepares its organized emigration
to America. It aims to found a sound communal life in the
New World, a healthy community conceived in the spirit
of the idea of mankind.

As the novel unfolds, the figure of Wilhelm Meister himself recedes further and further from the foreground. Until
his career in the theater fails he still appears as the hero of
the story, but when he joins the friends of the Tower he
becomes one of the group. During his wanderings he serves
as the agent through whom the reader learns about the
growing firmness of the community, the significance of its
ideas, and the advance toward their realization. *Wilhelm
Meister's Theatrical Mission*, the fragment of the early
eighties, was transformed after the Italian journey into the
Apprenticeship, finished in 1796. The consolidation of Goe-

the's personality and convictions is reflected in the transition of his inner form and style from *Werther* through the *Theatrical Mission* to the *Apprenticeship*. Goethe criticized the epilogue of the fragment on Nature for its lack of understanding of the morphological laws of polarity and intensification. It is such an ascent from the subjective level of inward experience to the integration of experience in the cognition and presentation of the typical that the sequence of the three novels reveals. *Wilhelm Meister's Theatrical Mission* is still an autobiographical novel even though the author takes the position of third-person narrator, which he avoided in *Werther*.

Werther's helplessness in the face of the ambiguous character of nature, his failure to break through his self-centeredness by building a firm and lasting way of communication with the "thou" of his beloved friend, and, finally, his despair over his inability to give a constructive meaning to his existence—all these lead him to suicide, through which he hopes at last to find harmony with the universe. The hero of the *Theatrical Mission* accepts life. His evolution is the core of the tale and it is reflected in his experience of the world of the theater. In the *Apprenticeship* the impact of Goethe's morphological studies is evident in the increased firmness with which he describes the stages of Wilhelm's development. And whereas the fragment presents the outer world in the light of its relationship to Wilhelm's personal growth, the *Apprenticeship* shows Wilhelm's growth into this world. In sequence these three novels reveal an intensification leading from the subjective to the normative, from the individual to the community. The last stage of this intensification is represented by the *Travels*, the idea of which was conceived as early as the writing of the *Apprenticeship*.

Wilhelm's family name, "Meister," alludes to the system of craft education prevalent in Europe. This was organized in three stages: "apprentice," "journeyman," and "master." Here it symbolizes the stages of growth and initiation. After the first publication of the *Travels* in 1821, Goethe introduced into the enlarged version of 1829 the plan of emigration and Wilhelm's resolution to become a surgeon; the figures of Hersilie's uncle and of Makarie were given deeper relief and heightened significance; the novel was brought to its conclusion with the meeting between Wilhelm and Felix. Goethe reinforced the utopian element by transforming the migration into an exodus, and strengthened the cosmic symbolism by giving a central place to Makarie's wisdom and to the reunion of father and son.

Within this plan, the stories which Wilhelm hears or is given to read present love as a heightening or endangering power. Love and hatred, hope and fear, are conditions within our "troubled inward being" which make us, like Werther, look toward the light or the dark side of life.[1] Consciousness of the universal significance of the human situation is the precondition of constructive freedom, in which passion and reason attain a balance. Each of the stories told in *Wilhelm Meister's Travels* presents a typical picture and a typical solution, either negative or positive, of the tension between love and reason: love is the impulse toward reconciliation; at the same time it is potentially destructive. It must not be suppressed, but it ought to be given its proper place in the economy of life.

The overwhelming force of passion transforms the hero of the fairy tale "The New Melusina" into a dwarf until he returns to his innate knowledge of himself. In "The Dangerous Wager" and in "Not Too Far" we witness the destruction of life resulting from a moment of error in which self-centeredness has its way. In "Who Is the Traitor?" and "The Man of Fifty Years" the entanglement is resolved through chance, self-observation, and the courage to face the truth. The figures of Hersilie and Susanne, interwoven with the main theme through their relations to Wilhelm, Felix, and Lenardo, reflect the contrast between a hesitant toying with love and a serene and responsible acceptance of life—an *amor fati*—which turns out to be the precondition of stable love. Wilhelm's own experiences are mirrored in those of others, and this mutual reflection elevates them from the personal to the universal.

As Goethe himself said, the novel is not all of a piece but it has a unified meaning.[2] It presents a panorama of existence which, refracting life into many individuals and relations as light is refracted into colors, sets forth the universal significance of man's wandering. Out of this wide-ranging panorama a life of culture arises under the guidance of friendship. The basic issue of the epic is the possibility of such a culture. *Wilhelm Meister* presents the art of cultured living, the way in which it can be learned, and the principles fundamental to a society in which it can thrive.

Out of the old society a new one emerges, whose institutions are subordinated to the end of man's self-education. The founders of the new community form an independent concept of man's position in the universe and take an independent attitude toward past and present. They are the pioneers of a new beginning. The historical aspect of existence is relegated to the fringes of the tale, and its cosmological significance is revealed through the figure of Makarie, whose diary must be regarded as an integral part of the whole.[3] In *Faust*, human life appears as a trial, tragic in its course and brought to a conclusion by grace. Wilhelm Meister responds actively to his situation, as does Faust, but Wilhelm succeeds in solving the riddle of human existence through self-resignation. In the end, he has grasped the idea and the spiritual significance of love, and he reconciles his individual life with that of the others and of the community by obeying the truth inherent in man's nature.

The historical world of Goethe's time is visible in only a few scenes of the novel. The social distance between the aristocrat and the burgher accentuates the narrowness of the bourgeois life which Wilhelm tries to escape by turning to the theater. An incident of war ruins his first theatrical undertaking. The resolution of the friends to emigrate is the result of their insight into the disintegration, both spiritual and political, of modern society. On his wanderings Wilhelm becomes aware of the threat of the rising machine age. Goethe views these historical realities from a calm, epic distance: Wilhelm finds his way to himself, and his community embarks upon its new venture, without antagonistic passion or self-alienating fancy, but with resolution based upon a realistic view of contemporary affairs. Goethe kept the tension between the historical and the ideal elements of the epic as small as was compatible with his purpose.

Wilhelm Meister presupposes both Goethe's cosmological and historical thought. Goethe's inner and outer experience crystallized around the plot and characters to form a synthesis with his philosophic thought and his didactic judgment. It is meaningless—and impossible—to trace whatever characteristics of friends and acquaintances he consciously or unconsciously imparted to the figures of the novel. A number of them, such as the Abbé, Jarno, Makarie, and Wilhelm himself, convey the conceptions of man and nature basic to Goethe's literary, scientific, and administrative work. In its social aspects the novel touches upon the educational, economic, and political problems with which society has had to contend since the rise of industrialism and the breakdown of the *ancien régime*. Hardly any other work of Goethe so richly reflects his own contacts with society, both as a man of action and as an observer.

Again, it was with a normative intention that Goethe faced these problems of modern society. The leading figures of *Wilhelm Meister* seek a constructive solution to these problems as soon as they become aware of them. The principles of their community are opposed to any Machiavellianism. The novel shows how to aim at a fruitful peace. It demonstrates the religious and ethical preconditions of peace in the individual and the community. Napoleon had called the demonic immensity of world affairs the incarnation of destiny. It was precisely this demonism of power which Goethe excluded from his image of the good life. He conceived of the good life as that which offers man a chance to bridle the unruly elements of existence. Wilhelm's profession—that of a surgeon—is symbolic of Goethe's intention to help man to a sound and healthy life in spite of the errors and accidents that beset his path.

Goethe lived through twenty-five years of almost uninterrupted war and political unrest and in the midst of it resumed work on this novel; hence the exclusion from its plot of political power is in itself important. Goethe sided neither with the Revolution nor with the reaction. For instance, he criticized the ruling bureaucracy through the reform-minded Odoard, and the introduction of disturbing economic practices through the story of the repair-man, the *Geschirrfasser*. In common with the revolutionary movement, Goethe's understanding of *Humanität* involved an impulse toward freedom and a general concern for man. Aware, however, of "the monster dwelling in man," he was unable to share the optimism of revolutionary theory. In the freedom of the individual he saw the precondition of his membership in a society of free men; in a community of men of insight and good will he saw the precondition of a free state. In principle, he considered positive law an emergency measure. Freedom, he thought, should be attained gradually through the self-discipline of groups devoted to freedom. The revolutionary theories of society, which postulated institutional change rather than self-education, appeared to him a retrogression rather than an advance. He found his view borne out by the discrepancy between the professed ideals of the Jacobins and their practice of terrorism. He saw only one way to support a life of culture in the face of the inertia of established custom, the inroads of economic selfishness, and the demonism of violence; namely, the union of men of good will.

The community of *Wilhelm Meister* is presented as such

a union. The mutual confidence which holds it together is built on reason and faith. The ground out of which it grows is the art of friendship. This art helps Wilhelm achieve his education. He is granted friendship and practices it, and thus learns to translate his personal experience into clear and firm convictions. Were it not that Goethe had denied Wilhelm the spark of genius, we could see Goethe's own course reflected in this development of a promising individual into a self-resigning personality within a nucleus of friends who plan to build a world association.

At the beginning of the novel we meet Wilhelm, a well-built youth with a keen and independent mind, a sensitive heart, and an active imagination, whose many-sided talents and interests make it difficult for him to find his way. Most important, however, he is a thoroughly normal human being. He attracts our attention by the repercussions of life upon him rather than by specific traits of character. There is nothing demonic about him. He commits the errors and falls into the temptations that are normal to adolescence. It is only the spontaneity of feeling, thought, and action with which he gives rein to his innate interest in his fellow men that distinguishes him from others. He knows what the work of the poet means to the world, but he soon despairs of his own creative capacities, for he has enough sense of poetic quality to recognize his limitations. He dreams of the stage as a noble sphere where God and nature are glorified, and sees himself as the founder of the much-desired national theater. But neither as an actor nor as a director does he show sufficient promise, and he is level-headed enough to realize in time the deceptive aspects of the stage and its life. Wilhelm is evidently a personality more simple than complex; susceptible to the beautiful although not averse to the useful; on the whole, well-intentioned but without direction. How such a creature, lovable and loving, may become master of himself instead of being governed by something he vaguely calls fate is the problem of the *Apprenticeship*.

Wilhelm does not remain alone on his dangerous road of inward independence. The Abbé and Jarno keep their eyes on him, as on Natalie's untamable brother Friedrich, the lover of the actress Philine. In decisive moments, the friends of the Tower warn him or come to his aid; they permit him to learn through error but they protect him from damage. As his relation to them grows closer, he abandons step by step his drifting way of living and, together with it, his self-centered sensitivity. He becomes aware of the need for co-operation among men of good will if the problem of life is to be mastered at all. His tormented inwardness gives way with growing confidence to freely chosen subordination to the community, which then receives him as an equal. His personality grows firm and clear. As his apprenticeship ends with his resolution to live a self-resigning and fruitful life, so his travels end with the first testimony of his mastery of his vocation, the *Meisterstück*. As a surgeon he saves the life of his own son. Goethe sketches the outlines of his future as a useful member of the community, part of which is already sailing to the new continent.

When, in the novel, institutions develop from the nucleus of friends, the importance of the individual characters diminishes. True to the common principle of resignation, it is the relationship of the characters which is considered essential, rather than the individuals themselves. Only through his integration into the community does the individual attain value. The code of human relations governing the community is metaphysically grounded and forward-looking. Life is regarded as a process of reconciliation. When Jarno explains to Wilhelm that the discrepancy between his dream of the theater and its reality is merely a reflection of human life in general, he leads him toward understanding his own life in terms of the universal polarity of existence. Man must continue on his way despite his failures; his errors should be rendered productive; his transitions are crises, and "is not a crisis like a sickness?"[4] This term suggests that man must summon the resolution and the courage to become healthy.

The first requirement toward this end. is that of facing one's self and one's reflection in the mind of others. In their art of knowing each other, the friends of the Tower reveal the responsible and constructive character of their relationship. When Wilhelm is told that the countess is Lothario's sister and that his own relations to her had a fateful impact on her decisions, his first impulse is to flee. The experienced Jarno simply replies that no one should put another to shame unless he is ready to speak in front of a mirror.[5] When he reads the biography of himself written for the Tower's files, Wilhelm realizes that its authors had observed more sharply than he had and that their judgment was supported by so understanding an interpretation that it would not shame him.

For the first time his own figure was presented to him; not indeed as in a mirror, a second self; but as in a portrait, another self: we do not, it is true, recognize ourselves in every feature; but we are delighted that a thinking spirit has so understood us, that such gifts have been employed in representing us, that an image of what we are exists, and may endure when we ourselves are gone.[6]

The courage to face one's life without self-delusion is one of the pedagogic demands of the Abbé. He believes that a man's way of acting reveals his personality and the stage of his development. To form an image of one's friends and to have them face it constitutes an essential act of friendship if done in the way which Goethe portrays, namely, with both clarity and love. This attitude of the friends toward each other is maintained beyond the stage of education. Natalie and Therese are aware how much their personalities and their educational methods differ; therefore they are able to help each other. Each takes in charge the children most fitted to her personality.

Therese's procedure is to drill; Natalie's is true education. But without envy Therese leaves to Natalie the more gifted pupils. The organic order of the future settlement is prepared by such achievements of self-resignation among the friends.

We may note the characteristic difference between the way in which the members of the community of the Tower exercise friendship and the mutual confessions of the pietists. In pietism, scrutiny of conscience is cultivated in order to arrive at inner peace. Wilhelm Meister's friends form a mental image of each other's personalities and therefore are able to help each other: the younger ones in their growth, the older ones in their active responsibilities. Their respect, or, in terms of the Pedagogic Province, their reverence for each other gives stability to their friendship and makes it possible to strive for a common goal. Personal affection or sympathy, which is also at the basis of their relationship, becomes less important as their friendship gains in productivity. They are able to combine toleration with judgment and criticism with love. They are as averse to doctrinaire moralism and self-tormenting introspection as to ethical negligence.

Men of widely divergent characters, talents, and opinions are united in mutual confidence by a few fundamental convictions. Each measure that is taken, each obligation that is imposed, is accepted either because its significance is understood or simply out of confidence. This mutual trust makes it possible for Wilhelm to subject himself to conditions the meaning of which he can realize fully only after having experienced them. In the Pedagogic Province we will observe once more this principle of learning through experience whose final meaning is not at first understood. The pedagogue who has learned to see the entelechy of the child and to act accordingly is trusted. As reason is held superior to intellect because it is directed toward becoming, confidence is the precondition of learning; the experienced pedagogue knows that any other way is self-delusion. The social relations among the men of the Tower and in the Province are built upon mutual trust. The guiding spirit of this community is the Abbé. Quietly he helps the individuals to understand and respect each other. This he does in such a fashion that he leaves to each the particularities of his personality in so far as they are productive and do not cause disturbance. The individual should free himself from slavery to his ego by realizing that he is part of a greater whole and is called upon to serve through his personality rather than simply to enjoy it. This communal spirit of the Abbé is the foundation of his action in the *Apprenticeship* as in the *Travels*.

Jarno is presented as a cool-headed intermediary between Wilhelm and the Abbé in the *Apprenticeship;* in the *Travels* he is the agent through whom the contrast between the new community and the world at large first becomes evident. As the spiritually guiding figure, the Abbé recedes into the background as the undertaking grows. His position is due to no outer authority. It is the intrinsic weight of his personality that gives him his place among the friends.

At a time when Wilhelm is not yet able to understand fully the Abbé's intentions and is inclined to feel that he is interfering with his self-determination, Jarno comes to his aid and, charged by the Abbé himself, gives an explanation of the man and his thought.

What gives him such a value in our estimation, what in some degree secures him the dominion over all of us, is the free keen eye that nature has bestowed upon him for all the powers which dwell in man and are susceptible of cultivation, each according to its kind. Most men, even the most accomplished, are but limited: each prizes certain properties in others and himself; he favors these alone, and these alone will he have cultivated. Directly the reverse is the procedure of our Abbé; for every gift he has a feeling; he delights in recognizing and forwarding every ability.[7]

Just after his engagement to Therese and after Mignon's death, Wilhelm, haunted by sorrow and struggling against his fate, is little disposed to hear repetitions and interpretations of the sentences which the society of the Tower gave him when receiving him into its midst. But Jarno chooses precisely this moment of increased sensibility to plant in his friend the most essential parts of the Abbé's philosophy of life:

It is all men that make up mankind; all powers taken together that make up the world. These are frequently at variance: and as they endeavor to destroy each other, nature holds them together and again produces them. . . . Every ability is valuable and ought to be unfolded. If one encourages the beautiful alone, and another encourages the useful alone, it takes them both to form a man. The useful encourages itself, for the multitude produce it and no one can dispense with it; the beautiful must be encouraged, for few can bring it forth and many may need it.[8]

The manifold entelechy of human nature calls for recognition, respect, and support. Thus Jarno opens Wilhelm's eyes to the excellence of Lothario and the quite different virtues of the physician. He reminds his friend that only by taking himself in hand will he attain freedom and achieve results in his life.

It is your affair to try to choose; it is ours to aid you. A man is never happy until his unconditional striving has itself marked out its proper limitation.[9]

The spirit in which the individual is reconciled to himself and to society is that of the community over which the Abbé watches. It is most clearly expressed by Lothario in his conversation with Wilhelm at the end of the *Apprenticeship:*

Since we came together so miraculously, let us not lead a trivial life; let us together become active in a noble manner! It is inconceivable how much a man of true culture can accomplish for himself and for others if, without attempting to rule, he can be the guardian over many; can induce them to do in season what they are at any rate ready enough to do; can guide them to their objectives, which in a general way they see with due distinctness although they miss the road to them. Let us make a league for this; it is not merely enthusiasm, but an idea which can be executed very well; which indeed is often executed, though not always with clear consciousness, by good men.[10]

The friends look toward the world and plan a common action; yet they are aware that the most cherished gifts of life are products of nature itself. It is not by accident that in the same conversation Lothario calls Natalie "unrivaled in the conduct which nature has prescribed to this pure and noble soul."

An ethics of responsibility and reverence governs the conduct of the Abbé and his group. This ethics is explained as a consistent whole in terms of educational and religious principles when Wilhelm brings his son Felix to the Pedagogic Province. The figure of the Abbé is merged with the sphere of the "generic," as Goethe called objective wisdom, in contrast to the "specific," which he developed through the other characters of the novel. The Abbé stands, so to speak, behind the other figures. We know his profession but not his name, and the religious connotation of his title may be taken as a suggestion of the religious source of his thorough insight into the universal context of life and nature. He belongs to "those wise and good to the highest degree," although he masters worldly and even tricky situations with ingenuity. His humane objectivity and inner independence give him the highest culture. Simple in speech and keen in observation, he is asked for advice and is ready whenever he is needed.

From this cultured group the new community has its inception. Connected with all domains and levels of life, the friends are surrounded by the culture of the past and are awake to the events of the present. On Lothario's estate Wilhelm finds the art collection of his grandfather which, as a boy, he had with deep regret seen his father give away. Then, he had found in works of art a mirror of his sensitive subjectivity. Now, he learns that the good work of art embodies a standard of perfection which demands recognition and imitation. In the hall of the past, where Mignon dies and is buried, Wilhelm sees the statue of Lothario's uncle on his sarcophagus and reads the inscription which, in one brief phrase, expresses the response that is demanded here to the temporal character of human existence: *Gedenke zu leben*—"Remember to live." This variation of the *Memento mori* is the quintessence of the architecture, sculpture, and paintings which make this hall into one monumental unity. By it the visitor is led beyond awareness of time toward reverence for a life which mirrors the timeless in the temporal. Whoever entered this hall, Goethe says, felt lifted beyond his individual self and experienced, through this symphony of the arts, "what man is and what he is able to be."

How this hall of the past is alive! One might equally well call it the hall of the present and the future. As it is here, everything was and everything will be. Nothing passes except the one who enjoys and watches.[11]

Ever-recurring images of existence are depicted on the walls: the simple relations of man to himself and to those close to him, and the solemn acts by which kings and peoples conclude the covenant with their gods. The proportions and colors of the architecture make Wilhelm feel that they are a symbol of unfathomable truth translated into clear forms. A cosmic order is mirrored in the work of man.

He who has arrived at such an awareness of the past's revealing of timeless truth faces life without attachment but with devotion. The *Schöne Seele* said of Natalie, for whom as a child she had felt admiration and even reverence, that she had the gift of being active without being in need of activity. The friends try to live in this way, the way of freedom and of a productive happiness which is not dependent on their action but lends it calm and responsibility. Thus they take in view the totality of the human situation when they make their decisions.

A merely social or economic aspect of life is never significant by itself. Some of the leading figures belong to the aristocracy. They intermarry with descendants of bourgeois families. Schiller at once recognized the importance of the three social *mésalliances* of the *Apprenticeship*, by which Goethe, "without losing a word, reduced birth and social status to their perfect nothingness."[12] Goethe agreed with Schiller as to the need of keeping the "aristocracy" of *Wilhelm Meister* free from merely social connotations; the best human beings should appear among them. Lothario's resignation of certain feudal privileges emphasizes his freedom from social prejudice. Social justice is furthered without any sacrifice of human or cultural quality, and the rule of *Humanität* is brought about by the victory of pure humanity over differences of social status. A hierarchy of values—wisdom being the highest among them—is established. The individual is not brought down to a general level. As a moral being he is an equal among equals and he is judged according to the degree to which his personality has attained freedom.

The inner structure of this group of friends was anticipated, on the level of contemplation, by the figures of Goethe's poem "Die Geheimnisse." The society of the Tower expands into the world. It faces concrete domestic, economic, and even political situations and is bent upon active service. The monastery of the "Cross in Roses" is, however, removed from the world. The recluses' past appears only in the tale of their former experiences. The Abbé might well be one of the twelve knightly monks who joined together under the leadership of Humanus. He shares their conviction that, in fact, there is only one truth behind the diversified forms by which men approach it. Moreover, Tower and monastery represent communities ruled by the spirit of responsible friendship and devoted to the transmission of their experience to a younger generation.

The poems "Die Geheimnisse" and "Zueignung" were conceived and written at the same time and originally were to form a whole. In the genesis of Goethe's poetry, the dedicatory poem has a decisive position because of its content and its form. The strict rhythmical pattern of the stanza and its tone of solemn serenity could be mastered only by a soul resolved to win composure. The poet, to whom truth is revealed through the veil of his muse, expresses the urge to transmit his insight to others. The goddess, though she seems to smile at his zeal, gives him the veil, which means that she restricts him to the symbolical medium. Poetry, used for the benefit of future generations, becomes the agent of "the desire for the highest formation of man."

Such love of the idea of man is the common ground of the brotherhood of the "Cross in Roses." Goethe called their monastery "my Montserrat" after Wilhelm von Humboldt had told him how "two unforgettably beautiful days" at the Spanish monastery had reminded him of the landscape and meaning of Goethe's "Geheimnisse," written fifteen years earlier.[13] "Zueignung" announced the prophetic mission of the poet in relation to truth. "Die Geheimnisse" went a step farther in ascribing to poetry a universal scope and social significance. The community of *Wilhelm Meister* ultimately transfers the brotherhood of the "Cross in Roses" to the plane of active co-operation. The friends of the Tower maintain a distance from the world at large. Within its own ranks the union has a strictly binding power. Negative figures unsuitable to its ends are excluded.

In the tradition of Christian spiritualism, the evangelical communion of Christ's disciples was regarded as the climax of history; its renewal remained a chiliastic hope. The Abbé has faith in such an evangelical communion, and works for its realization in the present. He believes in the possibility of expressing its requirements in principles of wisdom and of giving it a durable social form. While a common spirit holds together the leaders of the developing society, the group is not sectarian, since it is open in principle to every sound human being. The tested will to resignation is the condition of acceptance.

Lothario and Lenardo both have attained peace within themselves before they embark on the new venture. By turning away from the theater Wilhelm had made a decision of principle; to exchange semblance for reality, self-enjoyment for a productive existence. Brother Friedrich must use some effort to convince the Abbé that he should be taken in. He and Philine have to discover some way of making a useful contribution. Odoard becomes the ally of the men of the Tower by taking the initiative for social reform at home. His action reveals that the spirit in which the Abbé prepares the settlement abroad is not confined to any closed social group.

It is a sound type of person which this community attracts and tries to educate. The religious ethic on which it is built is in harmony with reason; the intellect is subordinated to the values it is to serve; the totality of body and mind is the object of education. In the *Travels*, the wanderers are called *die Entsagenden*, those who renounce themselves. What is demanded of them is an asceticism that is neither easy to learn nor painless to bear. The sor-

row of resignation engenders the lyrical tone of Epimetheus in *Pandora*. The conflict between this sorrow and
the fear that the wound causing it might not heal is essential to Ottilie's crisis in *The Elective Affinities*. The whole
of our life experience, Goethe thought, calls upon us to
resign ourselves.

Our physical as well as our social life, customs, habits, prudence, philosophy, religion, and many an accidental event, all
tell us that we must learn resignation. We may not bring forth
into the open much that belongs to our innermost self. We are
often deprived of that which we need from the outside to
supplement our being, whereas, on the other hand, much is
imposed on us which is as alien to us as it is burdensome. We are
deprived of that which we acquired with great effort, of what
was permitted in friendly fashion; before we are aware of it,
we find ourselves compelled to give up our personality, at first
piece by piece and then altogether.[14]

Goethe considered the effort to resign one's self wholly,
once and for all, in the conviction of an everlasting necessity, a superhuman demand. And yet the characters of
Wilhelm Meister are shown as coming to fulfillment only
by integrating necessity into their own lives. Hersilie,
Hilarie, and in the end even Felix are led toward this
resignation which the Abbé regards as the basic requirement for a fruitful existence.

The individual is to sacrifice his subjective desires to
universal ends. The good life is the goal of this asceticism
"within the world." The spirit in which it is lived is called
Weltfrömmigkeit by the Abbé—a piety within the world
rather than one tending beyond it; one which demands
that the art of living be directed toward the rhythm of
thought and action. In the parable of the charcoal pile,
Jarno explains to Wilhelm how man's emotional life can
be productively integrated into the totality of existence.
If the individual regards himself as a specimen of mankind,

his piety will embrace the whole, he will be able to exercise *Weltfrömmigkeit*.

The commandment of resignation is what most sharply distinguishes Goethe's ideal community from any romantic dream. He conceived his image in anticipation of the social and intellectual crisis predicated, in his mind, by the very structure of his time. When he demanded of the wanderer that he live for the present without reflecting about the past or the future he intended to counteract inclinations which inevitably weaken man's power to accept and mold his situation. When Goethe gave his community a simple but firm religious foundation which was in harmony with the demands of reason, he once more drew on the spiritualist roots of his faith. Lenardo's and Hersilie's uncle is presented to us as the grandson of a companion of "the eminent William Penn." Penn's is the only modern historical name mentioned in *Wilhelm Meister*. Arising from a common ancestry in religious spiritualism, the basic convictions ruling Goethe's ideal community, its practice of toleration, and its sense of active responsibility are indeed akin to the ideals of the great Quaker.

The wanderers accept necessity and try to render it productive; they spiritualize love by recognizing its universal significance; and they experience the unpredictable element of chance. Lenardo, when he is led into the community by Wilhelm, turns out to own American property adjacent to Lothario's. Such unexpected widening of future possibilities we may take as an element of "guidance" as we know it from Christian nonconformist groups. Goethe tells of guidance as he experienced it in his youth, and he includes chance—*Tyche*—as among the inescapable constituents of human existence. Wilhelm elicits the Abbé's criticism as long as he confuses fate with the uncontrolled feelings and wishes that are mixed with the occurrences on his way. As soon as he obeys "the demand of the day," the elements of human conduct take on a different and sound balance in him. Until then he was lucky in spite of his awkward errors and misfortunes; now the acquired art of resignation is accompanied by good fortune.

Goethe created his mythical image of the emigrating community as ultimately independent of any historical situation; as a symbol of the norm, accessible to faith and reason, and a reflection of the energy of hope. His fundamental demands on man crystallized in the poetic form of the "Symbolum,"[15] which he wrote for his Masonic lodge more than a decade before the completion of the *Travels*. The poem describes man's wandering and counsels him to go forward intrepidly on his way through the temporal under the guidance of the timeless toward a future which only discloses itself step by step. From behind the awe-inspiring veil of the unknowable, the voices of the spirits and of the masters of the past encourage man to put his trust in exercising the forces of the good and call him to the duty of active hope.

I 2

Error and Truth

The Meaning of Truth—The Productivity
of Error—The Test of Wandering
Mythical, Philosophic, and Spiritualist
Ways of Living—Profession
and Community—A Sibylline Book

IN THE EPIC OF the growing community, we learn of Wilhelm's individual growth into a personality capable of productive association with others. The novel of human development, *Entwicklungsroman*, forms a part of the novel of community, *Gemeinschaftsroman*. The stages through which Wilhelm has to pass confirm the Abbé's conviction that men who are capable of education arrive at truth only through error. "There are men who never err because they make nothing reasonable their purpose."[1] Wilhelm errs when, as though enveloped in the cloud of his subjectivity, he tries to find and to pursue his purposes at the same time. Yet the solution of precisely this paradox is the aim of the Abbé's watchful influence in the *Apprenticeship*. He is averse to theory and refrains from imposing rules of life from without upon any of his pupils. Only personal experience, if properly thought through, will wield a lasting influence upon the personality. The Abbé could not think otherwise, since his ideas reflect Goethe's conception of man as exposed to the polarity of life. The truth which the Abbé has in mind is an experienced truth.

In harmony with his organic view of nature and man, Goethe regarded truth as ultimately "a supertemporal good, independent and beyond all human support."[2] Man, however, has an inner feeling for truth which, as a sense of exactness, is the basis even of mathematics. This truth, which man can express only through signs and symbols, becomes manifest also through error. The recognition of error is the first step toward truth. The feeling of guilt follows recognition of the violation of truth and gives it an emotional emphasis. Striving for truth is a constructive response to error and guilt, and it was in this sense that Goethe could say: "The fruitful alone is true."[3] The integration of Wilhelm's personality into the universal norm inherent in it, is the theme of the *Apprenticeship*.

At the opening of the novel he appears as an enthusiastic youth, in conflict with the orderly bourgeois spirit of his family and yet supported in his poetic desires by his warmhearted mother. He lives in the enjoyment of his first love and in expectation of renewed hours of passion, and his mind is focused upon ennobling this relationship and his beloved partner. From then on, he goes through the experiences of deception and error until, with the aid of the friends of the Tower, he finds his balance. Because his development comes to a fortunate conclusion, we must not be deceived as to the moments of despair and danger through which he passes. The Abbé sees man threatened inwardly and outwardly by so many dangers that it is a miracle if he reaches his destination.[4]

Wilhelm progresses through good intentions and false actions, self-delusion and consequent suffering. None of these stages can be passed over, lest, as the Abbé says, we be led past the goal into endless errors.[5] The men of the Tower first make their spirit felt in the conversation which Wilhelm has with the art expert in the first book. On the boat the Abbé meets Wilhelm in the company of the actors. Later, in the third book, the performance in the castle brings Wilhelm into contact with Jarno, who impresses him by his cool but clear and outspoken knowledge of the realities of life. Toward the end of the fifth book Aurelie asks Wilhelm to read the diary of Lothario's aunt, the "Confessions of a Beautiful Soul." This manuscript consoles Aurelie before her death and introduces Wilhelm to the personalities and the religious background of the Tower. Then finally the moment comes for him to face these friends in person.

Wilhelm had been attracted by Mariane not only as a person but also as an actress. From the outset we are made aware of the conflict within him between the universal longing of his sensitive inwardness and the narrow life which his social origin prescribes. He tries to solve it by escaping to the stage. At first he founds a mediocre theater with Melina, an inferior actor who no longer believes in his profession. Wilhelm's compassion for the plight of the girl whom Melina loved had brought them together. He travels in their bohemian company. The group widens and, finally, Wilhelm finances Melina's enterprise. By another act born of the feeling for justice, he saves Mignon from barbaric hands; she and the harpist join him and she accompanies him as though she were his better self. On the boat the Abbé explains Wilhelm's situation to him clearly enough, although in general terms. He is sorry to see Wilhelm in bad company:

One who, in his early years, has lived in bad and insignificant company, will always long for it even though he may later have better companions. For the impression of his former company is lasting, since it is connected with the memory of youthful enjoyments which only seldom can be repeated.[6]

Even to frivolous Philine, the Abbé, the mysterious man who disappears without taking leave, looks "like a human being."[7]

Enriched in experience but bitterly disappointed in Me-

lina and his associates and conscious of his responsibility for
their misfortune—since he has persuaded them to travel
through the danger zones of war—Wilhelm joins the sea-
soned impresario Serlo. The ideal of the theater as the institution which, mirroring the totality of existence, educates
the totality of man, seems to come close to realization under
Serlo's guidance. Wilhelm's self-delusion is, however, once
more destroyed. After the performance of Hamlet, his en-
chantment with his dilettantism is gone. He hardly needs the
note left in the ghost's veil by the mysterious actor who
played Hamlet's father to induce him to flee.

Wilhelm's personality is contrasted with that of the phi-
listine Werner, his faithful friend and brother-in-law. Lacking in deeper insight, Werner represents all the narrowness
of the bourgeois world which Wilhelm seeks to escape.
Only occasionally does Werner try to romanticize his honest but merely practical activities as an efficient businessman.
Despite a serious and not unsuccessful effort, Wilhelm cannot resign himself to a life which, he feels, would cut him
off from the most intense yearnings of his inner self. His
longings are reflected in the impression which noblemen
make upon him. The form and freedom of their conduct
make him aware of the impulse which he has had since his
earliest years to form himself according to his innate potentialities. After his father's death, he seizes upon the chance
to do so. The burgher's son seeks on the stage the freedom
and universality which, he observes, are the nobleman's by
birth.

What good is it for me to manufacture perfect iron, while my
own breast is full of dross? What would it avail me to put my
properties in order, if I am at variance with myself? To say it in
one word: the cultivation of my own self, wholly as I am, has
from my youth onward been constantly though dimly my wish
and my purpose.[8]

Writing thus to Werner, Wilhelm for the first time interprets his own past in terms of a firm insight. His desire is to be fulfilled through experience and guidance, though in a way quite different from what he expects. His inward humanness is the source of his charm as well as of his errors. His future friends see in it the promise of his ultimate achievement. Before he is able to join them, however, Wilhelm has to learn that humane feelings are not enough and that dilettantism leads astray. He had used a world of semblance as an escape. The dying Aurelie shows him the truth.

Wilhelm's problem is to leaven his inner humanness with judgment. When he comes to Lothario's castle with the intention of presenting, not without a moralizing purpose, Aurelie's last letter to Lothario, her former lover, he finds men and situations thoroughly different from what he expected. Aurelie's truth was not the whole truth. Arriving in order to teach, he finds himself in need of being taught.[9] The end of his apprenticeship begins in this productive moment. Yet when he enters the group with which he is to establish a lasting bond he is still the object of fate rather than its master.

Wilhelm proved as helpless in love as in his general judgments and decisions. It had been a passionate dream that drove him into Mariane's arms. In Philine he encountered a playful adventuress of love whom he did not respect and yet did not know how to resist. He unwittingly caused a fundamental change in the lives of the count and countess by a moment of play and a moment of sudden passion. In Aurelie, on the other hand, he found a friend whom he respected but could not love. She made clear to him that love calls for responsibility—an awareness that dwelt within him but was not yet confirmed by consciousness. He errs once again in his relation to Therese, but this time, significantly, because he silences his heart, subjecting himself to Therese's judgment. When he first meets Natalie again, he is not sure whether or not she is the amazon who once saved him and later appeared in his dreams. When he discovers his love for her, he is unable to take the situation into his own hands. His friends, and Natalie herself, act for him.

Before Wilhelm reaches the stage when his thought, his self-knowledge, and his personal relations form a constructive unity, he is warned by the fate of others. In Melina an inhuman selfishness is joined with despair as to life's meaning, for which his cleverness is only a cloak. Wilhelm's very nature is repelled by this nihilism:

Nay, have there not been men so totally devoid of all feelings of existence that they have held the life and nature of mortals as nothing: a painful, short, and tarnished gleam of being?[10]

Even before he grasps the bearing of the Abbé's thought, an inner feeling for life gives Wilhelm the certainty that the existence of man is meaningful. His healthy capacity for faith expresses itself as compassion when he offers assistance to the unfortunate harpist. Even Mignon cannot draw him into her sphere of longing renunciation. While she loves him and acts as his conscience, he appears at times insensitive. A resilient strength—expressing itself as an ironical touch in his character—prompts him to accept life, whereas Mignon flees from it. His nature is not inclined toward the overrefinement which Natalie observed in the character of her aunt, the *Schöne Seele*. Wilhelm's innate soundness supports him in becoming what he potentially is.

Mignon's death and burial make clear to him the deeper significance of his instinctive acceptance of life. Slowly he learns to apply to his own existence the teachings of the indenture which was given him when the friends of the Tower considered the first phase of his education complete.[11] He leaves the theater, symbol of a life of self-delusion. His future promises to become clear when he joins the community of friends who had broken away from conventional ways of living for better reasons than the actors. His emotions are now tempered by his firmer comprehension; he begins in earnest to live a second life, that of the mind.

It is Natalie who draws him on to this last stage of his apprenticeship. In contrast to Wilhelm, who has to become what he is, she *is* what she is. Her personality awakens him to truth, neglect of which had hitherto made his life restless. From the fleeting moment when he first saw the amazon, her image has dwelt in him. But even now he is not strong enough to distinguish among his impulses nor confident enough to act on them. The capacity for intelligent action, which is Werner's excellence and limitation, is weakest in Wilhelm when he most needs it. Therese shows understanding of him when she decides to marry him out of inclination rather than passion, and in order that her power of reason may come to the aid of his heart. Nature speaks clearly in him, as well as in Natalie, in the terrible moments of Augustine's death and Felix's danger. Wilhelm needs Therese's clarity and Lothario's firmness to help him break through the barrier of his sensibility and find the truth of nature. He must still be led to the truth; he cannot grasp it himself. And rightly does Friedrich, the foolish brother, welcome him with the word: "You resemble Saul, the son of Kish, who went out to seek his father's asses and found a kingdom."[12]

Natalie is drawn to Wilhelm because of his genuine humanness. Passion, reverence, and reason are combined in his relation to her. He feels that his love for her is as all-encompassing as the love he had once had for Mariane. In fact, he now feels a responsible conviction instead of the delusive dream of his first passion. As he owed his physical health to Natalie when she called the surgeon to his aid, so his union with her puts him on his way to health as a human being. The impact of her personality "re-creates" him. It is not Mignon who ultimately is the agent of his maturity, nor the image of the Fair Saint, nor the experienced advice of Aurelie, but a human being whose spirit is in perfect balance with her nature and whose piety is incarnated in her being and action. Her image, no longer removed into the distance of an elusive dream, becomes a symbol of the life which Wilhelm now consciously accepts as the essence of that which nature intends for man. His reverence for Natalie opens his mind to the full significance of reverence. Resolved to become and to remain sound, he takes his future firmly into his own hands. Natalie's innate mastery of herself guides Wilhelm in acquiring his own.

The *kairos* with which his apprenticeship ends is the climactic moment of Wilhelm's life. On his travels, he lives in the spirit of this moment which had finally given him the certainty that existence is significant beyond the individual, beyond his temporality and the contingencies that beset him. With this *kairos* his "Hamlet-period" was ended. The errors of his apprenticeship are not repeated in the *Travels*.

You are saved; you are on the way to the goal. None of your follies will you repent; none of them will you wish to repeat. No happier destiny can be allotted to a man.[13]

In these words, spoken to Wilhelm by the Abbé before he received the indenture, Goethe expressed his ideal of the personality who has discovered the law inherent in man and is on his way toward realizing it in himself. Wilhelm's integrated personality is tested on his wanderings. He experiences the world in the light of the universal significance of existence which friendship and love had helped him to recognize. He becomes a help to others, shares in preparing the common future, and finally joins the exodus of the new community. He is accompanied by Natalie's image, and the distance between them is broken only by a few letters which remind us of his faithfulness to the moment of fulfillment.

The cultural landscape of the *Travels* is the counterpart of that of the *Apprenticeship*. Some of the figures in the *Travels* are akin to others we already know. The image of the *Schöne Seele* helps Wilhelm to understand Makarie. The character of the antiquarian resembles that of the

Abbé. Lenardo is akin to Lothario as a man of action; he is his opposite as a lover. By the reflection of the characters of the *Apprenticeship* in the new figures of the *Travels*, Goethe intended to reveal once more the morphological types of life.

The conditions to which Wilhelm submits on his travels are related to the errors of his former life. He is not supposed to stay in one place for more than three nights nor to repeat a visit within the year. He must refuse to be drawn into the concrete situations of life; rather he must master them by the objective recognition of their generally human aspect. His former role is reversed. Now he can be helpful, whereas before he was in need of help himself. The errors of his adolescence are repeated in Felix, Hersilie, and Hilarie. It is Wilhelm who helps Lenardo toward a reconciliation with his conscience and prepares him for participation in the community. He is in accord with the Abbé in his attitude toward others and in his convictions, and, ironically, he fails precisely where the Abbé's own guidance proved limited. The Abbé had no power over Friedrich; Lenardo and Susanne find their way to each other in spite of Wilhelm's precautions. Nature does not submit to calculation—not even to that prompted by the best intentions.

On his wanderings, Wilhelm learns that various forms of living meet the demands inherent in the human entelechy. As, in Western civilization, the cult of the church shares the function of guidance with philosophic reason, so Wilhelm encounters a mythical way of living in St. Joseph II and a philosophic one in Hersilie's uncle. Makarie's spiritualist universality comprises both. These three stations on Wilhelm's travels introduce him to energies of the mind as they formed historical styles of living in the modern world. Corresponding to Goethe's conception of the epochs of the mind, the mythical, the philosophic, and the spiritualist way of life can be in harmony with each other. It is only when the self-emancipated intellect exchanges a mechanical for an organic conception of nature and severs the bond with reason that the approach to the normative is barred and nihilism becomes inevitable.[14]

On the first station of their travels Wilhelm and Felix meet Joseph, Maria, and their children in the mountains. The second flight into Egypt is a true image of the first, in imitation of which Joseph's small family lives under the universal law in faithful and simple devotion. The fulfillment of daily duties in the service of the patron saint is a source of perfection and happiness in a narrow realm which, nevertheless, comprises the totality of life, work and art, meditation and action. This archaic image of culture is one succinct expression of the meaning of culture as the lived realization of faith.[15]

The visit to Hersilie's uncle, the philanthropic landowner, brings Wilhelm into a thoroughly different world. The uncle governs his extensive properties like a small state, on the basis of clearly formulated principles which the visitor finds written on the walls in the form of proverbs. He bans mythical imagery because he feels that it encourages man's inclination to escape from his active calling into a realm of fancy. In his art gallery Wilhelm finds the portraits of men of substance, chosen mainly from the sixteenth century. The uncle recognizes his ownership as a responsibility; he devotes his property to the common weal. Since his thinking is concrete, he formulates his maxims in the light of what he considers possible. He intends to bring "to the many" what is desirable, instead of doing "the best for the greatest number." For, he says,

the greatest number cannot be found or known, and even less can we establish what is the best. But surely there are always the many who surround us. We come to know what they desire; we reflect about what they should desire, and so something significant can always be done and created.[16]

He surrounds himself with men of self-reliance and free

judgment, and he counts on their spontaneous and reasonable co-operation. He looks at the useful as a guide to the true and for him neither the one nor the other can be a contradiction of the beautiful. He upholds the tradition of his father, who contributed to the freedom of religion in colonial America. He himself returned to Europe, the seat of a culture thousands of years old, instead of "playing Orpheus and Lycurgus across the ocean, centuries late."[17] He considers the community church a place devoted to maintaining public ethics, whereas religion proper remains the concern of the individual. He urges the members of his family to examine themselves each Sunday and to confess to a friend of their choice. He himself chooses Makarie as his mother-confessor. The uncle likes to be alone. He tries to master life by his independent reasoning, and he understands his community as the co-operative enterprise of self-contained individuals who have common ethical principles. His bond with Makarie brings his inner self into a wider range of experience.

Wilhelm proves capable of understanding Makarie's existence more deeply even than the members of her own family. A dream which he has about her is interpreted by the astronomer, Makarie's physician and companion, as a symbol of her innermost being. This dream becomes a clue to his insight. Makarie is a person of universality. She combines an active with a contemplative life. It is a useful and necessary service which she renders to the neighborhood by educating girls on her estate, and a similarly active and helpful interest in the lives of her family and friends turns her attention to the outside world. She sees her relatives "as though she penetrated the inner nature of each through the individual mask surrounding him." She regards them *sub specie aeternitatis*.

The figures known to Wilhelm stood before his soul as if transfigured; the sympathetic insight of this invaluable woman had removed the shell while enlivening and ennobling the sound kernel.[18]

Makarie's attachment to life is not opposed to her devotion to cosmological thought. Taken to the tower by the astronomer, Wilhelm feels overpowered as he senses the immensity of the universe and, under the impact of Makarie's conversation, he recognizes the correspondence between microcosm and macrocosm. At this station of his travels, Wilhelm is initiated into Goethe's philosophy of nature, man, and the universe. He responds to it as though such thoughts were inherent in his own being and were only now being released. In fact Makarie's own wisdom is explained to him by the analogy of poetical anamnesis.

One says of the poet that the elements of the moral world are hidden in his innermost nature to develop, step by step, out of him, so that nothing in the world comes to his intuition that was not already present in his inner sense. Likewise, it seems, the proportions of our solar system were fundamentally innate in Makarie, at first latently, then developing step by step, and later becoming more clearly alive.[19]

With this sudden and momentous insight into the ultimate unity of the universe and its reflection in human existence, the education of Wilhelm's mind is completed; he has made the central tenets of Goethe's thought his own.

Makarie's synthesis excludes neither the simple life in observance of the mythical image nor the activity of reason. Reverence for universal law, whether it be interpreted by symbolical or conceptual signs, is the common ground of both ways of life. The initial aphorisms of Makarie's archives, which Wilhelm was supposedly given, deal with the discrepancy between human wisdom and the order of nature, with the paradox that the only access to the infinite is through the finite, with the heuristic character of human existence, and with the relation of the prophetic to human nature. Prophecy recognizes the hidden in the patent, the future in the present; the living, not the dead, and the meaningful, not the meaningless.[20]

The sibyl's papers are represented as containing the crystallization in living conversation of a continuous mediation between the particular and the universal. Art and science, the religions of past and present, dwell in the mind of this most prophetical of the figures through whose masks Goethe conveyed his thought. For Wilhelm, however, Makarie's universalism clarifies the deepest impulse of his nature. Thus he can respond to her cosmic views by the simple word: "Great thoughts and a pure heart—this is what we should ask from God."[21] The most universe-embracing thought is close to the simple wisdom latent in the purity of the human being.

Makarie represents a possible synthesis of the divergent mental forces of the modern world. In her mind the liturgical life of the mythical epoch is reconciled with philosophic reason, the sphere of the beautiful with that of the holy, the revelation of nature with that of the spirit, the life of action with that of contemplation. There is present in her personality a wide horizon of human culture, to be received by the generation that is to build its communal existence upon the ground of such universal wisdom.

The consequences which Wilhelm draws from this experience of the typical forms of cultured life and of its cosmic significance, help him to build his own life. After his visit to the Pedagogic Province, he travels to the region of Mignon's origin, and, no longer in need of restrictive obligations, he asks for his release from the conditions of his wandering and learns the profession he is to exercise in the new community. He has become a man of culture and firm character. He did not acquire these qualities like Jung-Stilling, of whom Goethe, in *Poetry and Truth*, remarks that he sought his salvation in society in his own way, and thereby "attained a truly natural culture."[22] Wilhelm brought with him all the necessary gifts, but guidance and good fortune alone were able to carry him the long distance to the consolidation of his nature in the highest culture of the personality "which is capable of balancing its passionate wishes."[23] Through his life with his friends he realized that the art of living "consists in abandoning ourselves to gain ourselves."[24] His personality has gained a focus.

The teachings of the Abbé and Makarie have become a part of him. His personality no longer reveals selfishness or a gap between thought and existence, and therefore the impression he makes on others is convincing and he is received with confidence. This change in Wilhelm's character is evident in his attitude toward Susanne, which is a result of his own judgment alone. The daughter of the indebted tenant who was expelled over Lenardo's objections when the uncle needed money for his nephew's travel, had become a burden on Lenardo's conscience. When he finds her, Wilhelm discovers that she has made the best out of her situation, although the pietism from which she came had lost its significance for her. Her religious thought has lost in firmness; her worship has become conventional. Wilhelm aids her in the search for genuine convictions.

Goethe's conception of the human situation and the ethics which he developed from it, find another expression in the letter which Wilhelm leaves. He explains to Susanne the heuristic character of human existence, the limitation of man's insight, and the art of finding a sound rhythm of action and thought by facing the duties of each day. He concludes with this advice:

Continue to pursue the immediate duties of the day and thereby examine the purity of your heart and the firmness of your spirit. If, then, in a free moment, you take breath and find space to lift yourself upward, you will certainly win a proper attitude toward the sublime, to which we owe reverent devotion in every way, reverent observation of every event and recognition of its inherent higher guidance.[25]

It is a genuine and unsentimental piety which is here demanded, and one that is true to Makarie's conviction that the course of life itself discloses its universal relatedness. Piety and culture indeed come to be identical in Goethe's understanding. The former is sound only if merged with the conduct of life; the latter is possible only on a religious ground. "Piety is a means toward the highest culture rather than an end in itself."[26] "Only those who are truly religious have culture."[27] The *memento vivere* of Mignon's burial is echoed in this conception which bars the dissolving effect that religious feeling might have if used merely as an escape.

As Susanne's example shows, culture is by no means contingent upon an elevated position in society. Although she is the daughter of an expelled tenant, she is called "the beautiful and good" by her friends. She deserves this epithet by which the Greeks defined the highest possible achievement of the human entelechy, the *kalos k'agathos*, for she has succeeded in building a good life among the poor weavers of the mountains, beginning with the lowest level of labor and yet finding her way to mental freedom. The purely human finds in her an expression which is essential to Goethe's view and criticism of modern society, and it is through her that Goethe illustrates the dangers which threaten this society.

Wilhelm takes upon himself the way of life, with all its limitations, in which he confirmed Susanne. Jarno is instrumental in bringing about his last step of resignation. Wilhelm finds him as Montan, making use of the years before the emigration can start to practice the craft of geologist and mining engineer in which he had grown up. Even here, the world-experienced Jarno mercilessly continues to confront Wilhelm with the facts of society. In the past he had told him that he had no talent for the theater; now he has him face the fact that he must choose a craft. Precisely through his one-sidedness Jarno proves indispensable to Wilhelm. Contemptuous of words, skeptical about men, the test of action means everything to him. Under the cover of his taciturn self-control dwells, however, the respect for human perfection; he expects, by resolute work, to heal the suffering of a soul.

Jarno agrees with Wilhelm's own ideas when he suggests that he become a surgeon. "No one is more in need of a surgeon than the healthy."[28] The symbolism of this decision draws the meaning of the whole work together. Wilhelm had acquired the instruments of the surgeon whom Natalie called to his aid when he first saw her. He cherished them as a token of the turning point of his life. Now, in a letter to Natalie, he recalls the scene when his first boyhood friend was drowned although a skilled hand might have saved his life. Thus he chooses the skill which is meant to restore nature's highest creature to his preordained health; he resolves to learn the profession symbolic of the theme to which Goethe's novel is devoted. In the last scene he uses his skill on his son Felix. The son's life is saved, and we see father and son "embracing each other and standing, like Castor and Pollux, brothers who meet on the road from Orcus to light."[29]

The Abbé is not averse to Wilhelm's decision, although he is not as critical of general education as is Jarno. His criticism is directed against any ambiguous and dissipating pedagogy which

makes men uncertain; it awakens wishes when it should be animating tendencies; instead of forwarding our real capacities, it turns our efforts toward objects which are frequently discordant with the mind that aims at them.[30]

The Abbé understands the totality of education to be the harmonious relationship between reason and emotion rather than any versatility of the intellect. Character is the object of his care, and Jarno-Montan differs from him only in the high expectation he sets upon the ethical achievement that can be attained through the mastery of a single definite field. Here we find the educational conviction of Goethe's classical period integrated with his later ideas. In the circle of those who resign themselves to productive service, the concept of *Meisterschaft* includes vocational perfection. The new community demands this perfection from every one of its members. It is seen as a society in which culture and labor are reconciled.

Not only Wilhelm but Philine, Friedrich, and Lydie practice a craft. That the most modest occupation, such as Lydie's tailoring, is honorable and has an enlivening significance is shown when Philine and Lydie set out to work in Makarie's home. According to the sound conceptions of the *Travels*, work is the foundation not merely of the economic life of the new community, but also of its ethical structure. When the Abbé gives his consent to Wilhelm's plans, he announces an important decision of the community of the Tower:

We must bring our honest human intentions into a practical relationship with the widest realm and not only support those next to us but, at the same time, carry with us all mankind.[31]

The society which is growing out of the Abbé's group is seen here as a general answer to the dangers in which civilization finds itself. His concern for the sound development of the individual had led the Abbé to realize the indispensable service which friendship renders if it is wise and responsible. The tales of the *Travels*, outlining the manifold perturbations of the human heart and its restoration to health, tell also of the healing effect of friendship. Flavio and Hilarie, in "The Man of Fifty Years," praise it in their verses. The association of friends achieved the purely human within their own group. Now the Abbé seeks to build upon it a wider community that stands over and above the dissolving tendencies of the time.

The *Apprenticeship* had dealt with the dangers threatening man from within. All the care given to the harpist failed. The horror of nothingness which man may have to face could not be more drastically presented than by his fate. The friends who surround him seem about to succeed in starting him out on a new life, but chance brings back his unfathomable anxiety. In full consciousness of these depths of human nature, Goethe gives an answer to their threat. His image of the good life is conceived in terms of obedience to laws inherent in man. They postulate the acceptance of life, and forward its fulfillment through the self-mastery and understanding of the individual supported by reasonable friendship; they interpret marriage as the highest consummation of friendship and common responsibility, and as the foundation of culture; they oppose a despotic relation of father to son, by one of brotherhood; they demand that property be administered for the common good; they relate man's dignity to his work.

The wisdom of the *Apprenticeship* is historically significant because the existing objective culture no longer possessed its former binding validity. Enlightened patriarchalism could not prevent the collapse of feudal society, first on the mental, then on the political, and finally on the social level. The dogmatic conflicts of theological theory had alienated organized religion from its living purpose. Science had either encouraged the opposition to dogmatic religion or had furthered its neglect. The art of living seemed as much endangered as the standards of art, because of the license which the Romantic individual assumed. The answer which Goethe gave in *Wilhelm Meister* grew out of the same motives that prompted his defense of classical form and his criticism of contemporary art and thought. This stand he took in common with Schiller. His conception of education for freedom, formulated in response to the French Revolution and systematically expressed in Schiller's *Letters on Aesthetic Education*, constituted a first step toward his utopia.

The post-Napoleonic era could not deceive Goethe by its semblance of calm, nor could the constitutional debates and

the rising intellectual rationalism afford him consolation. A
volcano seemed to dwell below the surface, which Wilhelm
felt in himself when going through his first passionate sorrow. The mythical age was gone, the theological was
doubted; in poetry and philosophy dispersive tendencies
were at work. The serene activity of the old Goethe, his
continued social contacts, and his encouraging co-operation
with his helpers and friends were duties which he loved,
convinced that he ought to bestow his constructive powers
even on insignificant moments.

Through his experienced sensitivity, however, the octo-
genarian was aware of social dangers inherent in the modern
world, and he saw them a half-century before they entered
the common consciousness. The sterile chaos of the end
which he prophesied with a warning voice in his "Epochs
of the Mind," he saw foreshadowed by unmistakable signs
in both the social and the intellectual tendencies of his time.
The frequency of Goethe's critical utterances is all the more
significant because his attitude toward the negative took on
more and more the form of Jarno's reticence during the
time when, "in his fortress," he continued to exercise his
craft with only occasional complaints that the best he had
to say was becoming almost "incommunicable."[32]

The second part of *Wilhelm Meister* was given its ultimate form in 1829 in response to this view of the contemporary scene, and it points directly to the danger in which
modern man finds himself. Organic nature constituted a
holy secret, on which Goethe's thought in poetry and science was centered. His love was devoted to the living. He
conceived of the universe as an energy of life in infinite motion, and of the spirit of man as the guiding power bestowed
upon this part of nature by the creator of the whole. His
innermost being was offended wherever he saw reverence
for life relegated to oblivion and denied by an "emancipated" intellect. Here, we feel, is the ground common to
all his polemics. For the same basic reason he turned against

supernaturalism in theology and against mechanistic physics, and even the defense, sometimes ironical, sometimes impatient, of his whims, such as his aversion to drums, eyeglasses, and telescopes, hints at the same serious motif. Yet the basic problem was one of his oldest themes. His Mephistopheles is not a demonic power such as Lucifer, the fallen archangel. In Goethe's modern Satan the intellect has freed itself from reason. It is on that account that Mephisto acts merely negatively, although he is cynically aware of the limitations of his power within the universe and with men who are "on the right path."

When he is taken into the confidence of the artist-anatomist, Wilhelm once again experiences this tension between the organic and mechanical views of existence, between understanding by reason and understanding by intellect. He shares the anatomist's aversion to dissecting a beautiful body. The anatomist sees a universal and symbolic significance in his own struggle against dissection, and he predicts a conflict of life and death between "dead and living." "We gain more information by constructing than by destroying, by connecting than by dividing, by reanimating the dead than by further killing what is already killed."[33] If the anatomist's opposition to dissection in favor of his "proplastic" procedure borders on idiosyncrasy, the conflict which Goethe intended to symbolize by this incident is real. Shall science deny respect for life, and thereby its own possible meaning to human culture, its ethical responsibility and universal significance? A hundred years after Goethe's death the question had become critical to the future of the human race.

Through a variety of "repeated reflections" the cultural realm is disclosed by which Goethe's *Wilhelm Meister* presents the problems of life. As the *Travels* reflect the *Apprenticeship*, so Wilhelm finds his own errors repeated by Felix; the faithfulness of St. Joseph II is reflected in the

uncle's tenacity in adhering to his principles; the innate perfection of Natalie is mirrored by Hersilie's growth through
error to truth. This manifold picture is intensified and integrated by Makarie's universality and embracing wisdom.
In her, the cosmos and the universe of her human world
mirror each other. Along the thread of Wilhelm's road to
mastery we are shown original phenomena of human existence, mutually explaining each other and together forming
an image of the entelechy of man, of the norm inherent in
it, and of the dangers threatening its realization.

Such a reflection of man's self in that of others, of the
world in the work of the poet, of the past in the present, of
one literature in all literatures was, in Goethe's view, a "way
toward higher aliveness," bringing us closer to the ever-
recurring forms which the course of man's culture produces. It was, Goethe saw, the law of intensification that
rules the realm of nature repeated in the kingdom of man.
He liked to think of these repeated reflections in terms of
the multiple refraction of colors, in the same way in which
he likened the relation between the phenomenal world and
the reality of its *noumena* to that between the one universal light and its manifold refractions through the world of
colors.[34]

The interlacing network of human life, as Goethe presents it in the figures and events of *Wilhelm Meister*, ultimately serves to illustrate the rise of the new community
out of the spirit of friendship. We leave Wilhelm as one
among many; as one who is aware of the universal significance of the whole which he serves, who has resigned himself to the mastery of his craft and is open to the simple
human value of each of his associates. He is a part of the
image of truth by which Goethe tried to oppose the errors
of the individual and the time. In this image his sound observation of the realities of life, his art of creating symbols
of the normative, and his faithfulness to the spirit, all

merged together. The strength of his confidence in the lasting and regenerating power of the spirit is borne out by one of Makarie's sayings:

There will always remain a minority in support of the truth, and should it withdraw into one single mind, this would not matter. In stillness and seclusion he will continue to pursue his work, and a time will come when one seeks him and his convictions, or when these convictions may venture into the open once more, in a new all-pervading light.[35]

Out of faith in the spirit and out of love for the idea of man, Goethe wrote the book which he himself called sibylline.

Education for Reverence

Ultimate Convictions—The Education for
Reverence—The Universal Religion
Art and Community Spirit—*Humanität*

WILHELM MEISTER had received help from his friends in his own growth. He entrusts his son to the Pedagogic Province to which the community of the Tower looks for the best possible education of future associates. The image of man underlying this pedagogy is conceived in the spirit of the Abbé. Its end is the harmony and totality of the pupil's character and his preparation for fruitful service in communal life.

How in human relations the spontaneity of genius could be reconciled with the exigencies of common living, was the central problem of *Tasso*. *Wilhelm Meister's Apprenticeship* integrated Wilhelm's individual growth into the realm of the Tower precisely at the point where the novel took up the thread of the fragment, *Wilhelm Meister's Theatrical Mission*. Wilhelm attains maturity within the community of his friends. In the *Travels* these friends act as the founders of a new world and give a universal significance to their undertaking. At the same time the convictions at the basis of their action are expressed through the principles and practice of an educational institution.

In his last years Goethe abandoned his customary reticence about his innermost beliefs. Standing, "so to speak, outside of time," he now felt capable of presenting himself more purely than before.[1] In his presentation of an ideal scheme of education he expressed convictions which he had thought through for many years. Once more the wisdom that underlies the whole conception of the novel is reflected by the Pedagogic Province. Here it is given the concreteness of pedagogic practice.[2] Within this framework Goethe presented in a new and succinct version his religion of reverence and the ethics developing from it. The wisdom of the Abbé and of Makarie is shown in the daily reality of an educational institution built upon Goethe's conception of the "original" religion.

Goethe's pedagogic thought is based on principles he had in common with Johann Amos Comenius,[3] the seventeenth-century Moravian brother whose *Orbis Sensualium Pictus* Goethe used as a boy. Comenius conceived pedagogy as a religious service to mankind, which is intended to attain unity and peace in the community of saints. From his equally spiritualist basis Goethe arrived at similar conclusions, colored by his convictions about the function of the arts and crafts in the growth of man.

The debate about education and its underlying anthropology had never ceased since the exciting impact of Rousseau's *Émile*. Pestalozzi had become the protagonist of a social conception of education in theory and practice. Fichte, in his *Addresses to the German Nation*, had proposed the isolation of the young generation from all contacts with the past world of bad habits and unphilosophical ways of living. From such a pedagogic segregation he expected the national and human recovery of the Germans. The discussion about the purposes and methods of education developed into legislation and pedagogic experiments, just as liberal ideas had taken the lead in reform during the Napoleonic wars. The tension between freedom and authority, *Humanität* and nationalism, liberal and orthodox religious conceptions in education continued during the stalemate of the Restoration Period following the Congress of Vienna.

In this situation Goethe presented his own ideas about the ends and means of education. In decisive points they are strictly opposed to the main tendencies of his time. Indirectly they are connected with his own experience in supervising the academic institutions of the duchy of Weimar, a branch of administration with which he was still concerned even after he gave up his other public duties. The few but decisive characteristics by which Goethe outlined the education of the future citizen of the new community are derived from his deepest convictions. He still holds that education should aim at the free self-mastery of man, but this aim is shown as attainable only on the basis of a religious reverence which enables man to live well in community with his fellows.

Goethe did not share Rousseau's romantic view of man's original goodness or his criticism of civilization for degrading it. Consequently he could not approve of educational maxims which reduce the responsibility of elders or superiors for the child to the task of protecting him from damaging himself. The pedagogues of his Province go so far as to impose upon their pupils an order which they will understand only later, after they have grown in experience. Goethe had in common with Pestalozzi the freedom from social prejudices. He objected to Pestalozzi's methods where he felt that they cultivated the intellect in a one-sided fashion and thereby tended to engender a deceitful insolence.[4] In contrast to Fichte's scheme, Goethe's pedagogic institution is international rather than national and it is interwoven with the daily life of the region in which it is located rather than isolated from it.

In a sense, the Pedagogic Province is like a residential school in a healthy country environment. Despite the firmness of the principles which govern it, the Pedagogic Province anticipates the central position which Ruskin gave to the crafts in the educational process, and the methods used by the pedagogues are practically those of the modern *Arbeitsschule*.[5] The religious convictions which in Goethe's thought form the condition of human culture are fundamental for the life and organization of the Province. It aims at training man's capabilities rather than his theoretical knowledge; its vocational training is designed to be an education for living also; and it establishes a community spirit among its pupils which is to prepare them for their future life.

When he arrives at the Province with Felix, Wilhelm is surprised at the gestures the boys use to greet the supervisor who accompanies the visitors.[6] A ritual gives outward expression to an intangible inner attitude and at the same time indicates the grade of moral education at which each pupil has arrived. Three forms of greeting indicate the three kinds of reverence which the pupil is taught, step by step, to grasp and to express. With the exception of expulsion, the only disciplinary measure of which we are told is withdrawal of the privilege of observing the signs of reverence. By the ritual of the religion of reverence Goethe emphasizes that the supreme aim of education in the Province is ethical rather than intellectual or professional.

As a part of the pedagogic methods, the ritual implies the basic conviction that man ought to bring his inner attitude and its outward manifestations into harmony. Therefore the opportunity given for expression by gesture should be conducive, conversely, to an increasing comprehension of the inner meaning of the gesture. The pedagogues of the Province hold that it is not only acceptable but necessary to encourage the exercise of these forms of expression although they may not yet be fully understood. The doctrine of reverence is imposed upon the pupils in accordance with the principle *credo ut intelligam*. Using the adopted signs will teach their meaning. Since these signs represent the fundamentals of any religion, unconditional observation of them involves the practice of toleration. The required form is intended to help the pupil avoid misplacing the "absolute" by attaching it to objects of secondary or false significance. This minimum of ritual is upheld with the utmost firmness in correspondence with the requirements of the original religion. It is regarded as essential to education for freedom.

Each pupil begins with the first grade of reverence. He is granted or refused permission to ascend to higher grades. This means that the pupil's education is built upon his sense of honor, and his honor is connected with his status in regard to the central religious and ethical goal. The decision as to the pupil's educational status rests with his supervisor, whose disciplined objectivity is fully trusted. The educators of the Province are mature men who, through their self-education in resignation, have succeeded in objectifying their own personalities. The system Goethe describes is social and humane, since it is based on the precondition that the educators live up to the requirements of the Province. Not only are subjective prejudices counteracted by the emphasis upon one basic criterion, but differences of intellectual capacity are eliminated from the elements causing a differentiation of the pupil's status, since this is determined by his ethical conduct. Highest among his achievements rates his self-co-ordination with others. Only when he has learned to respect others can he respect himself and attain freedom. If one understands democracy as the theoretical affirmation and practical maintenance of the ethical equality among men, Goethe's system is the most democratic that can possibly be imagined.

The stipulation of an equal ethical chance and an equal educational goal for all is, however, combined with the cultivation of individual differentiation. It is expressed by a variety of clothing, the choice of which is left to the individual in accordance with the Province's strict opposition to uniformity. Wilhelm is told that even should a tendency toward uniformity appear among the pupils, its realization would be rendered difficult by unobtrusive means.[7] The community spirit of the pupils is encouraged at its religious and ethical roots. Reverence is considered the foremost agent of the education for man's freedom within the community. Goethe elsewhere explicitly stated that it is one of man's innate desires.[8] This capacity for reverence must, above all else, be most carefully developed. It is imperative that it be consciously guided and formed, since it depends mainly on this fundamental aspect of education whether or not the pupil becomes human in the full sense of the word. As the foundation of the pedagogy practiced in the Province, this religion of reverence corresponds to Goethe's concept of the original and universal religion, even though Christian forms and symbols prevail in the educational practice.

Reverence is an inner attitude that needs to be understood in order to grow firm and reliable. The three grades which compose it relate man to the things above, to the things below, and to the things around him. The first grade is reverence for the sphere above. A gesture indicating it is prescribed for the minors. Thus they testify "that there is a God who is manifested through the images of parents, teachers, and superiors."[9] Educational authority is conceived of as an office. It is authority, however, and the ultimate guarantee against its abuse is the spirit in which it is exercised and controlled by the superior and his three helpers. This authority has the purpose and the result of drawing the adolescent's attention to the limitations of human existence: there is always something superior to man.

The second grade of reverence is directed toward the sphere below man. The gifts of the earth make human life possible and give man both joy and pain. Danger from "below" accompanies him throughout life. Recognition of the positive and negative aspects of his relation to the sphere below is fundamental for gaining a balanced attitude toward it. But "as soon as possible" the pupil is freed from concentrating on this theme to turn to the third grade of reverence: reverence for others. "We call him to collect himself, to turn toward his fellows and orient himself toward them. . . . Only in connection with those equal to him does he face the world."[10] Reverence for others is the condition of fruitful community with them in that it breaks down any self-centered isolation.

Out of the combination of these three kinds of reverence the fourth arises, reverence for one's self. Before the adolescent can become a person he has to understand and accept for himself the three limitations of the individual. Practicing reverence for one's self presupposes a distance from one's self not unlike that of a portraitist from his subject. Here Goethe teaches what he practiced. Taking it as a given task, he viewed with creative self-criticism his own individuality, its limitations and its possibilities. It is through the ethics of reverence that the individual is to be reconciled to the resignation demanded of him. His pride is put in the right place. A man is limited from above and from below. He does not have more worth than others and only in community with them is he able to render his service. If the ethical value of man forms the criterion of his self-respect, his awareness of individual limitations should not humiliate him.

The three stages of reverence reappear in the three religions taught in the Province. They are called the ethnical, the philosophic, and the Christian; paintings on the walls of the main building illustrate them.[11] The ethnical religion is presented by the Old Testament stories and by parables from Greek mythology. The essence of man's historical existence, as mirrored in the fate that typically befalls whole peoples, is their object. Their educational aim is support of reverence for the sphere superior to man. It culminates in the veneration of the omnipresent creator-God. Historically, and at the same time on principle, this religion represents "the first beneficial severance from a low fear. All the so-called pagan religions are of this kind, whatever name they may have."[12] In the Pedagogic Province no religion that is based merely on fear is respected.

The second hall shows the life of Christ. It represents the religion which is based upon reverence for that which is equal to us. The pictures representing this "philosophic religion" end with the Last Supper. They extol the mediating mission of the human being by presenting Christ as the incarnation of the Logos, the *incarnatio verbi.*

The philosopher who sets himself in the middle must draw down to himself everything that is higher, and up to himself everything that is lower, and only in this central condition does he deserve the name of wise man. Since he now sees through the relation to his equals and therefore to the whole of mankind and to all other earthly surroundings, both necessary and accidental, he lives in the cosmic sense in the truth alone.[13]

It is the sage Christ, the supreme incarnation of wisdom among those "good and wise to the highest degree," who is celebrated here as a model for imitation. He is the mediator, *kat' exochen,* and as such he is called the Sage. Significantly, the image of the original Christian community concludes this series of didactic paintings, which correspond to the third grade of reverence. The confirmation of the spirit of community is the central aim of this third stage of achievement.

The pictures illustrating the third religion—which corresponds to the second grade of reverence—are shown only when the mature pupil leaves the Province. They adorn the "Sanctuary of Suffering," and we are told that they are devoted to the suffering and crucifixion of the Savior. A deep veneration for these sufferings causes the pedagogues to cover them with the veil of secrecy in order to avoid any precocious play with the ineffable ground "in which the divine depth of suffering is hidden."[14] There are domains of life which must be withdrawn from intellectual or fanciful curiosity. Before he leaves the Province the pupil is equipped with whatever knowledge of suffering he may need in the future course of his life.

The wise Christ forms the center of this education.

The life of this divine man has no connection with the world history of his time. Here the living wisdom is pronounced, the wisdom which does not cause strife; it is not an opinion about what is right or wrong; irrefutably it is the right or wrong itself. He shows to all those who are concerned about maintaining a certain elevation in wisdom and living what they have to expect from the world.[15]

Thus Christ, as the wise God-man, becomes the model for imitation. From the ethnical understanding of religion the pupil is guided to comprehension of the spirit as manifest in Christ. At first the historical realm of religious institutions is explored to its foundation, faith in the creator. Then the inwardness of the loving and creative spirit is evoked. The pupil is called to understand, to appropriate to his innermost self, and to practice, this spirit of reverence. Christ is seen as its highest incarnation. Finally, the pupil is shown where, if necessary, he may deepen his reverence for the sphere below man. It is in harmony with Goethe's conception of the mediating role of the human being that everything is done to prevent a negative or evasive attitude toward life, whether by overemphasis on its suffering or on its sinfulness.

As all three kinds of reverence together result in the fourth reverence for one's self as a creature, so all the three religions together compose the one true religion.

Man, when he has achieved his highest potentiality, may consider himself the best that God and Nature have brought forth; indeed, he may dwell on this height without again being sunk into the ordinary by conceit and selfishness.[16]

Reverence, as Goethe understands it, is also the means by which man overcomes anxiety. Such victory over fear enables him to cope fruitfully with the task of living. Neither "awe" nor "respect" renders correctly the meaning of the German *Ehrfurcht*, which combines fear with affection and signifies warmth coupled with distance.[17] The ultimate object of all the four dimensions of reverence is the creation, including its inner antagonism, the mediation of which is the life task of man. The dynamic quality of life makes vulnerable the entelechy of the creation. The cognitive component of reverence enables man to face this dynamism and to distinguish between those factors of life that endanger its end and those that call for support in view of its end. Through its emotional component the cult of reverence binds man's personality to the living of reverence. It results in bringing man's faculty of reason to bear upon his conduct and in introducing to him the higher guiding power of the spirit.

Goethe named and defined an experience of normative character in the religion of reverence, which is both metaphysical and ethical. In harmony with his cosmology, it presupposes both the transcendence and the immanence of the divine. Based upon the recognition of the finiteness of human existence, reverence touches upon the divine and accepts life as it is, not out of necessity but out of freedom. The inwardness of reverence distinguishes it from mere respect. As the commandment governing man's relation to his fellow men, it becomes an ethical force. In consequence it strengthens the sense of justice. It removes the decisive criterion from the outward semblance or deed to the basic ethical quality. It restores to man the proper evaluation of mental faculties and therefore acts as an agent of cognition. Thus it corresponds to Goethe's subordination of the intellect to reason and stands in agreement with his demand that the cognitive mind shall ultimately grasp the inner meaning of things. It even teaches men how to face the deepest suffering and become capable of a response to it.

The ultimate source of this reverence is the experience of

the numinous. The outward forms by which its significance is stressed are designed to make the pupil attentive to this inner experience, to which the highest value is imparted. The resulting asceticism is inner-worldly in that it accepts the world and compels man to resign himself to it while strengthening his best capacity for the task of mediation between the ideal and the phenomenal.

In the light of the religion of reverence, the leading figures of the Tower community gain in stature. The Abbé's wisdom and love and Jarno's relentless clarity are built on it. In Makarie, reverence is not only the basis of her guiding position within an ever-widening circle of devoted friends; it becomes an agent of cosmological inspiration. Makarie's feeling of the stellar system within herself is the strongest of those passages in Goethe's work which relate the human microcosm to the universe. In Natalie reverence is nature. In Susanne it grows through mastery of adverse and favorable circumstances toward the poise expressed by her beauty. Reverence protects one from the temptation to indulge in emotions or to take pride in intellectual brilliance. It lifts love above mere passion and integrates it into reason. It defines the positive aspect of that same process of education which is negatively expressed by the term "resignation." It is to be the nerve-center of the new community.

As a formulation of Goethe's "original religion" the wisdom of reverence is interreligious and universal. It represents the idea of the *una sancta catholica* in the sense of the spiritual church. It leaves undisturbed the historical varieties of devotional forms, and toleration is its necessary consequence. But this toleration comes to an end where the universal basis of religious conduct is endangered or abandoned. By no means shall the art of resigning himself leave man and society defenseless against breach of the law. The wisdom of reverence is the all-pervading spirit of conduct, and therefore also the source of legislation and of the preservation of law. Thus within the novel the significance of the religion of reverence extends far beyond its role in the Pedagogic Province. The chance for survival of the institutions of the new community depends upon the faithful observance of the commandments of this universal religion. From it springs the sober and unsentimental serenity of the emigrants.

Since religious and ethical education is the primary aim of the Province, intellectual pursuits are given only a secondary importance. The realm of theory appears to be reserved almost exclusively for the superiors. They master the art of saying no more in any particular situation than they deem conducive to proper understanding and fruitful action. The guide who receives Wilhelm knows exactly the limits to which he is permitted to go when explaining what Wilhelm wonders about.[18] In other words, man's cognitive faculties are not given an independent position and value. They are integrated into the purpose of the life which they serve. Intellectual insight is facilitated in the moment when life experience needs it to grow firm. It is discouraged as long as it is not balanced by such experience.

Goethe's aversion to any merely ideological procedure finds an expression in this principle which he himself practiced in his relations with others. His conversations as related by friends and visitors reflect not only his partners' degree of perception but his own way of attuning his statements to their receptivity. The counterpart of Goethe's inclination to hide behind his world of symbolical forms was his readiness to follow the flow of communication as soon as his partner encouraged it by adequate responsiveness.

The subordination of knowledge to living does not contradict Goethe's firmness in advocating the freedom of knowledge in instruction and research.[19] To him scholarship and art are, as we saw, built upon the religious foundation which is also basic to the Pedagogic Province. Because of the constructive character of scholarship and art they

will, by virtue of their own strength, prove superior to mis-
leading conceptions if the freedom of production and debate is guaranteed. The pedagogy of the Province, however, implies a philosophic anthropology which, beyond a
definite view of the laws governing human development,
demands an order of values complying with Goethe's conception of the position of man in the universe.

The educational practice of the Province is organized
into different "regions" to which, according to their inclinations, the pupils are assigned. A vocational education is
built on the basis of the common spirit. To ward off the
danger of one-sidedness, balancing measures are taken
within each region. The aim common to all branches of
education and training is mastery of the subject. It is attained through active trial and experience. Thus Felix is
taken into agriculture and he has to serve an apprenticeship
by advancing from the lowest forms of work upward. To
balance the rough agricultural labor, he learns languages.
Here again, the aim of teaching is the mastery of language
in speech and poetry; the method of teaching is concentrated upon practice to the extent that one foreign language
is taught exclusively over a given period of time, during
which only this language is used.

Thus all the fields of knowledge are treated as arts. A
working mastery of their proper methods, rather than the
abstract knowledge of method, is the goal throughout. So
in the region of the fine arts emphasis is laid on the activity
of creative imagination and its control; the pupils are asked
to reproduce on their own, through the medium of their
craft, some precise event which has been briefly described
to them.[20] Every measure taken is devoted to kindling the
initiative before criticism is encouraged.

The Province is designed to be a mirror of life. The
achievements of each region are of significance for the
whole. The buildings, for example, are erected by the Province's own craftsmen and are decorated by its own artists.

The region of the artists is distinguished from that of the musicians by its splendor.

Creative artists must be housed like kings and gods; how should they otherwise build and decorate for kings and gods? In the end, they must lift themselves above the ordinary to such an extent that the whole community of the people may feel itself ennobled in and through their works.[21]

The social function of the artist is manifestation of his inner world through visible forms; that of the musician, the translation of his inwardness into tone. Both live in a competitive relationship with the poet, and each supports the other by confining himself to the laws inherent in his particular medium. The fundamental conception of art is common to them all. The enjoyment of its achievements rests in the reflection of the divine through the beautiful work of man's hand. Art is praise and *sacrificium*. This common end constitutes the brotherhood of the artists.

> *Tausendfach und schön entfliesse*
> *Form aus Formen deiner Hand,*
> *Und im Menschenbild geniesse,*
> *Dass ein Gott sich hergewandt.*
> *Welch ein Werkzeug Ihr gebrauchet,*
> *Stellet Euch als Brüder dar;*
> *Und gesangsweis flammt und rauchet*
> *Opfersäule vom Altar.*[22]

The community spirit is manifested and strengthened by common singing. The serene simplicity which distinguishes the compositions of Goethe's friend Zelter is characteristic of the songs of the Province. The song with which the *Novelle* culminates is in the same style as the songs of the artists and emigrants in the *Travels*. Everyone is capable of sharing in this common undertaking which forms another part of the community's liturgy. As in the organization of the orchestra, the co-operation of the individual in the community singing leaves to each participant his selfhood while co-ordinating him into the whole action. Thus the music sung in common mirrors the solution of any social problem by the community. Zelter's compositions left the rhythmical body of the poetry intact while heightening and musically determining the tonality inherent in the poem. In consequence, his music was fit for self-subordinating co-ordination with Goethe's poetry. Zelter was reluctant to use the song as a manifestation of dramatic and emotional conflict. He conceived of it rather as an agent to crystallize and reaffirm constructive emotion joined to forward-looking and even didactic thought. This anti-Romantic tendency corresponded, in the realm of music, to Goethe's all-pervading principle of resignation. For the same reason Zelter's music came closer to the requirements of Goethe's community than that of any other composer of the time. Goethe's predilection for Zelter corresponded to his neglect of forms which, while richer in musicality, had, he felt, a dispersive rather than an integrating impact.[23]

The realm of education is by no means separated from the adult world but forms an organic part of it. The miners' festival to which Wilhelm is led during his second visit to the Province reflects through another medium, as it were, the social spirit of its education.[24] The work of mining, an epitome of communal co-operation, goes on during the year in secret below the surface. It is made wholly visible at the festival. Life itself matters rather than knowledge of it. Thus the miners' festival forms a part of Wilhelm's initiation into the wisdom underlying the whole community and, significantly, it is on this occasion that Jarno-Montan reveals to him the reasons for his aversion to "useless strife and idle remembrance,"[25] for his resolution to keep his deepest convictions to himself rather than to make them the object of aimless discussion. Jarno's attitude accentuates once more that of the superiors of the Province. Unless related to action, knowledge is worthless; unless connected

with experience, it is shallow. The educational practice in
the Province is devoted to the rhythmical correlation of
thought and experience essential to the crafts and to the
arts metaphorically demonstrated by the life of the miners.
Thus its role of service to communal life is once more restored to the intellect.

The same ascetic insistence on serious and fruitful activities causes the pedagogues to ban the theater from their
realm. This "frivolous art," Wilhelm is given to understand,
requires a lazy audience to which the born mime is inclined
to present his delusive tricks.[26] When used by the theater,
other arts deteriorate. Pupils who show an irresistible inclination to dramatics are removed from the Province and sent
to theaters outside. At this juncture Goethe refers with
irony to the many years he himself devoted to the theater.
He seems to have abandoned altogether the hope that the
theater might fulfill an educational mission. Certainly he
banned it from his utopia: for the community which cel-
ebrates the universe and man's position within it through
the serene earnestness of its daily action is not in need of
any delusive play of fancy which remains without consequences and, therefore, detracts from the task of life instead of furthering it. The verdict of the old Goethe against
the theater is analogous to that of Plato against the poets.

Devoted, on the educational level, to the realization of
the ideal society, the Province does its work in the original
branches of labor. Mining, agriculture, building, and weaving are basic. Sculpture, painting, speech, poetry, and music
represent its cultural intensification. This division of labor
is simple. Goethe's opposition to general education, the
allgemeine Bildung which Jarno loathes, is directed against
its theoretical character rather than against Goethe's own
earlier postulation of harmony and totality. As we learn
from Felix's assignments, the teachers counteract one-sidedness in the individual pupil. The totality of character stands
in harmony with the mastery of a special branch of work.

All the interrelated branches have in common an ethical significance. A common spirit holds together the manifold talents, individualities, and services; it conveys its power to each member and guides all toward the one great goal of a healthy common life.

It seemed as though no one achieved anything by his own power, but as though a secret spirit was intensely alive in them all, directing them toward one single great goal.[27]

The elimination of the theater, the absence of mechanical production and of the corresponding intellectual disciplines, the emphasis laid upon arts and crafts, and the specific role of the numerically small intelligentsia governing the Province, indicate the opposition to nineteenth-century tendencies which Goethe expressed through this image of an education for a future culture. The humanistic content of the educational program is merged with its basis in the original religion. Goethe could reduce this image of a utopia of education to the simplest fundamentals of wisdom necessary for the way of living he intended to describe.

These educational principles are in harmony with his aim of establishing and maintaining standards. This is the task of the superiors of the Province. What he had in mind was not knowledge about culture but the creation of culture. For this, the art of living in fidelity to accepted values is decisive. It is precisely this faithfulness which relates the Province to the image of St. Joseph II and to that of the Persians in the *Divan*, who observe the legacy of their founder as the guarantee of their life of culture. The life of the Province is deliberately designed in opposition to the tendencies of modern society. The pupil is educated for an exodus, be it by emigration or inner resistance. Rather than to adjust himself to a given social reality, he is taught to obey the norm inherent in himself as a human being.

The religious bases of education in the Province are as wide as Goethe's conception of original religion. They are universally human in character. By the image of the Pedagogic Province, Goethe translated into terms of pedagogy his concept of *Humanität* and showed the firmness and the wide range of its religious foundations. They enable the superiors to disregard traditional boundaries of religious confession or of nationality and, at the same time, to be rigid in attending to their central task. Once more we recognize in these men the features of the men of wisdom who form Goethe's evangelical communion. Within the small domain of their poised and considerate activity they educate for the Abbé's world association. Instruction and even practical training are not ends in themselves, but serve in the formation of the pupil toward self-mastery within the common life. The realm of aesthetic beauty mediates between the daily duties of man and the religious significance of his existence. The varying forms of art reflect the manifold creation through which the divine spirit reveals itself. The quintessence of cultured life is man's response to the creation, and through the most beautiful symbols he is to praise the ultimate truth. To one who, through the medium of art, thus possesses the sense of truth it is granted to live in calm expectation of "the light of highest clarity."

> *Wie Natur im Vielgebilde*
> *Einen Gott nur offenbart,*
> *So im weiten Kunstgefilde*
> *Webt ein Sinn der ewigen Art;*
> *Dieses ist der Sinn der Wahrheit,*
> *Der sich mit dem Schönsten schmückt,*
> *Und getrost der höchsten Klarheit*
> *Hellsten Tags entgegenblickt.*[28]

14

The New Community

The Exodus—A Utopia of Constructive Humanness
Power and Society—The Critique of
Modern Civilization—The Myth of Renewal

THE PEDAGOGIC PROVINCE reflects the spirit which is to guide the emigrants in the foundation of a sound communal life overseas. We become acquainted with this central undertaking of the friends of the Tower in the moment when Lenardo organizes the emigration and gives Wilhelm an insight into the principles of its future government. To those who decide to remain in the old country, Odoard offers at the same time his project of inner colonization.[1] Both these plans are presented as forms of an exodus from the existing problematic society, and in both of them the inner meaning of human association is seen as a constructive life of peace.

The association is formed by the free resolution of each participant. Lenardo prepares the conclusion of the covenant and interprets its motives and institutions to the associates. Some of them at once express their understanding and approval; for the spirit that is to govern the new community is that of man's healthy nature, and the details of the planned institutions arise from the consensus of those present. *Ubi homines sunt modi sunt*, the proverb on the door of the assembly room, hints at human relationship as the source of all forms by which men like to be and to remain together. It is the life from which institutions arise that they are to serve.[2]

Wilhelm realizes that a common spirit is already in the making when he meets the first among the associates, two young carpenters who ask him for a poetic text in order to sing it. They quickly grasp his wanderer's song; they improvise on it, others fall in, and the next day the full meeting sings the refrains which express the common situation, the melancholy anticipation of departure and the joyful acceptance of worldwide wandering. It is a society governed by the spirit of art to which we are thus introduced; in it poet and artist are a part of the people, their product is part of the common life. The community song, uniting all in independence and co-operation, reflects "the significant purposes of life."[3] It is love and action that Wilhelm's song praises. The simplicity of its rhythm corresponds to the simple clarity of the common purpose. It mirrors the bond of religion and ethical awareness which, "in the end, hold men together." Art and thought are not ends in themselves. They serve the purely human which gains reality in this association.

Lenardo subordinates himself to the laws required by the common purpose and practices them in uninhibited fashion.[4] He transforms into a thoroughly humane art of leadership the patriarchal talent of his uncle. He considers himself merely the bond holding these emigrants together. As Natalie's brother Friedrich could become a member of the society only because he was able to offer a service, so the barber is accepted only on condition that he forego his professional vice of gossiping, and he does so with a joyful self-irony. Resignation is required from all if the gap between the people and the intelligentsia is to be bridged. The principles of communal life developed by the Abbé are translated by Lenardo into social and political organization. He is the right person for this task because of the ethical sensitivity which, as we know, he evidenced in his relations to Susanne.

A free convention has decided the basic laws of the new

community. Some of the rules, at the moment when Friedrich explains them to Wilhelm,[5] "still circulate as problems within the society." The new order is understandable only from its spiritual basis. In contrast to modern constitutions, there are few guarantees of rights and privileges. They are superfluous where the spirit of *Humanität* is developed into communal responsibility. It is the foundation of the new community on this spirit that constitutes the core of Goethe's image. It is from the spirit that he expects a good order to emerge; by the spirit it will be maintained. The humanness of the new community is the opposite of the impersonal immensity of modern society, which began to develop in Goethe's time. Goethe's ideal community is intended to refocus attention on the purpose of any social organization to serve not its own but generally human ends.

At the moment when each emigrant must finally decide whether or not to go abroad, Lenardo appraises the undertaking. He makes the participants aware of the universal significance of their action. Although he begins by praising the quiet and steady flow of life within the small confines of family land, he points out that wandering is a fundamental phenomenon of historical existence. Man's home is not confined to a definite place, but is rather to be found in his way of living. Alone, the individual is helpless; with the aid of others, he can act on the basis of knowledge and reasonable foresight. In this sense Lenardo feels the new community to be included in a "world association." "The conception is one of simple greatness; through reason and energy its execution is easy."[6] The cherished values of life are to be found in man himself wherever he may wander, rather than in circumstances. The original religion, conceived in terms of the *Credo* and practiced through the cult of reverence, gives him the strength of toleration and the certainty of ethical judgment.

Lenardo interprets the common undertaking as essentially human and, therefore, universal. Wandering is the lot of man; it carries with it the chance for either happiness or a curse. With horror Lenardo reminds his audience of the barbarism of the conquerors, but he mentions by name "the noble imperial wanderer Hadrian, who . . . traversed the inhabited world subjected to him and thus took full possession of it."[7] With his praise of the Roman emperor, Lenardo comes closest to expressing the universal significance of the emigration. The spirit in which it is undertaken is directed toward universal peace, the cause of the emperor, the *Pax Romana*. The hope of two millennia, expressed both in the Antonine conception of the *imperium* and in the catholicity of the medieval Christian idea of empire, stands on the horizon of the new community.

Then the speaker returns to the practical issue. In man himself the foundation is to be laid for the organic community among all men. His religion and his ethics are human rather than restricted to the narrow confines of nations, groups, or races. Theoretical stipulations are reduced to a minimum, since good organization is regarded as the assured consequence of the confident friendship which engenders a sound conception of life. If thoroughly understood, the community spirit will become manifest through daily action. Aware of its purpose, the new community shall proceed, through its simple daily services, to translate into reality the entelechy of man which is understood as *Humanität*.

Thus the emigrants are described as pioneers. They leave a world which "lives from the past and perishes under it."[8] They exchange it for a common life built upon the practice of the spirit of reverence. All the details of its formation are subordinate to the religious and ethical basis of the undertaking. Essential to the pioneering character of the enterprise is the original religion, which stands beyond dispute. Protestants and Catholics are given freedom of worship: the religion of the new community is Christian in so far as the wisdom of Christ takes a central and paradigmatic part in it; all must accept the fundamentals of the religion of reverence. The religious tenets of the new community, however, are not to be construed as a "Christian" ideology in the name of which un-Christian conduct might be justified.

The exodus is shown as a simple, modest, and practical action. The most universal of purposes is pursued by the most concrete and realistic of deeds. The good life has no more to do with its location at Herrnhut than it has with America as the site of the new community. Rather, the good life is "right here"; that is, in the men who resolve to live it.[9] The beginning and the end of human existence are "drawn into one" by this translation into the concrete of Goethe's original evangelical communion. The task of bridging over the dualism inherent in the nature of man is viewed in a thoroughly unromatic fashion. It is neither to better themselves nor to satisfy their desires nor to escape from reality that the emigrants come together. Intent upon living *sub specie aeternitatis*, they obey the ethical command revealed by the voice within man as well as by the study of man's nature. This ethical commandment is given reality through meeting "the demand of the day."[10] Goethe's ideal community is neither a romanticism of the past nor of the future. It pleads for the *ritornar al segno*, the conversion to a simple but timeless truth through sound living.

This ultimate result of Goethe's lifelong concern with the problem of the human community forms an organic part of his philosophic conceptions and his social thought. It is almost idle to ask how far he was stimulated by contemporary ideas and to which one of the social philosophies of the nineteenth century his own view came closest. He was certainly acquainted with Saint-Simonianism and received that sect's journal, *Le Globe*. He read the diaries of Prince Bernhard of Weimar,[11] which included reports on Robert Owen's settlement at New Harmony. But the significance of the ideal world which Goethe himself constructed consists in the inner logic by which it grew out of his fundamental convictions. It was the religious basis of the new community that lifted it above the ideological conflicts which came to dominate the nineteenth and twentieth centuries and are rooted in the historical events of Goethe's lifetime.

Aware to an extraordinary degree of the intellectual and social dismemberment prior to, during, and after the Napoleonic era, Goethe anticipated many of its future consequences. It was in response to this foresight that he created the image of the new community. The issue he thus raises is still significant for our time because Goethe was more than an exponent of his own time; he was a thinker who incessantly strove beyond historical contingencies toward metahistorical truth. Goethe's image of a constructive and humane way of common life is meant to be a challenge to the human being and his capacity to modify the form he has received from nature. When Wilhelm Meister learns that precisely "by giving up our existence we come to exist,"[12] he is led from the "I" to the "we" of his community with others. The freedom for which this community as a lawgiving authority strives is identical with the norm which Goethe seeks in his morphological study of man. The dynamic nature of man and its limitations demand that life and freedom be conquered anew day by day.

> *Nur der verdient sich Freiheit wie das Leben,*
> *Der täglich sie erobern muss.*[13]

With the dream of standing on free soil in the midst of his free people, the dying Faust ends his earthly course. His legacy of freedom is mirrored in Goethe's image of the new community. This image opposes and challenges Goethe's time and ours; it belongs with, and is the last of, those utopian images of the good life which, much more than wishful fantasies, are symbols of the idea, the original phenomenon, of human existence. The history of the utopia "forms a part of the history of the faith in the spirit."[14]

The utopian novel is intended to liberate the reader from the habitual and the degraded by showing him the opposite: the ideal of communal life in the state of realization. Such an image need not remove itself from so-called reality, since one's inner self may live in tension with outer conditions. Goethe kept his desirable community within the limits of the probable. His will to reform begins with man's relation to others and to himself. On the formation of man depend the institutions which he builds. In Goethe's novel, the institutions of the new society serve as illustrations rather than as a model. They are designed to help man on the road toward pure humanity and presuppose his resolution to pursue it.

The highest good which the old Goethe deemed accessible to the individual was that calmness of soul which results from the everlasting power of idea and love. Meaning is imparted to man's love, and fruitfulness is granted to his life, if he devotes himself to the realm of the idea which becomes evident through the phenomenal world. The human community and its organization are to serve this "cosmic" meaning of human existence. To this end the rule of a wise order which has binding power is needed. In Goethe's work a variety of such forms of communal order is presented. As the *summum bonum* is manifest to the human mind through a variety of formulations, so the conduct of life, which obeys the advice of nature and spirit, can be organized in many different ways. But each of these forms requires faithfulness to the law of *Humanität*, the original religion. Each of these forms may give expression to it in its particular terms while preserving the law common to all possible forms of the ideal community: the self-resignation of the members in order to serve the common human good.

The religious community of "Die Geheimnisse" is devoted to the contemplation of the universal significance of human existence, as manifested through the varieties of re-

ligious experience and articulation. The state of the "Vermächtnis Alt-Persischen Glaubens" is founded on faithfulness to a simple legacy which integrates the daily duties into
their universal context.[15] St. Joseph II lives in devotion to
the sacred image which is model and mirror for the small
domain of his existence. The personalities of Humanus, the
Abbé, and Makarie hold the life around them to its center
of gravitation. The commandments which the old Persian
gave to his people include liturgical forms which visibly
express and confirm the relation between the temporal and
the eternal. Hersilie's uncle, the enlightened puritan, also
lives for the sake of his chosen standards. It is on the faithful
art of translating the highest convictions into the conduct
of life that Goethe places his emphasis. Each of the above
figures seeks truth rather than novelty, constructive action
rather than dispute. Each, within the limits of the possible
to which he has resigned himself, has found and tries to fulfill the desirable.

Even such ethical resolution, however, does not dispose of
the problem of power. As we have seen, Goethe regarded
power as the reality of the demonic whenever it emancipates
itself. In the figure of Timur, which mirrors Napoleon, he
described in unmistakable terms the vicious circle of violence which, in the end, ruins those who are possessed by it.
Goethe's new community, when embarking for a new
world, answers the challenge of the demonic by the religious ethics on which it is built, by the asceticism with
which it resolves to live, and by the institutions which are
to serve it. It is the determination of the emigrants to control the danger of self-annihilation which threatens the human world by checking the demonic immensity latent in
human nature. They know that ultimately the only valid
defense against the threat of power from within and without is resoluteness of spirit.

The emigrants consider it their main concern to take
overseas the advantages of civilization and leave the dis-

advantages behind.[16] What we are told of their future life
reveals an extreme of simplicity, motivated not only by the
pioneering stage of the new settlement but by the intention
of stressing the essentials from which culture is to arise.
When Goethe took occasion to put under a ban overseas
what he disliked at home, such as saloons, lending libraries,
or uniforms, he meant to combat false ways of "intensification" which give men stature and self-confidence from
without rather than from within. Jarno's scorn of general
education is directed against the semblance of learning by
which knowledge is turned into ambitious chatter. It is only
genuine and creative mentality that finds encouragement.
The giant St. Christoph—thus named because he carries
heavy loads over the mountains—tells the fable of the dangerous wager. The barber in the red coat who forsook his
gossiping in order to join the new community, tells the
story of "The New Melusine."[17] The number of intellec-
tuals in the group of emigrants is restricted, at least at the
beginning. We find ourselves among agriculturists, craftsmen, and artists; and when Odoard puts arts and crafts on
an equal level, he acts in the spirit of the others. If, for a
moment, we recall Ardinghello's utopian island of art and
beauty in Heinse's novel,[18] we feel all the more strongly the
sober and ascetic realism of the Abbé's scheme.

The decision to build a sound and healthy life demands
the renunciation of habits cherished by any sophisticated
civilization. There is no enjoyment of disputes; on the contrary, they are avoided. The intelligentsia is not an end in
itself; the artist is equal to the craftsman; meaningless entertainment is excluded; nothing is done simply to pass the
time; superfluous talk is ridiculed. Compared to life in a
modern city, Goethe's new community looks almost as simple, or even barren, as one of the primitive societies which
are the object of modern man's nostalgia. Everybody works;
but, true to Goethe's conviction that "sheer aimless activity,
of whatever kind, in the end makes bankrupt,"[19] work is

considered the means toward a good life. The warp and woof of its culture is formed by art and music, in which each member of the association can actively participate. Strict exclusion of distracting elements is the counterpart of the serene and vigorous spirit we find among the associates. They themselves consider their community as only one cell of a worldwide association of men of good will. Their purpose reaches beyond the ephemeral, and for this reason social distinctions disappear and human relations are honored.

The supervisors live in the same style as the other members of the community. They do not reside in a capital, the rise of which is considered an evil; they move about as the ancient German emperors did "in order to preserve unity in fundamental matters, and to let everybody have his will in secondary matters."[20] "The greatest need of a state is a courageous government."[21] Such a government is to arise from the life in pursuit of the common purpose. The eldest of the superiors alone is to have the right of disapproval and blame; he is called the acknowledged superior, *der anerkannte Älteste*.[22] Goethe implies that in an association of free men such recognition can be withdrawn. The role of the highest authority is conceived as similar to that of the eldest of the pedagogues: he is everywhere and nowhere; his government is immediate, his interference is not restricted except by the ethical presuppositions which make him fit for the office and include the principle of reducing interference to the minimum. "That government is the best which teaches us how to govern ourselves"—this maxim of Goethe's is valid also for the art of government in the new community.

When Goethe devised his utopia, he had witnessed a half-century of discussion about the legal constitution of government. That he passes over this question can only be interpreted as intentional. We may presume that he resolved not to take sides in this issue because he considered the success of any kind of government contingent upon the ethical agreement on which it was built. Thus the organic view of constitutional growth, as Möser and Burke expressed it, is transformed in Goethe's community into the interpretation of constitutional organization as the result of human relations, which are stabilized by the common view of life. The fundamental law is religious in character. Inevitably it will have consequences for administration and legislation. The community may tend to make increasingly strict laws, but legislation is considered as functionally related to life rather than abstractly preconceivable in detail.

Goethe toned down precisely those issues upon which nineteenth-century continental Europe laid the main stress. Where society is built upon a common ethical ground, where its superiors receive recognition on account of the ethical quality of their character and wisdom, the institutions designed to give constitutional protection to the individual may be neglected, and for this reason they are neglected in Goethe's community. Moreover, it is a question which hardly can be answered in an affirmative sense, whether any constitutional protection can be sufficient when the spirit from which it arose and which it serves has lost its binding power. It was Goethe's conviction that there is no ultimate protection from the abuse of power other than ethical strength.

By his anthropology, Goethe placed man between cosmos and chaos, sin and virtue. The new community is a symbol of the constructive possibilities given to him in this dynamic situation. Positive law must take into its purview the worst possible aspect of human nature. It is on the basis of the best possible side of man that the novel presents the universal end of human society. Without deluding himself about the reality of the demonic and the absurd in the course of history, Goethe formed a constructive vision which gives weight to man's chance for virtue.

The opposite aspect of man's nature, however, leads Goethe himself to the provision of some definite safeguards[23] against the abuse of freedom, although he does not recognize any ultimate guarantee against it save in the spirit. The police of the community is governed by the rule that nobody should become a nuisance to anybody else. The directors of the police are guided by a liberal conception of their service. They may admonish, blame, or remove those whose conduct becomes intolerable. It is left to their discretion when to call a jury and how large a one to call. Again, on the level of police action, the ethical personalities of the directors of police are trusted, rather than any detailed rules. Police action is devoted to serving the interests of the community as a whole. The organization of the judiciary branch of government refers, on the other hand, to the individual.

Goethe's text indicates that the separation of police and judiciary is maintained. "Punishment may be decreed only by an assemblage of jurors."[24] The protection of peace, for which purpose supreme power is vested in the state, is served by both police and judiciary. This functional justification of government implies that government involves a risk as soon as this function is no longer fulfilled. "We do not ask what right we have to govern: we govern. We do not care whether or not the people have a right to recall us: we are only cautious so that they may not be tempted to do so."[25]

The order provided by the law shall be strictly maintained. Goethe's insistence on legality of procedure results from the ethical basis of his concept of right, and is in harmony with his apology on behalf of reason and his distrust of uncontrolled passion. In other words, he is guided by his conviction that society is to pursue an educational end; he is as averse to breach of the law as to revolutionary action because of the demonic qualities and effects which, even against man's intention, sever the bond between his action and the idea of justice. Violence in any form shall be excluded from the new community. Police and judiciary act merely in defense of the social order, and, significantly, preparations for warfare are justified only by considerations of self-defense. The application of force is permissible in such eventualities. This precaution does not conflict with the resolution of the world association of the wanderers to work for the increasing limitation of the demonic forces.

Goethe gave more detailed indications of his constitutional convictions through his support of the principle of equality and his skepticism about majority rule. He considered privileges to be contradictory to the exigencies of association. He advised the individual to avail himself of the advantages of society by resigning his inborn claim to privilege.[26] This formulation of the third commandment of the religion of reverence transforms it into a social rule which implies voluntary subordination to the ethical law. Social and political equality, however, drastically restricts the liberty of the individual. The principle of equality is a moral one. It requires the free resolution to abandon selfishness and to be intent upon service rather than upon exception or immunity.[27]

Since Goethe holds that error is inevitable, he by no means takes reason for granted and is therefore skeptical about majority rule. He goes so far as to approve of it for ordinary affairs, whereas he announces his specific distrust of it in decisive moments of crisis. His suspicion comes close to negation when, in his aphorisms, he speaks of the formation of a majority out of "a few leaders followed by opportunists, men of weak judgment who assimilate themselves, and the masses who trail behind without knowing in the least what they want."[28] The partisan spirit which Goethe strikes at with the word *Parteigeist*, he considers the result of self-centeredness. "Man hates what he feels has not been done by himself; therefore the partisan spirit is so eager."[29] The political tensions following the Napoleonic era led Goethe to the bitter statement: "Nobody is capable of imagining that one can construct or support something except for the purpose of forming a faction."[30] The deeper

cause of this verdict must be sought in Goethe's conception
of reason and freedom. A free man should not influence
what he cannot responsibly judge. It is not even sufficient
that he is trying to think reasonably. It should be his self-
resigning intention to have reason as such govern. He should
want the desirable, not what he himself desires.

The partisan spirit which tends to prevent the understanding of any but one's own point of view stands in the
way of reason. In its extreme and disciplined forms it pre-
cludes any constructive debate. It is not surprising therefore
that the defenders of modern party dictatorship find it difficult to accept the views of a man who was so acutely aware
of the dangers inherent in the party spirit, to which they attach a monopoly of coercive power. Already those among
Goethe's contemporaries who were inclined to absolu-
tize party opinion, whether revolutionary or nationalistic,
blinded themselves to the deeper understanding of Goethe
and therefore branded him a "reactionary."

Actually, Goethe was "conservative" precisely and exclusively in upholding the one demand that public organization
serve the whole entelechy of man and society. Therefore
he could be skeptical with regard to partial views of society,
particularly when they were defended with conceited ar-
rogance in terms of general ideologies. Instead, he would
"honor the old foundations without abandoning the right,
again at some point to make a new beginning."[31] Goethe
held that each institution can be defended by interpreting
its rational inception and by claiming at the same time that
"what was true about it in the beginning, is still true now."
He also recognized, however, that institutions undergo a
change of meaning and function. Similarly, "great ideas
have a tyrannical effect as soon as they appear, and therefore, all too early, the advantages they bring about are transformed into the opposite."[32] The observation of history
taught Goethe how man's actions may estrange him from
his intentions. His distrust of ideologies, mirrored in the

figure of Jarno, justified him in maintaining a certain distance from the predominant political issues of his last decades. Without the common spirit, the institutions of any
community are empty; from the spirit embodied in the men
of the Tower the institutions of Goethe's ideal community
receive their meaning.

Like the political, so also the social organization of the
new community results from its supreme purpose. Goethe
was convinced that the main source of confusion among
men is "their treating the means as an end," and that therefore, with all their activity, "nothing is achieved, or perhaps
even something adverse is brought to pass."[33] The organization of property in Goethe's ideal state is to serve the ends
of the whole. As we have seen, the distinction of social privileges is abandoned on the ground of the prevailing spirit of
Humanität. The property of Lenardo, however, remains
his. He practices his uncle's maxim, "ownership and common property," by putting his domains to use on behalf of
the emigrants. Furthermore, he considers ownership justified "by the use made of it rather than by the way it was
acquired," and thus he remains faithful in his opposition to
the indivisibility and public protection of estates.[34] The
property of all the emigrants is expected to increase. In
other words, the social conditions which later came to be
termed proletarian are to be eliminated. This central tenet
of the new community is the inevitable consequence of its
religious and ethical foundation. It is not alone concern
about her own future and that of those entrusted to her
which makes Susanne afraid of the threatening proletarianism of the weavers, nor is her aversion to the machine caused
only by her sense of the more artistic nature of the work
done with hand tools. It is rather the inhumane impact of
anonymous economic forces that causes her anxiety.

Goethe was far from having any illusion that a change of
outer conditions could in itself bring about a change of
human attitude. He keeps his utopia above the issues of the

modern class struggle, which, from his point of view, appears as a deadlock because it tends to distract the participants from the central problem, which is ethical rather than economic. Since Goethe, during his early administrative experience, had observed the hosiery workers in Apolda, he was aware of the social tensions which became acute during his lifetime and foreshadowed the severest problems of the nineteenth century. In the *Geschirrfasser*[35] he personified the anonymous ruthlessness of technical and economic progress. Werner is the epitome of a one-sided businessman who attains higher usefulness only by his ultimate integration into the community of friends. In the hope for a form of existence worthy of the human being, Susanne moves away from her valley and the others decide to emigrate. The spirit that governs the new community and the character of Lenardo are the guarantees against abuse—personal guarantees which, in Goethe's eyes, are stronger than any legal protection could possibly be.

Also in regard to the problems of social structure, the appeal to ethical sensibility is the quintessence of Goethe's image. Since every person, with each of his actions, is measured by the service rendered, the outstanding quality of an individual can be accepted without disturbing the principle of human equality. As is demonstrated in the Pedagogic Province, talent and achievement will be recognized without envy when man's moral character is the criterion and object of his self-respect. Neither political nor economic necessities shall dominate the new community and allow its members to develop into "masses." Instead they shall remain individuals devoting themselves to the common weal. The end of human existence ought also to govern the economic means of sustaining it.

It is in harmony with his view of man and society that Goethe directs his criticism against the tendency of modern Western civilization to alienate man from the measures set for him by nature itself. While accepting as a historical fact

the destruction of the old and the insecurity of the new institutions of Europe, Goethe remained opposed to the tendencies which came to dominate the century of his death.
Averse to the optimistic belief in technical and material
progress, he saw in ascendance a way of living "in which
the next moment devours the preceding one," in which the
rhythm of the machine is imitated by man's conduct in society, in which day-by-day judgment, *der Tagesgeist*,[36] endangers the calm pursuit of man's personal growth and
communal service. The immensity of outer conditions to
which in modern times each individual is exposed, meant to
Goethe the result of the emancipation of the intellect. To
the individual, he gives the advice to "make neither dispro-
portionate demands on the world nor to let himself be determined by it." Threatened by the spirit of the day, man
should make haste to realize for what ends his will should
strive.

In the story of Susanne, as one example, Goethe anticipated the human significance of modern economic change
and the conflict between technical rationalization and human nature. The very fiber of his thinking compelled him to
be suspicious of any development tending to restrict man's
responsible freedom and to make him a functionary of an
anonymous mechanism. He judged the tendencies toward
immensity as demonic and considered the machine a potential agent of enslavement.[37] At a juncture when the modern
world was about to fall prey to man's own products, Goethe gave to his ideal community a small range within which
human relations could remain decisive. His image of society
reflects the opposition of his organic conception of nature
to a mechanistic interpretation of it.

The opposition to technical innovations among workers
who are threatened by them is as old as the machine itself.
In Goethe's time, however, the human implications of the
technical age had not yet been so clearly stated in relation
to their economic and social aspect as in *Wilhelm Meister*.

The technically minded Lenardo tells us that he "was less favorably disposed toward the machine than to immediate craftswork by which we exercise power and feeling in combination."[38] He sees the craftsman with the eye of the artist. Susanne is concerned about the ethical consequences of the threatening machine age. Whereas others in her valley fear nothing but unemployment, she foresees the annihilation of that flourishing life which had developed in her mountains for centuries. She realizes, however, the irresistible character of the impending industrialization. Although for herself she decides not to do what is economically advantageous but ethically doubtful, she sees in the repairman, the *Geschirrfasser*, who prepares the introduction of machines to the valley, the guilty-unguilty agent of an anonymous process.

When Goethe chose a weavers' community to demonstrate the disrupting impact of modern economic progress, he turned to a symbol which he had often used before to epitomize the fruitful social organization. In the image of weaving, we remember, he mirrored the organic community which, in its turn, he likened to the universe. Weaving is "the oldest and most magnificent art which, in fact, first distinguished man from the animal."[39] At the time when Lenardo is made aware of the plight of the weavers he had just been remembering the description that Wilhelm gave of Susanne's life:

A homelike situation, based upon piety, enlivened and preserved through industry and orderliness, not too narrow and not too wide, with the most favorable proportions between duties and capabilities. Around her, the cycle of handicraft moves in the purest original sense; there is both seclusion and contact with distant scenes, prudence and moderation, innocence and activity.[40]

What is threatened is the good life which harbors a universe in itself.

Goethe's criticism of the machine age implies his skepticism about mechanized labor, his aversion to social change, and his opposition to the "economic man." As may be indicated by the foundation of the furniture factory undertaken after the emigrants left, the machine as such is not a radical evil although it endangers the relation of man to his work.[41] The social change brought about by the new methods is worse, for it undermines the continuity needed for the meaningful building of life. Continuity of work and growth is demanded by man's nature and is essential to his culture. Against the catastrophic fluctuations of the rising industrial system, Goethe shares Lenardo's and Susanne's preference for small associations grouped around a common complex of work. There "one exists with the purest feeling of a living whole." Against the modern nomad, Goethe holds man's consciousness of being a link within the chain of generations.[42] The repairman, finally, embodies the most inhuman aspect of the modern age, the merely "economic man." His figure announces "the coming thunderstorm," and with despair Susanne realizes that "nobody has the determination to make a wholesome move."

Goethe's social thought does not comply with any particular doctrine of his time. He did not share the romantic expectations of the Saint-Simonians concerning the historical mission of industrialism. In the case of the repairman he seems to turn against free enterprise, but figures such as "the tested friend Werner" prove the contrary. The new economy is "planned" both abroad and at home, but it is built on the initiative of individuals and of free associations. The worldwide symbolism of the exodus separates it from any national conception of economy. Goethe did not think in terms of economic theory or particular institutions. He conceived of life in its human totality and centered his ideal community on the ethical wisdom of the spirit of friendship. He opposed the impending disintegration by an image of a culture, simple, devoted to work, and worthy of man. He was inclined to believe that "across the ocean certain convictions worthy of man are in continuous ascendance,"[43] but his new community was intended to indicate a generally human remedy rather than an individual or collective escape.

Within this new community the main responsibility is laid upon the family, especially in the pioneering stage of the new beginning. Although the Abbé is to undertake its general organization, it is in the family that education is centered. The Abbé's method is that of a workshop where "teacher and pupil are formed at the same time."[44] Servants are taken for granted, but they form a part of the family and, to judge from the servants surrounding Makarie, the humane purpose of living includes them on an equal basis. In a society which attributes value to each individual according to his service, no service is in itself dishonorable. An unskilled laborer, such as St. Christoph, attains an outstanding position among the emigrants. On the other hand, a nobleman or landowner is not unfit for leadership in the new undertaking simply because of his ancestry or his capital.

All the details of the political and social structure which Goethe gives to his new community serve to illustrate the central intention of its author, the presentation of *Humanität* as the enduring norm of human association. He warned against reading into *Wilhelm Meister's Travels* a systematic theory,[45] because the primary emphasis of his work is on the conversion which the reader must undergo as the precondition of any wholesome life. In contrast to the morally elusive nature of ideologies, it was such a conversion which Goethe considered effective.

Goethe's image leads the reader from the community of the Tower to the first measures to be taken toward a sound education, a sound society, and a sound world. Inherent in the nature of man and accessible to his understanding, a religious ethic forms the guiding spirit of this exodus to the promised land. This spirit lives in the self-denying Abbé, in the sibylline Makarie, in the taciturn Jarno-Montan. The search into nature is reconciled with man's religious sense, clarity of judgment with the strength of faith, the individual with the community.

The new commonwealth, its spirit, and its figures are within the range of the probable. The whole undertaking grows out of circumstances which are by no means extraordinary. It is based upon friendship, the need and desire for which are indestructible. Its aim of reconciling personal, social, and religious conflicts expresses the deepest longing of modern man, even when he is convinced that the exigencies of modern reality deprive this aim of any chance. Viewed against the background of our twentieth-century skepticism, Goethe's image of the fruitful community discloses its constructive character. A sage who had grown old in the faithful pursuit of his mission, transmitted by this novel, with a light hand and through symbolic hints, his vision of the reverence, the self-resignation, and the freedom of man in a free community. In itself a creation and an act of love, this image shows love at work for the sake of the idea, which Goethe saw as the intention of the creator manifest in the nature of man. This image is an ideal, since it was in the norm represented by the original phenomenon that its author sought the way toward rejuvenation; it is political in that it was born of the will for renewal; it is timeless in that it was left as a challenge to the future. Goethe left this "book with seven seals" as a legacy to posterity rather than to his contemporaries. He was well aware how little his time was ready to weigh and grasp the work he did in his "tower"—the work of his last years, which saw the completion of *Meister* and of *Faust*.

In the last scene of the novel, Goethe once more moves the classical symbol of the idea of man into the center and foreground. It was for its sake that Wilhelm Meister set out on the road of apprenticeship and learned to accept the lot of a wanderer. Now Felix, another prodigal son, returns to his father. Inwardly and outwardly wounded and in need of Wilhelm's art, he exclaims: "If I live, it shall be with you." Through him another generation renders its errors productive and, out of insight and free volition, joins the life of reverence and resignation. The healing forces of nature and the art of the surgeon bring Felix back to life. For a moment we see him lying on the ground, a most beautiful youth, "the magnificent image of God." The smile on his face reveals the calmness which he has regained; in the mild warmth of the sun the color in his cheeks announces that health is returning.

Are you ever to be brought forth anew, magnificent image of God! . . . and are you at once to be injured again, within and without. The coat fell over him, the miid glow of the sun gently and tenderly warmed his limbs, his cheeks grew red with health, he seemed to be fully restored.

With a myth of renewal Goethe brings his tale of the ideal commonwealth to its conclusion.

NOTES AND SELECTIVE BIBLIOGRAPHY

Notes and Selective Bibliography

Bibliographical data of pertinent publications are given in connection with each part or chapter and with emphasis on postwar publications. *Passages of Goethe's works* are quoted by the German title. Book, chapter, or act, and the beginning of the first stanza of poems are indicated. Thus, the reader will be able to use any edition of Goethe. The volume and page references to the *Jubiläumsausgabe* (Stuttgart, Cotta, 1902–7) are added. Passages not found there are quoted on the basis of *Weimarer Ausgabe* (Sophienausgabe), abbreviated *WA*. Reference is made to collections of aphorisms contained in the *Inselausgabe* (Grossherzog Wilhelm Ernst Ausgabe), *Naturwissenschaftliche Schriften*, Vol. I, abbreviated: *Insel* N 1.

ABBREVIATIONS OF GOETHE'S WORKS

Aus meinem Leben—Dichtung und Wahrheit	*DW*
Italienische Reise	*IR*
West-Östlicher Divan	*Divan*
Noten und Abhandlungen zum West-Östlichen Divan	*Noten*
Wilhelm Meisters Lehrjahre	*WML*
Wilhelm Meisters Wanderjahre	*WMW*
Materialien zur Geschichte der Farbenlehre	*MGF*

Maximen und Reflexionen are quoted according to the numbering of *Schriften der Goethe-Gesellschaft*, Vol. 21, ed. Max Hecker (Weimar, 1907). Abbreviation: *Maximen*.

Conversations are quoted by name and date, followed by the number of the conversation in *Goethes Gespräche*, Gesamtausgabe, ed. F. Frhr. von Biedermann (2d ed.; Leipzig, 1909). Abbreviation: *Biedermann*.

Letters and *Diaries* are quoted by the date: letters of Goethe by the name of the addressee, other letters by the name of both correspondents.

Publications of the Modern Language Association of America. PMLA.

Life and Vocation

GOETHE'S AUTOBIOGRAPHICAL WRITINGS

Aus meinem Leben—Dichtung und Wahrheit; drafted 1808–9; Parts I–III published 1814; Part IV posthumous.

Italienische Reise; published in parts 1816, 1817, and 1829.

Tagebücher und Briefe Goethes aus Italien an Frau von Stein und Herder. Schriften der Goethe-Gesellschaft, Vol. 2; ed. Erich Schmidt. Weimar, 1886.

Kampagne in Frankreich 1792; published 1822.

Belagerung von Mainz 1793; published 1822.

Aus einer Reise in die Schweiz 1797; published by Eckermann from diaries and letters, 1833.

Am Rhein, Main und Neckar 1814 und 1815; published in *Über Kunst und Altertum;* 1816 ff.

Geschichte meines botanischen Studiums; first formulation published in *Zur Morphologie,* 1817; in the German-French edition of *Die Metamorphose der Pflanzen,* 1831.

Materialien zur Geschichte der Farbenlehre. Konfession des Verfassers; published 1810.

Annalen oder Tag- und Jahreshefte als Ergänzung meiner sonstigen Bekenntnisse; finished 1825; published 1830.

Paralipomena zu den Annalen; posthumous.

Tagebücher. WA, III.

RECENT BIOGRAPHICAL LITERATURE

Fuchs, Albert. *Goethe: Un Homme Face à la Vie.* Essai de Biographie Intérieure I, Paris, Aubier, 1946.

Fairley, Barker. *A Study of Goethe.* Oxford, Clarendon Press, 1947.

Müller, Günther. *Kleine Goethebiographie.* Bonn, Universitätsverlag, 1948.

Buchwald, Reinhard. *Goethe und das deutsche Schicksal.* München, Münchner Verlag, 1948.

Goethe, Wisdom and Experience. Selections by Ludwig Curtius, translated and edited with an introduction by Herman J. Weigand. New York, Pantheon Books, 1949. (Contains a biographical introduction and outstanding translations of well-selected philosophical prose.)

CHAPTER ONE: PERSONALITY

1. *MGF.* Newton's Persönlichkeit; 40:263 f.
2. Ibid., p. 264; cf. *Maximen* 391–400.
3. To E. K. L. Ysenburg von Buri, May 23, 1764.
4. Kestner, May–June, 1772; *Biedermann* 32.
5. Jean Paul Friedrich Richter, June 17, 1796; *Biedermann* 487.
6. Friedrich Hölderlin, 1794–95; *Biedermann* 438; cf. also 435, 473a.
7. Wieland to Reinhold, 1796; *Biedermann* 502.
8. Schiller to Countess Schimmelmann; *Biedermann* 618.
9. Cf. Rudolf Kassner, *Das Neunzehnte Jahrhundert* (Erlenbach-Zürich, Rentsch, 1947); Faust und der Barockmensch, pp. 58–86.
10. Tagebuch, May 6–13, 1780; the "schools of fate," to Countess Auguste Stolberg, May 18, 1776; to Johanna Fahlmer, Nov. 22, 1775.
11. *DW*, I, 1; 22:15–27.
12. Ibid., II, 6; 23:15.
13. Ibid., I, 3; 22:92–94.
14. Ibid., II, 9; 23:207–8.
15. Ibid., II, 9; 23:208.
16. Elisabeth Goethe, *Biedermann* 1.
17. *DW*, II, 6; 23:16–19; quot., p. 17.
18. *Ibid.*
19. *Maximen* 391–400.
20. "Predigten über das Buch Jonas von Johann Kaspar Lavater." Review in *Frankfurter Gelehrte Anzeigen*, probably by Bahrdt, included in Vol. 33 of *Ausgabe letzter Hand* by Goethe.
21. *DW*, IV, 19; 25:106.
22. *DW*, II, 8; 23:144–46; cf. Goethe's letters of Sept. 8 and Nov. 24, 1768, Jan. 17, 1769, Apr. 29, 1770, Oct. 27, 1773, published first in *Braunschweiger Jahrbuch* (1922) by Paul Zimmermann.
23. In regard to *Werther*, cf. Herbert Schöffler, *Die Leiden des jungen Werther; ihr geistesgeschichtlicher Hintergrund* (Frankfurt am Main, Klostermann, 1938); and Stuart Atkins, "J. C. Lavater and Goethe: Problems of Psychology," in *Die Leiden des jungen Werther, PMLA*, LXIII (1948), 520 ff.
24. To Augustin Trapp, July 28, 1770.
25. Cf. Max Kommerell, *Gedanken über Gedichte* (Frankfurt am Main, Klostermann, 1943), pp. 28–30.
26. "Bedeutende Fördernis durch ein einziges geistreiches Wort" (1823, on occasion of Heinroth's *Anthropologie*); 39:49.

27. Cf. Erich Franz, *Goethe als religiöser Denker* (Tübingen, Mohr, 1932), Chap. II, "Religion und Ironie," 62–108.
28. "Aristeia der Mutter"; 25:213.
29. "Die Geheimnisse," 1:293 (Ein wunderbares Lied).
30. *Divan,* Buch Suleika; 5:76 (Volk und Knecht und Überwinder).
31. *Maximen* 829.
32. *Divan,* Buch des Sängers, "Selige Sehnsucht" (Sagt es niemand); 5:16.
33. Riemer, Dec. 29, 1812; *Biedermann* 1454.
34. *DW,* Vorwort; 22:4 f.
35. "Urworte. Orphisch," *Daimon;* 2:252 and Goethe's comments, p. 355.
36. "Seefahrt" (Lange Tag' und Nächte); 2:56.

Chapter Two: The Experience of Faith

1. "Trilogie der Leidenschaft, Werther" (Noch einmal wagst du); 2:206. *Torquato Tasso,* V, 5; 12:220.
2. "Selbstschilderung 1797"; 25:277 f.
3. Eckermann, March 3, 1831; *Biedermann* 2931.
4. "Des Ewigen Juden Erster Fetzen"; 3:232–41. Cf. Jakob Minor, *Goethes Fragmente vom ewigen Juden und vom wiederkehrenden Heiland* (Stuttgart, Cotta, 1904), and Erich Franz' criticism, *op, cit.,* 269–71.
5. "Von deutscher Baukunst, D. M. Ervini a Steinbach" (1772); 33:3–13.
6. Cf. Christian Sarauw, *Goethes Augen,* Historisk-filologiske Meddelser, Det Kgl. Danske Videnskabernes Selskab, II, 3 (Kopenhagen, Host, 1919), pp. 5–69: "Schauen und Sehen."
7. "Bedeutende Fördernis," 39:48.
8. To Charlotte von Stein, July 9, 1786.
9. *Zur Farbenlehre.* Didaktischer Teil, Einleitung; 40:70–71.
10. *Faust ll,* 5, vss. 11,296–97; 14:256.
11. *Gottfried Arnold, Auswahl,* hg. Erich Seeberg (München, Langen, 1934), p. 37.
12. To Langer, Jan. 17, 1769; cf. Eckermann, Mar. 11, 1832; *Biedermann* 3055, p. 443 (Christianity of inner intention and action).
13. *WMW,* II, 1; 19:184. Cf. Goethe to Herder, October, 1793 (evangelical communion), and Schiller to Goethe, Aug. 17, 1795 (abrogation of the law and its substitution by free inclination).

14. "Ephemerides," *WA*, I, 37:81 (Paracelsus), 82 (Bruno), 90–91 (Ad Fabricium), 98 (Kempis).

15. *DW*, III, 14;24:200–01.

16. "Paralipomena zu den Annalen," Lavater; 30:396. The letters exchanged between Goethe and Lavater; cf. *Schriften der Goethe-Gesellschaft*, Vol. 16, Weimar, 1902.

17. *DW*, III, 14; 24:221, 223.

18. Lavater to Goethe, July 28, 1782; Goethe to Lavater, Aug. 9, 1782. *IR*, Oct. 23, 1787; 27:134–36; *ibid.*, Oct. 5, 1782; 27:128–29, against Lavater, Jacobi, and Claudius as Herder's critics.

19. Cf. Franz Koch, *Goethe und Plotin* (Leipzig, Weber, 1925).

20. *Faust I*, vss. 1306–8; 13:53.

21. "Klassiker und Romantiker in Italien"; 37:125.

22. *DW*, II, 7; 23:83.

23. *Tagebuch*, Aug. 7, 1779.

24. H. G. von Bretschneider to Friedrich Nicolai (1775); *Biedermann* 126.

25. "Bedeutende Fördernis"; 39:49.

26. *DW*, II, 9; 23:186.

27. *Ibid.*, pp. 187 ff. On German Pietism, cf. Hans R. G. Günther, *Jung-Stilling; Ein Beitrag zur Psychologie des Pietismus* (2d. ed.; München, Federmann, 1948).

28. "Satyros oder der vergötterte Waldteufel," Drama; 7:103–24.

29. To Elisabeth Jacobi, February, 1774.

30. Cf. Ernst Beutler, *Der König in Thule und die Dichtungen von der Lorelay* (Zürich, Artemis, 1947).

31. *DW*, III, 15; 24:215. Goethe to F. H. Jacobi, Aug. 21, 1774; Lavater, *Biedermann* 59; Heinse, *Biedermann* 62. A poetic interpretation by Max Kommerell, *Gespräche aus der Zeit der deutschen Wiedergeburt* (Berlin, Holten, 1929), pp. 15–20.

32. Jacobi to Wieland, July, 1774; *Biedermann* 73; Zimmermann reports to Charlotte von Stein in January, 1775, an excerpt of a letter by Lavater of Aug. 27, 1774, quoted here. In the letter of Zimmermann: "Une femme du monde qui l'a vu souvent, m'a dit que Goethe était l'homme le plus beau, le plus vif, le plus original, le plus ardent, le plus impétueux, le plus doux, le plus séduisant pour le coeur d'une Femme qu'elle avait vu en sa vie." *Biedermann* 85.

33. "Gross ist die Diana der Epheser," Acts 19:39; (Zu Ephesus ein Goldschmied sass); 2:109. Cf. "Paralipomena zu den Annalen," Jacobi; 30:402 f. "We loved each other without understanding each other."

34. *Ibid.*, p. 403; cf. Goethe to Jacobi, May 10, 1812; to Knebel, Apr. 8, 1812.

35. To Jacobi, June 9, 1785.
36. *"Denn das Leben ist die Liebe*
    Und des Lebens Leben Geist."
Divan, Buch Suleika (Nimmer will ich dich verlieren); 5:97–80;
Noten, Allgemeinstes; 5:195; on the level of *Geist* (spirit) "all the
other qualities are united without any one of them insisting on its
particular right."
37. *Noten*, Israel in der Wüste; 5:248. The publication of the
letters to Langer initiated a re-evaluation of Goethe's religious
development. Cf. Hans von Schubert, *Goethes religiöse Jugendentwicklung* (Leipzig, Quelle und Meyer, 1925); Wilhelm Flitner,
Goethe im Spätwerk (Hamburg, Claassen und Goverts, 1947),
pp. 7–56. Cf. especially:
   I. "Goethes Alterswerke als religiöse und ethische Gesamtaus-
sage."
   II. "Die religiöse Jugendentwicklung Goethes."
Literature on the controversy about Goethe's religious thought: cf.
the author's article, "Goethe's View of Christ," *Modern Philology*,
XLVI (Feb., 1949), 172–202.

CHAPTER THREE: ART AND POETRY

1. To Lavater, Sept., 1780 (appr. 20th).
2. *WMW*, III, 11; 20:161.
3. *DW*, III, 12; 24:89. "Sturmlied" (Wen du nicht verlässest);
2:52–55.
4. *The Odes of Pindar*, tr. by Richmond Lattimore (Chicago,
The University of Chicago Press, 1947), p. 8 (Olympia 2). On
Goethe's relation to Pindar, cf. Otto Regenbogen, *Griechische
Gegenwart* (Leipzig, Koehler und Amelang, 1942), pp. 43–70:
"Goethes Pindar-Erlebnis."
5. To Herder, July 10, 1772.
6. *Divan*, Buch des Sängers; 5:13.
7. "Der Wanderer" (Gott segne dich, junge Frau); 2:91–97.
8. *Faust I;* 13:140 f.
9. *Noten*, Einleitung des Verfassers; 5:148.
10. *Divan*, Buch des Sängers, Hegire; 5:3.
11. "Dauer im Wechsel" (Hielte diesen frühen Segen); 2:243.
Cf. Emil Staiger, *Die Zeit als Einbildungskraft des Dichters* (Zürich
und Leipzig, Max Niehans, 1939), pp. 101–144: B. "Der Augen-
blick."
12. *Maximen* 955, 959.

13. *DW*, II, 10; 23:257–58.
14. "Paralipomena zu den Annalen," Herder; 30:397.
15. *DW*, III, 15; 24:231–32.
16. J. G. Hamann, "Aesthetica in Nuce," in *Schriften* (hg. Widmaier; Leipzig, Insel, 1921), p. 192.
17. *DW*, II, 10; 23:233.
18. *DW*, IV, 16; 25:9. "The practice of this poetic gift could be stimulated and determined by the occasion; it made itself felt in the most joyful and abundant fashion when arising involuntarily, or even against my will." To August Stolberg, July 17, 1777; the poem 3:87.
19. To Auguste Stolberg, July 17, 1777; the poem, 3:87.
20. "Von deutscher Baukunst"; 33:5.
21. *DW*, III, 12; 24:74.
22. *Ibid.*, 75.
23. "Zum Schäkespears Tag" (1771); 36:4. "Shakespeare und kein Ende" (1813 ff.); 37:37–50. *DW*, III, 11; 24:54–58.
24. "Einfache Nachahmung der Natur, Manier, Stil;" 33:54–59. Quot. p., 57.
25. *Maximen* 200.
26. "Einleitung in die Propyläen;" 33:108.
27. "Dritte Wallfahrt zu Erwins Grabe;" 33:44.
28. *Maximen* 183.
29. *IR*, Sept. 6, 1787; 27:108.
30. "Winckelmann" (1805), Schönheit; 34:17–18.
31. "Aus Goethes Brieftasche" (1775); 36:115.
32. "Glückliches Ereignis" or "Erste Bekanntschaft mit Schiller"; 30:391.
33. *Maximen* 433.
34. *Maximen* 1369.
35. *Urphänomen.* Cf. Collected passages, *Insel N1*, 93–97. Numinosum: *Maximen* 412. Cf. Erich Franz, *Goethe als religiöser Denker* (Tübingen, Mohr. 1932), pp. 110–18.
36. *Divan*, Buch Suleika (Ists möglich, dass ich); 5:68.
37. Cf. Helmut Kuhn, "True Poetry Is Praise," *Theology Today*, IV (1947), 238–58.
38. "Zueignung" (Der Morgen kam); 1:5; vss. 69–72.
39. "Einleitung in die Propyläen;" 33:115.
40. "Der Sammler und die Seinigen," 6. Brief; 33:176.
41. "Über den Dilettantismus" (together with Schiller and Meyer), *WA*, I, 47:299–326.
42. "Neue Unterhaltungen über verschiedene Gegenstände der

Kunst als Folge der Nachrichten von den Weimarischen Kunst-
ausstellungen" (1808). *WA*, I, 48:135. (Cf. "Ephemerides," *WA*,
I, 37:87: "Art is nothing but the light of nature.")
43. *Ibid.*, 137. "Allgemeiner Schematismus über Natur und
Kunst," *Annalen*, 1799; 30:65 (Dilettantismus). Cf. Schiller to
Goethe, May 29, 1799.
44. *Maximen* 328.
45. To Wilhelm von Humboldt, Mar. 17, 1832. On Goethe's
philosophy of art, cf. Curt Müller, *Die geschichtlichen Voraus-
setzungen des Symbolbegriffs in Goethes Kunstanschauung* (Leipzig, Mayer und Müller, 1937), Palaestra 211; Herbert von Einem,
Goethe und Dürer: Goethes Kunstphilosophie (Hamburg, Marion
von Schröder, 1947); Ernst Robert Curtius, "Goethe als Kritiker,"
Merkur (Stuttgart, Deutsche Verlagsanstalt), II (1948), 333–355.

Chapter Four: Government and World Affairs

1. *DW*, IV, 20: 25:138. *Egmont* II, 2; 11:273.
2. *Faust I*, vss. 1972–73; 13:78.
3. On Goethe's relation to Justus Möser, cf. Reinhard Buchwald, *Goethe und das deutsche Schicksal;* Grundlinien einer Le-
bensgeschichte (München, Münchner Verlag, 1948), especially pp.
20 ff., 50, 80.
4. Charlotte von Stein, March 7, 1776; *Biedermann* 143. "Why
his continuous lampooning, they are all creatures of the great Being
which tolerates them,—and now his indecent behavior with swear-
ing and vulgar, low expressions."
5. "Ilmenau" (Anmutig Tal!); 1:276–81.
6. "In das Stammbuch von Mr. Brak," Oct. 12, 1783; *WA*, I, 5,
2d part; p. 360.
7. Wieland, February, 1776; *Biedermann* 140. Cf. Wieland to
Lavater, January-February, 1776; *Biedermann* 141.
8. Merck to Nicolai, September, 1778; *Biedermann* 179; to
Lavater, *Biedermann* 180.
9. "Literarischer Sansculottismus" (1795); 36:141.
10. To Karl August, Mar. 17, 1788.
11. To Krafft, Sept. 9, 1779; cf. Fritz Ernst, *Aus Goethes
Freundeskreis, Studien um Peter im Baumgarten* (Erlenbach-
Zürich, Rentsch, 1941).
12. *Tagebuch*, 1776–80, is basic for the following passages.
13. *Tagebuch*, July 13, 1779.
14. To Lavater, Oct. 13, 1780.
15. Eckermann, Oct. 23, 1828; *Biedermann* 2635.

16. *Tagebuch*, Feb. 1, 1779.

17. Memorandum to Marshal Berthier about the institutions of learning in Jena and Weimar (in French); *WA* I, 53: 243–49.

18. To Charlotte von Stein, Mar. 6, 1779.

19. Cf. Hans Bürgin, *Der Minister Goethe vor der Römischen Reise* (Weimar, Boehlau, 1933); Fritz Hartung, "Karl August als Staatsmann," *Jahrbuch der Goethe-Gesellschaft*, IX (1922), pp. 297 ff.

20. *Die Vögel*, written July, 1780, performed Aug. 18, 1780; 7:279–308.

21. *Campaign in France*, Sept. 19, 1792; 28:60.

22. *IR*, Aug. 23, 1787; 27:97.

23. Eckermann, Jan. 4, 1824; *Biedermann* 2214.

24. "Über die Liebe des Vaterlandes," von J. v. Sonnenfels. *Frankfurter Gelehrte Anzeigen;* 36:67–70; Luden, Dec., 13, 1813; *Biedermann* 1529.

25. Eckermann, March, 1832; *Biedermann* 3051; cf. *Maximen* 690.

26. *Maximen* 682.

27. Cf. Wilhelm Flitner, "Reine Tätigkeit," *Goethe*, Eine Viermonatsschrift, Weimar, III (1938), 144 ff.

28. *Pandora;* 15:178, vss. 1071 ff.

29. *Tagebuch*, Dec. 14, 1778.

30. *Tagebuch*, Mar. 26, 1780.

31. *Tagebuch*, with regard to himself, May 13, 1780.

32. Feb. 24, 1784, published *Deutsches Museum*, January, 1785; 40:3–7.

33. To Jenny von Voigts, *née* Möser, who was to convey this message to "the old patriarch," June 21, 1781.

34. "Vorspiel zur Eröffnung des Weimarischen Theaters am 19. September 1807"; 9:194–203; quot., p. 198.

35. For a compilation of passages see Curtius-Weigand, *Goethe, Wisdom and Experience* (N. Y., Pantheon Books, 1949), pp. 279–89.

36. *DW*, III, 11; 24:49; Helvétius, 52. "We did not understand how such a book could be dangerous. It appeared to us so grey, so chimerical, so dead, that we could hardly bear its presence and felt frightened by it like by a ghost."

37. *Maximen* 353.

38. "Schwebender Genius über der Erdkugel" (Zwischen oben); 2:126–27.

CHAPTER FIVE: GROWTH AND ACHIEVEMENT

1. Eckermann, Mar. 10, 1830; *Biedermann* 2797.

2. "Gott, Gemüt und Welt," first published 1815; 4:1–7; quot., p. 4, repeated in "Zur Morphologie" I, "Zwischenrede" (1820); 39:353–54.

3. *WML*, II, 2; 17:91–92.

4. "Warum gabst du uns die tiefen Blicke" (Apr. 14, 1776); 3:83–85.

5. *Die Natürliche Tochter*, III, 4; 12:290, vs. 1583. Cf. Rudolph Alexander Schröder, "Ein Wort über Die Natürliche Tochter," *Goethe-Kalender 1938* (Leipzig, Dieterich), pp. 63–100.

6. *Iphigenie auf Tauris*, V, 6; 12:87, vss. 2142 ff.

7. Schiller, beginning of 1802; *Biedermann* 649.

8. *Torquato Tasso*, II, 1; 12:127, vss. 930 ff.

9. *Ibid.*, 12:130, vss. 995 ff.

10. To the Senate of the University of Jena, Nov. 24, 1825.

11. *Egmont*, IV; 11:308, lines 26 ff.

12. *Ibid.*, 311, lines 11 ff.

13. Cf. to Charlotte von Stein, July 9, Aug. 23, Sept. 1, Nov. 7, 1786; to Karl August, Sept. 2, Oct. 14, Nov. 3, 1786; to Elisabeth Goethe, Nov. 4, 1786: "I will return as a new man and live to the greater satisfaction of myself and my friends;" to Herder, Dec. 2 and 13, 1786 (rebirth).

14. J. D. Falk, July 17, 1792; *Biedermann* 380.

15. "*Römische Elegien*" VII; 1:159.

16. *WML*, VIII.

17. "Paralipomena zu den Annalen," Unterredung mit Napoleon, 1808; 30:411–16; quot., p. 414.

18. To Schiller, Jan. 17, 1804.

19. *Die Horen*, Eine Monatsschrift, von einer Gesellschaft verfasst und herausgegeben von Schiller. Öffentliche Ankündigung. Dec. 10, 1794. *Schillers Sämtliche Werke* (Leipzig, Insel), 7:193.

20. On Goethe, Schiller, and their relationship, cf. K. L. v. Woltmann; *Biedermann* 830.

21. To Zelter, June 1, 1805. "I ought to start out on a new way of living. In my age, however, there is no such way left."

22. Sonette; 2:3–13. Motto: "*Liebe will ich liebend loben; Jede Form, sie kommt von oben.*" The transition to Goethe's "old age": cf. Paul Hankamer, *Spiel der Mächte. Ein Kapitel aus Goethes Leben und Goethes Welt.* (Tübingen, Wunderlich, 1943).

23. To Zelter, May 11, 1820.

24. "Zahme Xenien," I–IX (VII–IX in the main part posthumous); 4:33–135.

25. "Götter, Helden und Wieland. Eine Farce" (1773). Wieland to Lavater, after having met Goethe, November, 1775; *Biedermann* 127. Quot., *Maximen* 396.

26. To Auguste Stolberg, Feb., 13, 1775. Metempsychosis: *Maximen* 403.

27. "Gott und Welt"; 2:260–63.

28. "Epochen geselliger Bildung" (1831); 38:232–33.

29. J. G. Cogswell, Mar. 27, 1817; *Biedermann* 1763.

30. Eckermann, May 2, 1831; *Biedermann* 2957. Kleist and Immermann, *Tagebuch*, July 11, 1827. Heine, Oct. 2, 1824; *Biedermann* 2286.

31. Eckermann, Mar. 10, 1830; *Biedermann* 2797, pp. 235–36.

32. Cf. 33:35. J. H. Meyer's essay "Neudeutsch religiös-patriotische Kunst" as a challenge: *WA*, I, Vol. 48, 1. Abt., pp. 21–58. "Hellenic-patriotic" in the sense of sound conceptions of art and mythology: cf. to Boisserée, Jan. 16, 1818. A general criticism of the insanity of the time": cf. to Rochlitz, June 1, 1817.

33. Translations: *Goethes Übersetzungen und Bearbeitungen fremder Dichtungen, Insel*, 11.

34. "Studien zur Weltliteratur," *WA*, I, 42, 2d part, pp. 491–505. "The seriously minded ones consequently must form a quiet, almost oppressed church, since it would be futile to withstand the broad stream of the day; one must, however, try to maintain one's position unflinchingly, until the trend has passed" (*ibid.*, 503). Cf. Fritz Strich, *Goethe und die Weltliteratur* (Bern, Francke, 1946).

35. *MGF*, Johann Kepler; 40:206.

About the unity of structure in Goethe's life, cf. L. A. Willoughby, *Unity and Continuity in Goethe* (The Taylorian Lecture 1947; Oxford, Clarendon Press).

An extensive commentary on *Divan*: Goethe, *West-Östlicher Divan*, Unter Mitwirkung von Hans Heinrich Schaeder, hg. und erläutert von Ernst Beutler (Leipzig, Dieterich, 1943), includes "Der Osten im West-Östlichen Divan" by Schaeder.

Pyritz, Hans. *Goethe und Marianne von Willemer*. Stuttgart, Metzler, 1943.

Milch, Werner. *Bettine und Marianne*. Zürich, Artemis, 1947.

Blume, Bernhard. "Kleist und Goethe," *Monatshefte* (Wisconsin, 1946), Vol. 38.

Sevin, Barbara. *Kanzler Friedrich von Müller*. Jena, Frommann, 1936. "Jenaer Germanistische Forschungen, Bd. 29."

Beutler, Ernst. "Johann Peter Eckermann," *Essays um Goethe*. Wiesbaden, Dieterich, 1947. II, 282–306.

Weniger, Erich. *Goethe und die Generale.* Leipzig, Insel, 1942. (Goethe's relations to and influence upon the German military leaders of the revolutionary era.)

Lukacs, Georg. *Goethe und seine Zeit.* Bern, Francke, 1947. (Wilhelm Meisters Lehrjahre," 31–47; "Der Briefwechsel zwischen Schiller und Goethe," 48–77.)

The Universe and Man

Weinhandl, Ferdinand. "Goethe," in *Das Deutsche in der deutschen Philosophie;* hg. Haering. Stuttgart, Kohlhammer, 1941. pp. 297–336.

Spranger, Eduard. *Goethes Weltanschauung;* Reden und Aufsätze. Insel, 1946.

Schaeder, Grete. *Gott und Welt;* Drei Kapitel Goethescher Weltanschauung. Hameln, Seifert, 1947.

Flitner, Wilhelm. *Goethe im Spätwerk;* Glaube, Weltsicht, Ethos. Hamburg, Claassen und Goverts, 1947.

Michel, Ernst. *Goethes Naturanschauung im Lichte seines Schöpfungsglaubens.* Wiesbaden, Dieterich, 1946.

Hildebrandt, Kurt. *Goethes Naturerkenntnis.* Hamburg-Bergedorf, Stromverlag, 1947.

Schlechta, Karl. *Goethe in seinem Verhältnis zu Aristoteles.* Frankfurt am Main, Klostermann, 1938.

Cassirer, Ernst. "Goethe und Platon," in *Goethe und die geschichtliche Welt.* Berlin, Cassirer, 1932.

Liebert, Arthur. *Goethes Platonismus;* Zur Metaphysik der Morphologie. Berlin, Pan, 1932.

Leese, Kurt. *Die Krise und Wende des christlichen Geistes;* Studien zum anthropologischen und theologischen Problem der Lebensphilosophie. Berlin, Junker und Dünnhaupt, 1932. (On the history of the concept of God-in-Nature: pp. 104 ff.)

CHAPTER SIX: COSMOLOGY AND COGNITION

1. Epistemological essays and outlines:

"Der Versuch als Vermittler von Objekt und Subjekt" (1792); 39:15.

"Erfahrung und Wissenschaft" (MS, 1798); 39:26.

"Einwirkung der neueren Philosophie" (1820) (on Kant's Aesthetik); 39:28.

"Anschauende Urteilskraft" (1820); 39:33.

"Bildungstrieb" (1820); 39:335.

"Analyse und Synthese" (MS, 1829); 39:55.

"Bedeutende Fördernis durch ein einziges geistreiches Wort"; 39:48.

Aphorismen; collected under epistemological points of view in *Insel Nı* ("Idee und Erscheinung," 85; "Das Besondere und das Allgemeine," 89; "Beobachten und Denken," 109; "Wissen und Wissenschaft," 123; "Ursache und Wirkung," 132; "Wahrheit und Irrtum," 134; "Wissenschaftsgeschichte," 141; "Mathematik," 154; "Philosophie," 159; "Symbolik," 165–69; "Empfindungsformen," 169–70).

Paralipomena, WA, II, 5, 2d part; *Nachträge, WA,* II, 13.

2. *Maximen* 619.

3. "Biographische Einzelheiten"; Wiederholte Spiegelungen; 25:221 ff. Cf. "Bezüge nach aussen" (38:137 f.) in regard to world literature.

4. For a recent treatment, cf. Hans-Georg Gadamer, *Goethe und die Philosophie* (Leipzig, Volk und Buch, 1947).

5. Johannes Falk, *Goethe aus näherm persönlichen Umgange dargestellt* (3d. ed.; Leipzig, Brockhaus), p. 69.

6. "Sprichwörtlich"; 4:14.

7. Cf. Wilhelm Dilthey, "Aus der Zeit der Spinozastudien Goethes," *Gesammelte Schriften* (Leipzig, Teubner), 2:391 ff. Spinoza essay, cf. 39:6 ff.

8. Kant's "adventure of reason," "Anschauende Urteilskraft"; 39:33.

9. Otto Kein, *Die Universalität des Geistes im Lebenswerk Goethes und Schellings* (Berlin, Junker und Dünnhaupt, 1933).

10. *Maximen* 1002.

11. "Anthropomorphismus der Sprache," *Insel Nı:* 167; *WA,* II, 5, 2d part, p. 298.

12. Poetry in the sense of *Dichtung* corresponding to Goethe's conception of the poet; cf. "Zueignung" (Der Morgen kam); 1:6.

13. *Annalen.* Bis 1780; 30:3; *ibid.* 7; Eckermann, Feb. 26, 1824; *Biedermann* 2230 (anticipation of the world in *Götz;* Byron and anticipation; analogy between inner sense and experience on the one hand, light and colors on the other hand); quot., p. 81.

Goethe transforms Linné's conception of anticipation ("Metamorphose der Pflanzen," XVII, 107–9; 39:290–92) into a general morphological law and makes it the basis of his theory of cognition. Marie Hendel, "Die platonische Anamnesis und Goethes Antizipationen," *Kantstudien,* XXV (1920), 182–95.

14. *Maximen* 1299.

15. *DW*, II, 8; 23:164–67, referring to Neo–Platonism, Hermes Trismegistos, Cabala, Mysticism, in connection with Arnold's *Kirchen– und Ketzergeschichte*.

16. *Faust I*, Studierzimmer; 13:50.

17. *Divan*, Buch Suleika, "Wiederfinden" (Ist es möglich); 5:88–89.

18. "Gesang der Geister"; 2:44; "Mahomet's Gesang"; 2:42.

19. 2:241–42. Cf. *Faust II*, 3, vss. 9506–74, and Werner Vordtriede, "Zu Goethes Morphologie," *Trivium* (Zürich, 1948), pp. 218 ff. (Goethe's last morphological poem).

20. *Entwurf einer Farbenlehre*, Verhältnis zur allgemeinen Physik, Num. 139; 40:83.

21. Cf. "Epirrhema" (Müsset im Naturbetrachten); 2:249.

22. *DW*, III, 14; 24:202.

23. "Beiträge zu Lavaters Physiognomischen Fragmenten," 33:20–35; 39:117–18.

24. "Von den oft nur scheinbaren Fehlschlüssen der Physiognomisten"; 33:24–26; quot., p. 25.

25. "Vorarbeiten zu einer Physiologie der Pflanzen," *WA* II; 6:301–2.

26. "Erster Entwurf einer allgemeinen Einleitung in die vergleichende Anatomie, ausgehend von der Osteologie"; 39:137; quot. from Chap. II; 39:137–160; quot. p. 140.

27. "Versuch einer allgemeinen Vergleichungslehre"; 39:131.

28. Ferdinand Bulle, "Zur Struktur des Pantheismus," *Euphorion* (Wien–Leipzig, XXI [1914], 159).

29. Cf. R. G. Collingwood, *The Idea of Nature* (Oxford, Clarendon Press, 1945), Part II, 1.

30. Cf. note 21; "Märchen"; 16:274 (the patent secret is the most important one).

31. "Nachträge zur Farbenlehre," 27. Der Ausdruck trüb, *WA*, II, 5, 394 ff.; "God counted on this perturbation," Riemer, Dec. 11, 1811; *Biedermann* 1451. "Turba" in *Pandora*, 15:379 (Schema der Fortsetzung).

32. *Entwurf einer Farbenlehre*, Verhältnis zur Philosophie, Num. 716; 40:77.

33. "Fragment über die Natur"; 39:3–6; comment 39:349–50; translation of the fragment in Agnes Arber, "Goethe's Botany," *Chronica Botanica* (ed. Frans Verdoorn; Waltham, Mass., X [1946] 63–126.

34. "Naturgedicht," *Annalen* 1799; 30:65; to Knebel, Feb. 14, 1821, and Jan. 22, 1822, about his translation of Lucretius; there,

and Müller, Feb. 20, 1821; *Biedermann* 1939 about L.'s religious views as motivated by the opposition to the fear of conditions after death prevailing in his time. "If men *en masse* were not so miserable, the philosophers would not need to be so absurd for the sake of contradiction."

35. "Die Natur," comment; 39:350; "Über die Spiraltendenz der Vegetation"; *WA*, II; 11:166.

36. Intensification through freedom and order: see "Die Metamorphose der Pflanzen," 2:247 ff.; "Die Metamorphose der Tiere," 2:247 ff.

37. "Betrachtung über Morphologie überhaupt" (um 1795); 39:133-37; zoonomy, 135; inner and outer form, 136. ". . . one might almost say, that the organic natures become the more perfect the less the mechanic principles are applicable to them."

38. "Über die Bildung von Edelsteinen" (*MS*, 1816); WA, II; 10:87. Cf. "Über die Bildung der Erde," outline of 1806; 40:31-38 (universe incomplete, 31).

39. "Zur Botanik," Probleme; 39:342.

40. Cf. Werner Heisenberg, *Wandlungen in den Grundlagen der Naturwissenschaft*, (4th ed.; Leipzig, Hirzel, 1943), pp. 58-76: "Die Goethesche und die Newtonsche Farbenlehre im Lichte der modernen Physik"; C. F. von Weizsäcker, *Zum Weltbild der Physik* (3d ed.; Leipzig, Hirzel, 1945); Bernhard Bavink, *Ergebnisse und Probleme der Naturwissenschaften* (8th ed.; Leipzig, Hirzel, 1944).

41. Schiller to Goethe, Aug. 23, 1794.

42. F. von Müller, Apr. 29, 1818; *Biedermann* 1838.

43. "Zahme Xenien," VI; 4:97.

44. H. Voss, Feb. 13, 1804; *Biedermann* 742. (Conversation about Plato's "Thaumazein," the revelation of God through the creation, the natural-supernatural miracle.)

CHAPTER SEVEN: THE NATURE OF MAN

1. "Schillers Reliquien" (Im ernsten Beinhaus); 1:285-86. Cf. Karl Viëtor, "Goethes Gedicht auf Schillers Schädel," *PMLA*, LIX (1944), 142-183.

2. "Deep in ourselves that creative power is latent which is able to bring about what ought to be." *WML*, VI; 18:150.

3. Eckermann, May 2, 1824; *Biedermann* 2254.

4. On the postwar discussion of *Faust*, which has become the carrier of a debate on principles of ethics, cf. Johannes Pfeiffer, "Zum Faustbild der Gegenwart," *Sammlung*, III, November, 1948. A new edition of *Faust*, erläutert von Franz Endres (Basel, Benno

Schwabe, 1949), Vol. 1 (running commentary). *Faust II:* cf. Max Kommerell, *Buchstabe und Geist der Dichtung* (Frankfurt am Main, Klostermann, 1944), pp. 9–131. Ernst Jockers, "Faust und die Natur," *PMLA*, LXII (1947), 436–471 and 707–734.

5. *Faust II*, 4; vss. 10,064–66; 14:209–10.

6. Cf. Konrad Burdach, "Die Schluss-szene in Goethes *Faust*," *Sitzungsberichte der Preussischen Akademie der Wissenschaften* (Philos.–hist. Klasse; XVII [1931], 603 ff.).

7. To Eichstädt, Mar. 10, 1815; to Knebel, Apr. 8, 1812.

8. "Bedeutende Fördernis"; 39:48.

9. Schiller, "Über die ästhetische Erziehung des Menchen in einer Reihe von Briefen," 4th letter.

10. *Maximen* 286, 1362. "Empfindungsformen," *Paralipomena*, *WA*, II, 13:457.

11. To Christian Schlosser, Feb. 19. 1815; cf. the same letter for the comparison of nature and subject and for Goethe's concept of totality.

12. *Faust II*, 1; vs. 4727; 14:7.

13. *Faust II*, 5; vss. 11,997–12,004; 14:282. For a new interpretation of Plato's *Symposium*, cf. Gerhard Krüger, *Einsicht und Leidenschaft; Das Wesen des Platonischen Denkens* (2d ed.; Frankfurt am Main, Klostermann, 1948).

14. (Was soll ich nun vom Wiedersehen hoffen); 2:206–11.

15. *Divan*, Buch des Paradieses, Höheres und Höchstes (Dass wir solche Dinge lehren); 5:127.

16. Riemer, Nov. 24, 1809; *Biedermann* 1230; *Maximen* 935.

17. Gottfried Arnold, ed. Seeberg, *op. cit.*, p. 342.

18. *Maximen* 504.

19. Eckermann, Feb. 13, 1829; *Biedermann* 2657. Cf. *Maximen* 555, and *MGF*, Autorität; 40:157.

20. *WMW*, II, 9; 20:25.

21. Schiller to Goethe, July 3, 1796.

22. *Maximen* 667.

23. *Maximen* 1107.

24. Grete Schaeder, op. cit., pp. 58–59 and 92, criticizes Goethe's religious faith on a basis which, in principle, is that of Jacobi, as "a mysticism without firm anchorage."

25. "Zahme Xenien," IX; 4:125.

26. Eckermann, Mar. 11, 1832; *Biedermann* 3055.

27. *Ibid.*, p. 444.

On the legislative function of man in ethics, religion, government, and science, cf. "Zur Morphologie," Probleme, *WA*, II, 7, 2d part, 75 ff., and the answer of Ernst Meyer, *ibid.*, pp. 78 ff. In "Bildungs-

21. "Ihro der Kaiserin von Frankreich Majestät," 1812; 3:128–29.

22. *Des Epimenides Erwachen*, 1815; the stanza quoted, 1816; 9:146.

23. Eckermann, Mar. 18, 1831; *Biedermann* 2939; the potentiality of demonic energies in Goethe himself: "If I left myself without restrictions, it might be in my nature to ruin myself and those around me," Eckermann, Mar. 21, 1830; *Biedermann* 2806.

24. "Don Alonzo, ou l'Espagne," von Salvandy, 1824; 37:283–89; quot., p. 288. On "radical evil," to Herder, June 7, 1793.

25. *"Fundamentum omnium virtutum."* Cf. Cicero *Pro Planchio* xii, 29.

26. Modern interpretations of reverence: see Albert Schweitzer, *The Philosophy of Civilization*, Vol. II. *Civilization and Ethics* (3d rev. ed.; London, Adam and Charles Black, 1946), Chaps. 21 and 22; Otto Friedrich Bollnow, *Die Ehrfurcht* (Frankfurt am Main, Klostermann, 1947): in regard to Goethe, cf. pp. 55 ff. and 71–73. Since Goethe does not consider man "autonomous," Bollnow's interpretation of Goethe's *Ehrfurcht* is unsatisfactory; cf. Chap. 13 of this book.

27. *WMW*, II, 7; 19:285; the passage in *Wilhelm Meister*, where this term is used, widens the concept of Hausfrömmigkeit, the piety toward the circle of relationships to which the individual in the community of the Tower belongs. "Upon it the certainty of the individual and ultimately also the firmness and dignity of the whole are based." The Abbé conceives of the necessity to think in terms of mankind with respect to the ethics and activity of his community. Cf. Chaps. 11 and 14.

28. Cf. Lilli Simon, *Verantwortung und Schuld in Goethes Roman* (diss. Erlangen, 1934), with emphasis on the Elective Affinities. As the religious problem of despair underlies *Werther*, the religious problem of guilt is essential for Faust from the earliest conception onward.

29. *DW*, II, 8 (conclusion of cosmology); 23:167.

30. "Novelle"; 16:333–59. Cf. Emil Staiger, "Goethes Novelle," *Trivium* (Zürich, Atlantis, I [1942], 4–30).

CHAPTER NINE: THE ARCHETYPE OF SOCIETY

1. Eckermann, Jan. 18 1827; *Biedermann* 2469. To Schultz, Jan. 10, 1829, about Novelle: "Man fühlt es ihr an, dass sie sich vom tiefsten Grunde meines Wesens losgelöst hat."

2. Count Alexander G. Stroganoff, 1825–30; *Biedermann* 3010, p. 410.

trieb," 39:335 f., Goethe takes up Blumenbach's form
nisus formativus as the ultimate urge that engenders the
of organic matter; "personified, it appears to us as a god,
and preserver, whom we are called throughout to adore,
and to praise."

CHAPTER EIGHT: THE RESPONSE TO LIF

1. *Maximen* 835.
2. *Maximen* 856.
3. Melina, *WML*, I, 14; 17:58–59; Lothario, *WML*, 18:172–74.
4. To Christian Daniel Rauch, Oct. 21, 1827.
5. *Maximen* 241; "In action one is always unscrupulous; n
has conscience but in contemplation"; conscience to be arou
to be assuaged, *WML*, I, 7; 19:94.
6. *Maximen* 382; against the mannerism of rhetorical brilli
cf. *Maximen* 508.
7. *Maximen* 493.
8. *Faust I*, Prolog im Himmel, vs. 32,829; 13:15.
9. *WMW*, I, 4; 19:41–43.
10. *Maximen* 477.
11. *Maximen* 474.
12. *Maximen* 711; *Divan*, Buch der Betrachtungen; 5:39.
13. *WMW*, II, 5; 19:241–42.
14. To Jacobi, Jan. 6, 1813: "Men are united through inne
intentions *(Gesinnungen)*, they are separated through opinion
(Meinungen). The former ones are something simple in which we
come together, the latter ones something manifold into which we
disperse ourselves." The relation of inner intention and thinking:
cf. *Maximen* 794. (Thought is aroused by *Gesinnung* and is shaped
by it.)
15. Eckermann, Mar. 11, 1828; *Biedermann* 2578; cf. also Eckermann, Mar. 2, 8, 18, 30, 1831; *Biedermann* 2927, 2931, 2938, 2948.
16. Eckermann, Mar. 8, 1831; *Biedermann* 2931.
17. Eckermann, Mar. 30, 1831; *Biedermann* 2948.
18. *Zur Morphologie*, Vol I (1817); *Insel N* 1:20–24; partly in
30:392 ff. (*Paralipomena zu den Annalen*, Erste Bekanntschaft mit
Schiller.)
19. Mignon's Exequien: *WML*, VIII, 8; 18:353–57; "Entflieht der
Nacht! Tag und Lust und Dauer ist das Los der Lebendigen,"
p. 354.
20 *Divan*, Buch Timur; 5:63–64.

3. Riemer, Dec. 11, 1811; *Biedermann* 1451.

4. *Pandora;* 15:140–78; Scheme of continuation: 379–81. First mentioned, *Tagebuch*, July 27, 1806, written November, 1807–May, 1808; published 1810. Cf. a recent interpretation by Paul Hankamer, *Spiel der Mächte, op. cit.*, 91–206. On the occasion of the performance in the *Schauspielhaus Zürich* in the fall, 1945, published by Oprecht (Zürich-New York) with an epilogue by Fritz Ernst, who emphasizes that Goethe, in the edition of his works, put *Pandora* "at the end of the last volume as a last word."

5. Christine Reinhard, May 30, 1807; *Biedermann* 1001.

6. "Noch ein Wort für junge Dichter," posthumous; 38:325–26.

7. *IR*, Apr. 13–14, 1787; 26:298 ff.; *Annalen* 1789; 30:7–9.

8. For instance, Sutor to Eckermann, about Goethe's feeling of the Messina earthquake of February, 1783; *Biedermann* 232.

9. See Note 27, Chap. 4; health: cf. "Zahme Xenien," I and III; 4:38 and 60. "Most of recent [literary production] is not romantic because it is new but because it is weak, sickly, and sick, and the ancient one is not classic because it is old, but because it is strong, fresh, joyful, and sound." Eckermann, Apr. 2, 1829; *Biedermann* 2672.

10. *Die Natürliche Tochter*, V, 8; 12:343.

11. "Vorspiel zur Eröffnung des Weimarischen Theaters am 19. September 1807"; 9:194–203. "Within eight days I invented and made it. . . . " To Knebel, Oct 7, 1807.

12. Schiller to Goethe, Aug. 17, 1795; cf. Eckermann, Mar. 11, 1832; *Biedermann* 3055.

13. *Maximen* 831–33. Natalie on laws, *WML*, VIII, 3; 18:297 (in favor of a definitely pronounced law, in view of the nature of man); "almost all laws are syntheses of the impossible," von Müller, Oct. 19, 1823; *Biedermann* 2172.

14. *Maximen* 471.

15. *Maximen* 367; 542.

16. *Eckermann*, Mar. 22, 1831; *Biedermann* 2942.

17. *Maximen* 216; cf. 217: "Wo man die Liberalität aber suchen muss, das sind die Gesinnungen, und diese sind das lebendige Gemüt." Cf. Note 14, Chap. 8.

18. Karl Jaspers, *Unsere Zukunft und Goethe* (Zürich, Artemis, 1948), p. 17; in regard to this essay, cf. H. Stefan Schultz, *German Books* (U. of Chicago, I [1948]), 306–8. Wolfram v.d. Steinen, "Um Goethes Grenzen," *Neue Schweizer Rundschau*. (Zürich [February, 1948], pp. 620 ff.)

19. "Symbolum" (Des Maurers Wandeln); 2:231–32. "Wir *heissen* euch hoffen."

CHAPTER TEN: CULTURE AND THE HISTORICAL WORLD

1. *MGF*, Zwischenzeit, Lücke; 40:151.
2. Jacob Burckhardt, *Weltgeschichtliche Betrachtungen* (Werke, Vol. 7; Stuttgart, Deutsche Verlagsanstalt, 1929), p. 208. (Engl. trans.: *Force and Freedom* (New York, Pantheon Books, 1943), p. 390.
3. *Noten;* 5:145.
4. "What would all history be if an inner sense did not come to its aid?" On the inner sense as the agent of conceiving the inner meaning on the basis of Schelling's philosophy of identity, cf. F. W. Schelling, *The Ages of the World;* tr. de Wolfe Bolman (New York, Columbia University Press, 1942), p. 87.
5. To Zelter, Dec. 4, 1827.
6. Müller, Mar. 31, 1831; *Biedermann* 2950.
7. Luden, Aug. 19, 1806; *Biedermann* 874, p. 436.
8. Müller, Mar. 31, 1831; *Biedermann* 2950.
9. To Niebuhr, Apr. 4, 1827.
10. Eckermann, Mar. 22, 1831; *Biedermann* 2907; Goethe's relation to Hegel is to be understood on the basis of Hegel's respect for Goethe's method in science and Goethe's aloofness from Hegel's system. Cf. *Annalen* 1817; 30:305.
11. "Zahme Xenien," IX; 4:124.
12. To Boisserée, Mar. 22, 1831. "I felt that all my life I had intended to qualify as a Hypsistarian; this is, however, no small effort. For, how could one, as a restricted individual, arrive at the awareness of the most perfect? In friendship at least we will not let ourselves be surpassed."
13. Hugo von Hofmannsthal, *Buch der Freunde* (Leipzig, Insel, 1929), p. 43.
14. *IR*, Sept. 6, 1787.
15. *Winckelmann und sein Jahrhundert*. In Briefen und Aufsätzen herausgegeben von Goethe (1805). Goethe's contribution, "Winckelmann," 34:3–48.
16. Luden, Oct. 1, 1812; *Biedermann* 1478.
17. "Winckelmann," Poesie; 34:38–39.
18. *Noten*, Israel in der Wüste; 5:247–268; quot., p. 248.
19. Cf. Konrad Burdach, "Faust und Moses," *Sitzungsberichte der kgl. Preussischen Akademie der Wissenschaften* (Philos.-hist. Klasse, 1912), pp. 358–403; 627–50; 736–89.
20. *Benvenuto Cellini;* Anhang zur Lebensbeschreibung des B. C. bezüglich auf Sitten, Kunst und Technik, XII: "Schilderung Cellinis"; 32:260–68.
21. *Ibid.*, X: "Flüchtige Schilderung florentinischer Zustände";

32:246–58. On the relation of the history of ideas to the level of general culture, cf. *Maximen* 793.

22. Cf. Collection *Insel N1*: 103–54; "Einleitung zu einer Morphologie," "Principes de Philosophie Zoologique." Discutés en Mars 1830 au sein de l'Académie Royale des Sciences par M. Geoffroy de Saint-Hilaire (Paris, 1830). "Hypothese über die Erdbildung." "Über Mathematik und deren Missbrauch, sowie das periodische Vorwalten einzelner Wissenschaftszweige." *MGF*, "Epochen der Wissenschaften."

On art in the Netherlands and on the lower Rhine, with a general outline of the rise of Western art out of the Christian religion, a characterization of the cultural realm of the lower Rhine regions and an analysis of the development of style and technique, cf. "Kunst und Altertum am Rhein, Main und Neckar"; 29:235–332, esp. 302–26.

23. *MGF*, Farbenlehre der Alten; 40:131–32.

24. Cf. Julia Gauss, "Die methodische Grundlage von Goethes Geschichtsforschung," *Jahrbuch des Freien Deutschen Hochstifts*, hg. Ernst Beutler (1932–33), pp. 163–283; about the project, pp. 192–98, 263–66 (reconstruction of the schema of the "work on Italy").

25. "Kunst und Handwerk," posthumously published, probably shortly after the return from Italy; 33:70; cf. 33:305 and *WMW*, as discussed in Chap. 14 of this book.

26. Baukunst, 1795. *WA*, I, 47, 67–76.

27. *MGF*, Farbenlehre der Alten; 40:140.

28. "Anzeige der Propyläen," 1797; *WA* I; 41:37.

29. "Einleitung in die Propyläen"; 33:120.

30. *MGF*, Farbenlehre der Alten; 40:140.

31. *Ibid.*, p. 141.

32. *Maximen* 1156; cf. 1155 and 1157.

33. *MGF*, "Zwischenzeit. Lücke"; 40:147 f.

34. *Ibid.*, p. 149.

35. *Ibid.*, p. 151.

36. *Maximen* 545.

37. *MGF*, Paralipomena, "Zwischenzeit. Lücke"; *WA*, II, 5, 2d part, 242.

38. *MGF*, "Autorität"; 40:158.

39. *MGF*, "Überliefertes"; 40:156; cf. *WA*, II, 3, 143.

40. *Zur Morphologie*, "Leben und Verdienste des Doctor Joachim Jungius, Rectors zu Hamburg," *WA*, II, 105 ff., quot., p. 115. Analogy between the development of Goethe's botanical studies and the history of botany: "Geschichte meines botanischen Studiums"; 39:299.

41. *MGF*, "Zwischenzeit. Lücke"; 40:148–49.
42. *Ibid.*, Farbenlehre der Alten; 40:138.
43. *Ibid.*, p. 140.
44. Humphry Trevelyan, *Goethe and the Greeks*, (Cambridge, The University Press, 1941), p. 283.
45. *MGF*, Paralipomena, "Zwischenzeit. Lücke"; *WA*, II, 5, 2d part, 244.
46. Karl Reinhardt, "Tod und Held in Goethes Achilleïs," *Beiträge zur geistigen Überlieferung* (Godesberg, Küpper, 1947), p. 255.
47. "Geistesepochen, nach Hermanns neuesten Mitteilungen," 1817; 37:102–5.
48. *IR*, Neapel, Mar. 5, 1787; 26:224; *Annalen*, 1794; 30:30.
49. *Maximen* 1155; 1175; 1220.
50. *MGF*, Überliefertes; 40:153.
51. Müller, Apr. 29, 1818; *Biedermann* 1838.
52. *WMW*, III, 11; 20:161. *Divan*, Buch der Sprüche, 5:55.
    "Mein Erbteil wie herrlich, weit und breit!
    Die Zeit ist mein Besitz, mein Acker ist die Zeit."
53. "Winckelmann," Schönheit; 34:17.
54. "Unterhaltungen deutscher Ausgewanderten"; 16:265. Märchen, 266–304, published 1795 in Schiller's *Horen*.
55. Riemer, Mar. 21, 1809; *Biedermann* 1165. Xenien 110; 4:167:
    "Mehr als zwanzig Personen sind in dem Märchen geschäftig.
    "Nun, und was machen sie denn alle?" Das Märchen, mein Freund."
56. "Versuch einer Witterungslehre, 1825; 40:55; cf. *Maximen* 619, and 297 about the interrelationship of constant and passing factors of history: "The thoughts return, the convictions are transmitted; the conditions irrevocably pass."

Meinecke, Friedrich. *Die Entstehung des Historismus.* München-Berlin, Oldenburg, 1936.
Cassirer, Ernst. *Goethe und die geschichtliche Welt.* Berlin, Cassirer, 1932.

The Ideal Commonwealth

Gregorovius, Ferdinand. *Göthes Wilhelm Meister in seinen sozialistischen Elementen.* Schwäbisch-Hall, Fischhaber, 1849; 2d ed.,

1855. An interpretation written, on the basis of romantic social-ism, in the atmosphere of the revolution of 1848; in its literary analysis the book depends on Gervinus; it touches upon pertinent questions, although Gregorovius does not recognize the unity of composition in *WMW* and is one-sided in regard to Goethe's social ideas.

Wundt, Max. *Goethes Wilhelm Meister und die Entwicklung des modernen Lebens-ideals.* Berlin-Leipzig, Goschen, 1913.

Hellersberg-Wendriner, Anna. "Soziologischer Wandel im Welt-bild Goethes." *PMLA*, LVI (June, 1941), 447–465.

Radbruch, Gustav. "Goethe, Wilhelm Meisters sozialistische Sen-dung," in *Gestalten und Gedanken.* Leipzig, Koehler und Ame-lang, 1944. Pp. 93–127.

CHAPTER ELEVEN: THE COMMUNITY OF THE TOWER

1. *Tagebuch*, May 25, 1807.
2. To Zauper, Sept. 7, 1821.
3. Cf. Wundt, *op. cit.*, 493–509.
4. *WML*, VII, 3; 18:185.
5. *Ibid.*, p. 183.
6. *WML*, VII, 1; 18:270 f.
7. *WML*, VIII, 5; 18:326.
8. *Ibid.*, pp. 326–27.
9. *Ibid.*, p. 328.
10. *WML*, VIII, 10; 18:393.
11. *WML*, VIII, 5; 18:313.
12. Schiller to Goethe, July 5, 1796.
13. Wilhelm von Humboldt to Goethe, 1800; *Goethes Brief-wechsel mit den Gebrüdern von Humboldt* (hg. Bratranek; Leipzig, Brockhaus, 1876), p. 166.
14. *DW*, IV, 16; 25:6.
15. "Symbolum"; 2:231 f. (written 1815).

The "Cross in Roses," cf. Karl Löwith, *Von Hegel bis Nietzsche* (Zürich, Europa Verlag, 1941), pp. 28–46, and Konrad Burdach, "Die Schluss-szene in Goethes Faust," *Sitzungsberichte der Preus-sischen Akademie der Wissenschaften* (Philos.-hist. Klasse, XVII; 1931).

CHAPTER TWELVE: ERROR AND TRUTH

1. *Maximen* 197. Note the difference in attitude toward error with Natalie, who helps instantly and prefers that men err accord-

ing to rules rather than under the compulsion of their nature (*WML*, VIII, 3; 18:297); Jarno, who considers himself a bad teacher because he cannot bear anyone's inept efforts without interfering (*WML*, VIII, 5; 18:324); and the Abbé, who believes that educational wisdom culminates in helping others to learn from their errors (*ibid.* and VII, 9; 18:257–58). But "strong, virile minds only are heightened and strengthened by the recognition of an error" (*WMW*, II, 5; 19:253). Getting rid of errors is costly but even then is good fortune (*Maximen* 323). "Certain deficiencies are necessary to the existence of the individual. We would not like to see old friends abandon certain peculiarities" (*Maximen* 18).

2. *MGF*, d'Ortous de Mairan; 40:272; the mathematician, *Maximen* 609; exactness as the consequence of the sense of truth, *Maximen* 607.

3. "Vermächtnis"; 2:246.

4. Cf. *WML*, V, 1; 18:81, "Much of our education and our civic institutions prepare us and our children for the absurd."

5. The community aims at "putting man on his own feet" (18:324) rather than imposing outward restrictions which, at any moment, he may exchange for "an unconditional liberty" (289).

6. *WML*, II, 9; 17:134–35; quot., p. 138.

7. *WML*, II, 10; 17:139.

8. *WML*, V, 3; 18:12–13.

9. *WML*, VII, 1; 18:169 ff., VII, 3; 18:184 ff. (error of the theater); VII, 7; 18:225 ff.

10. *WML*, I, 14; 17:59; cf. Augustin, the harpist, VII, 4; 18:187–88.

11. Indenture, Lehrbrief, *WML*, VII, 9, and VIII, 5; 18:259–60 and 322–29.

12. *WML*, VIII, 10; 18:396.

13. *WML*, VII, 9; 18:258.

14. Cf. the distinction of faculties above. Chaps. 7 and 10.

15. *WMW*, I, 1 and 2.

16. Hersilie's and Lenardo's uncle, *WML*, VI, and *WMW* I, 4, 6, and 7; quot., p. 6; 19:74.

17. *WMW*, I, 7; 19:92.

18. *WMW*, I, 10; 19:133; Wilhelm's visit, 131–147.

19. *Ibid.*, p. 145.

20. *Maximen*, "Aus Makariens Archiv," 617–789; quot., p. 627, pp. 621–32 are translated from Hippocrates' *De Victus Ratione*.

21. *WMW*, I, 10; 19:136.

22. *DW*, II, 9; 23:188.

23. *MGF*, Alchimisten; 40:181.

24. *Maximen* 302.

25. Lenardo's Tagebuch, *WMW*, III, 5 and 13; 20:82–98 and 173–98; Wilhelm's letter of admonition, 13; 20:186–87.

26. *Maximen* 519; by way of the "purest calmness of the soul."

27. Riemer, Sept. 26, 1807; *Biedermann* 1039. "Vernunftkultur" —culture of reason rather than of the intellect.

28. *WMW*, II, 11; 20:47.

29. *WMW*, III, 18; 20:226.

30. "Sheer foolish nonsense is your general education" (Jarno), *WMW*, II, 11; 20:47. The Abbé's way of building the personality upon innate inclinations by supporting capabilities rather than awakening desires: cf. *WML*, VIII, 3; 8:288–89. Danger of leaping over necessary steps of formation: cf. *MGF*, Farbenlehre der Alten; 40:140.

31. *WMW*, II, 7; 19:285.

32. "fortress," to W. v. Humboldt, Mar. 17, 1832 (Burg).

33. *WMW*, III, 3; 20:68. A memorandum to Peter Chr. W. Beuth, director in the Prussian ministry of commerce (February, 1832), on "Plastic Anatomy" indicates Goethe's seriousness about the literal meaning of the anatomist's ideas: *WA*, I, 49, 2d part, 64–75.

34. "Entoptische Farben" (Lass dir von den Spiegeleien), in "Gott und Welt"; 2:257,

> Spiegel hüben, Spiegel drüben,
> Doppelstellung auserlesen;
> Und dazwischen ruht im Trüben
> Als Kristall das Erdewesen.

Cf. the "methodical analogy" between the processes in the atmosphere and those in the eye as evidence of the interrelationship between all parts of the universe, "Chromatik," Entoptische Farben, XXIX, *WA*, II, 5, 2d part, 293. Rupprecht Matthaei, "Neues von Goethes Entoptischen Studien," *Goethe* (Viermonatsschrift der Goethe-Gesellschaft), V (1940), 71–96.

35. *WMW*, III, 14; 20:207. To Schultz, June 29, 1829.

CHAPTER THIRTEEN: EDUCATION FOR REVERENCE

1. *Maximen*, p. 342.

2. *WMW*, I, 11; 19:162–63, connects the antiquarian with the institution of which Lenardo speaks to Wilhelm as "a kind of utopia"; Wilhelm's visits: II, 1, 2, and 8; 19:173–94; 20:3–20.

3. Cf. Erich Franz, *op. cit.*, 145–48, including Comenius' influ-

ence on freemasonry in the 18th century: *Orbis Sensualium Pictus* (1654), *DW*, I, 1; 22:37; methodical qualities of Comenius' thought: *DW*, III, 14; 24:204.

4. On Pestalozzi, cf. *Biedermann* 1640, 1680, 1687 (visit to d'Aspée's school in Wiesbaden, 1815); overestimation of mathematics by Pestalozzi's method: cf. Müller, June 18, 1826, *Biedermann* 2423. The positive relation to Fellenberg, *Annalen*, 1817 and 1821; 30:312 f., 352.

5. Georg Kerschensteiner (*Begriff der Arbeitsschule*, 1912) was skeptical about "general education" in a sense similar to that expressed by Jarno in *WM*.

6. *WMW*, II, 1; 19:173–75; penalty, II, 2; 19:193.

7. *Ibid.*, pp. 175; 193–94.

8. "Salvandy's Alonzo"; 37:288.

9. *WMW*, II, 1; 19:180.

10. *Ibid.*, p. 181.

11. *WMW*, II, 2; 19:184–92.

12. *WMW*, II, 1; 19:182.

13. *WMW*, II; 1; 19:182 and 2; 19:190.

14. *Ibid.*, pp. 191–92.

15. *Ibid.*, pp. 188–89.

16. *WMW*, II, 1; 19:183.

17. Cf. "Symbolum," stanza 3; 2:231

18. *WMW*, II, 1; 19; 175, 179.

19. Freedom also of majority influence, *Maximen* 701–4.

20. *WMW*, II, 8; 20:13.

21. *Ibid.*, p. 11.

22. *Ibid.*, pp. 17–18.

23. Cf. Frederick W. Sternfeld, "Renaissance Music in Goethe," *Germanic Review*, XX (1945), 241 ff. About tone, word, and meaning: cf. *WML*, II, 11; 17:145.

24. *WMW*, II, 9; 30:21–26.

25. *Ibid.*, p. 25; cf. "Zahme Xenien," IX (Amerika, du hast es besser),

> *Dich stört nicht im Innern,*
> *Zu lebendiger Zeit,*
> *Unnützes Erinnern*
> *Und vergeblicher Streit.*

Cf. Walter Wadepuhl, *Goethe's Interest in the New World* (Jena, Frommann, 1934).

26. *WMW*, II, 8; 20:17–19.

27. *Ibid.*, p. 9.

28. *Ibid.*, p. 16; the song of the artists written in 1816; cf. to Schadow, Dec. 27, 1816; to Zelter, Jan. 1, 1817.

Chapter Fourteen: The New Community

1. *WMW*, III, 10; 20:146–47; and 12; 20: 165–70.

2. *WMW*, III, 1; 20:50. A sociological view of the rise of communities in contrast with the contract theory. Goethe explains the proverb by adding that wherever men associate with each other, the ways develop in which they intend to be and to remain together.

3. Singing as the basic level of education: cf. *WMW*, II, 1; 19:176 f.

4. Lenardo, III, 1; 20:58–59; III, 6; 20:99 introducing the "red coat"; speech about wandering, III, 9; 20:137–46.

5. *WMW*, III, 11; 20:160–65; quot., p. 165.

6. *WMW*, III, 9; 20:144.

7. *Ibid.*, p. 143.

8. *Maximen* 167; the burden of history: cf. 662.

9. Lothario, who fought in the war of Independence, to Jarno: "Here or nowhere is America! . . . Here or nowhere is Herrnhut!" *WML*, VII, 3; 18:182–83.

10. *Maximen* 443; cf. *WML*, III, 13; 20:187.

11. Goethe about Prince Bernhard's diary to Karl August, July 20, 1826 (asking for a copy of the passage about the "Shakers"); to W. von Humboldt, Oct. 26, 1826. Speaks about Jefferson's University of Virginia in Charlottesville with J. Burton Harrison, *Biedermann* 2809. Beccaria and Filangieri, representatives of 18th century humanitarianism, are mentioned as influencing Hersilie's uncle, *WML*, I, 6; 19:74; cf. *IR*, Neapel, Mar. 5 and 12, 1787; 26:223 f., 237 f. Goethe disagreed with Beccaria's decline of the death penalty, *Maximen* 685.

12. *Maximen* 302.

13. *Faust II*, 5, vss. 11,575–76; 14:267.

14. Hans Freyer, *Die Politische Insel*. Eine Geschichte der Utopien von Platon bis zur Gegenwart (Leipzig, Bibliographisches Institut, 1936), p. 21.

15. "Vermächtnis Altpersischen Glaubens," *Divan*, Buch des Parsen, 5:111–13; and *Noten*, "Ältere Perser," 5:158–62. Vs. 27:

> *Und nun sei ein heiliges Vermächtnis*
> *Brüderlichem Wollen und Gedächtnis:*
> *Schwerer Dienste tägliche Bewahrung,*
> *Sonst bedarf es keiner Offenbarung.*

16. *WMW*, III, 12; 20:164.

17. "Wager," III, 8; 20:130–36; "Melusine," III, 6: 20:100–27.

18. Wilhelm Heinse, *Ardinghello und die glückseligen Inseln* (Lemgo, 1787).

19. *Maximen* 461.

20. *WMW*, III, 11; 20:163–64.

21. *Ibid.*, p. 162.

22. *Ibid.*, p. 164.

23. Penalty of separation from society: cf. *WML*, III, 3; 20:72–73, with reference to America.

24. *WMW*, III, 1; 20:164, line 14; cf. Goethe's admiring statements about the "Magna Charta," *MGF*, Roger Bacon; 40:160. Both Gregorovius (*op. cit.*, 217) and Radbruch (*op. cit.*, p. 118) overlook this passage.

25. *Maximen* 683.

26. *Maximen* 949.

27. *Maximen* 950–54.

28. *Maximen* 604.

29. *Maximen* 868.

30. *Maximen* 870.

31. *Maximen* 548.

32. *Maximen* 541.

33. *Maximen* 463.

34. *WML*, VIII, 2; 18:272 f.

35. "Geschirrfasser" (repairman), *WMW*, III, 5; 20:92–94, 98; III, 13; 20:190–93.

36. *Maximen* 477–81.

37. On the concept of "immensity" (das Ungeheure): cf. August Raabe, "Der Begriff des Ungeheuren in den *Unterhaltungen deutscher Ausgewanderten*," *Goethe* (Eine Viermonatsschrift), IV (1939), 23–39.

38. *WMW*, III, 4; 20:81.

39. *WMW*, III, 5; 20:93.

40. *WMW*, II, 6; 19:264.

41. In *MGF*, Urzeit; 40:126–27, Goethe discusses the difference between stationary and technically developing peoples in regard to technique, explains the inimitable quality of "primitive" technique by the conservative slowness of the process, and distinguishes from it the quickness and precision of "the technically most developed peoples, where the machines become again reasonable instruments" (*verständige Organe*).

42. The desirable attitude toward the older generation: cf. *Maximen* 862: "to acknowledge the merits of older contemporaries

without being hindered by their defects"; Wilhelm Meister plans generations ahead, when, "together with the feeling of fatherhood he had acquired all the virtues of a citizen." *WML*, VIII, 1; 18:267. The whole novel extends over several generations.

43. *WMW*, III, 3; 2072. Jarno, to the contrary, expects that the new world is no better than the old one, *WMW*, I, 3; 19:35.

44. *WMW*, III, 11; 20:162.

45. Müller, Feb. 18, 1830; *Biedermann* 2782. To Rochlitz, July 28 and Nov. 23, 1829, on the intention to arouse feeling and thought and on having the impact of his writings continue (*ein Fortwirkendes*) in the future.

Pfund, Harry W. "Goethe and the Quakers," *Germanic Review*, XIV (1939), 258–69.

Jockers, Ernst. *Soziale Polarität in Goethes Klassik*. Philadelphia, University of Pennsylvania Press, 1942.

INDEX

INDEX